D0800229

RESCUE MEN

CHARLES KENNEY

RESCUE MEN

PublicAffairs
New York

Published in the United States by PublicAffairs™, a member of the
Perseus Books Group.

PublicAffairs books are available at special discounts for bulk purchases in the
U.S. by corporations, institutions, and other organizations. For more information,
please contact the Special Markets Department at the Perseus Books Group,
11 Cambridge Center, Cambridge, MA 02142, call (617) 252-5298, or email
special.markets@perseusbooks.com.

Library of Congress Cataloging-in-Publication Data

Kenney, Charles.
    Rescue men / Charles Kenney.
        p.   cm.
    Includes bibliographical references.
    ISBN-13: 978-1-58648-310-4 (hardcover : alk. paper)
    ISBN-10: 1-58648-310-2 (hardcover : alk. paper) 1. Boston (Mass.). Fire
Dept.—History. 2. Fires—Massachusetts—Boston—History. 3. Boston
(Mass.)—Officials and employees. I. Title.
TH9505.B7K45 2006
363.37092'274461—dc22
[B]
                                                              2006033290

First Edition

10 9 8 7 6 5 4 3 2 1

*This book is dedicated to my brothers—
Michael, Thomas, Patrick, John, and Timothy.
And, of course, to my father.*

"Withersoever Thou callest me, I am ready to go."

FROM A FIREFIGHTER'S PRAYER TO SAINT FLORIAN
BY RICHARD CARDINAL CUSHING, ARCHBISHOP OF BOSTON

Contents

Preface: A Family Story

My father, nearing age eighty, sits surrounded by boxes of files, notes, audio- and videotapes, photographs, and transcripts. All of this and more has made him one of the world's leading experts on the Cocoanut Grove nightclub fire of 1942. A couple of decades ago, my father set out to try to understand one of the worst fires in American history and eventually became intimately knowledgeable about an inferno that killed 492 people in minutes.

"I was just a firefighter doing something as a hobby," he says offhandedly. "I wanted to try and find out as much as I could."

My father was a rescue man on the Boston Fire Department. He followed in the footsteps of his father, who was also a rescue man and who had been at the Cocoanut Grove fire. In the process of research and investigation, my father gained an encyclopedic knowledge of the fire. He had never written a book, never written anything longer than a few pages, in fact, yet he had set himself the task of writing a history of the fire.

Now it is the winter of 2004, and we sit in his home in a small Cape Cod village. There is the quiet here of a summer place in the dead of winter. Sunlight slants through the sliding glass doors leading to the yard and my father sits with his boxes and files and notes and tapes, and he talks about the fire, as he has done since I was a child.

"The first person I called was George Graney," he says, recalling that day in 1987 when his research began. "He was at the Grove with my father. I called George at home in South Boston, Athens Street. He was long retired, I had not spoken with him in forty years. When I called, George said, 'I was just sitting here talking about your father. We were talking about the Cocoanut Grove and I was talking about how your father saved those people.'"

My dad recalls the conversation with a certain satisfaction, as though, yes, of course, when you call someone after forty years they would surely, *at that very moment*, be talking about your father and the fire at the Grove.

As part of the research he began in 1987, my father—nicknamed Sonny—called the Boston fire commissioner, Leo Stapleton, who invited him to fire headquarters. As young men, Sonny and Leo had fought fires together, and the commissioner greeted him warmly. At the commissioner's direction, an assistant led Sonny upstairs to the department files on the Grove, where he found tens of thousands of pages of documents buried away. To Sonny, the dusty files were a gift. He focused on the Form 5s—official reports filed by each Boston Fire Department officer after a fire. Here was every detail: which companies arrived when, what they did, and the name of every firefighter on the scene. Sonny also found the transcript of the official department investigation into the fire—a hearing that had been convened less than twenty-four hours after the fire and had continued for weeks. Sonny found the testimony from hundreds of witnesses, twelve volumes of transcripts in all.

He went home and read through the Form 5s. He read them a second time and then a third, comparing them, studying them, committing many to memory. Then he read the twelve-volume transcript of the investigation and when he was done reading every word, he read it again—then again. Using this mass of information, he calculated that within just eight minutes on the night of the fire, twenty-five engine companies had arrived upon the scene.

Sonny and I sit together on this frigid winter day in 2004, the sun bright in the sky, and I listen as he tells stories of the Grove. Soon, the subject of his book comes up. He sits and draws on a Lucky Strike, letting the smoke gather in his lungs, then slowly, languidly releasing it, letting it drift upward, creating a cloud that rolls and rises slowly through the slanting sunshine. "All of the reports, the testimony, everybody said that the fire did not behave as an ordinary fire," he muses. He had known that at the time, of course, from his own father. But this thought has stayed with him through the years, puzzling him, eventually haunting him. He turns his face toward the sun streaming in and says softly: "The fire that got me didn't behave in a normal way, either."

The Cocoanut Grove fire defined our family in a way. It was, as Sonny once put it, "the magnetic center of our attraction to firefighting." For Boston, the Grove was a moment in history and we were part of it, forever connected. My paternal grandfather—who was known as Pops—was with one of the first companies to arrive on the scene, and he was able to save numerous lives. Through the years, the legacy of the Grove has been passed down through three generations in our family. Pops was badly injured at the fire. Notwithstanding what happened to him, Sonny was drawn to follow in his footsteps. Later, to Sonny's eternal satisfaction, my brother Tom not only followed them—the third generation of Kenney rescue men—but proved to possess something of a genius for the work, engaging in a series of rescues through the years that would please Sonny as nothing else could.

When my father brings up the subject of the book he wants to write, I believe I know what is coming. For my father sits in the sunlight, enjoying his stubby, filterless cigarette, his white wavy hair pushed back, surrounded by his treasure trove of research and revelations—and he tells me that the book . . . well, there is no book. We sit in silence for some time. I have questions I want to ask but I remain silent, hoping that he will reveal something to me. He is careful with his thoughts and emotions, even stingy at times. And soon, as I persevere in the increasingly brittle silence, he speaks.

"There were so many interruptions," he says, frowning, trying to explain. "There was Nana's illness," he says, referring to his mother, Molly. "Theresa's death," he says—his second wife. Then he pauses and catches himself, shaking his head as though scolding himself.

"That's an *excuse*," he says. "The truth is I didn't have the drive. I didn't have the discipline to do it." His words hang in the air. His jaw is fixed in a frown.

But I wonder whether there isn't more to it. I wonder whether, along the way, he saw inside of the history, saw the arc of a story that began and ended with the Grove but contained within it the story of our family. Perhaps he realized that to tell the story of the Cocoanut Grove in the context of his own family would require revealing history better left undisturbed. I wonder whether during his work he caught a glimpse of the story he would have to tell and flinched—the story of how bedrock institutions, including the U.S. government in the form of the federal courts and the Roman Catholic Church, betrayed him and his family, leaving him confused, angry, and hurt. How would he write about the loss of his closest boyhood friend? His first wife? His father? How would he handle the loss of the only job he ever truly loved? The dark period where he lost his way and sought refuge in alcohol? How would he describe his fear when his son Tom was sent as a rescue man to Ground Zero on September 11, 2001?

Perhaps he focused only on the difficulties and challenges and did not see the determination that he, my grandfather, my brother, and all of their fellow rescue men displayed—the determination and courage that are essential elements of their stories.

As I sit with him, I realize that in the Grove and its story—inside its mystery—he has sought a kind of redemption. It always bothered my father that the official cause of the fire, how and why it moved with such murderous speed, had never been determined. After months of investigation, including interviews with technical experts and dozens of eyewitnesses, the fire commissioner concluded in 1943 that the Cocoanut Grove fire was "of undetermined origin." Could my father somehow find a clue to solve this half-century-old mystery?

I look at his wrinkled brow, his bony fingers, the cane leaning against his chair; and I realize what I must do. I must take all of this and do what he set out to do: record the history of this event. To me, it is a mystery story, a story about a cultural tradition, about the fraternity of firefighting and rescue men, the story of a man's struggle and determination. I suppose, ultimately, this is the story of how my father's devotion to the fire and its history would prove to be his salvation.

And so I will pick up where he left off. I tell him this and he nods, for just as I knew what he would reveal, he knew I would take this on, knew I would finish what he started.

He smiles, draws on his cigarette, and he tells me stories about the Cocoanut Grove.

1
Fire

On the night of November 28, 1942, my grandfather—Pops—was working on Rescue 1 of the Boston Fire Department. Shortly before 10:00 PM, an alarm sounded for a fire at Stuart and Carver Streets in the city's South End, about a half mile from the firehouse. Rescue 1, along with trucks from Engine Companies 7, 22, and 26 and Ladders 13 and 17, roared into the night, sirens wailing, speeding through a densely populated warren of old commercial and residential buildings. After a brief ride, the trucks pulled up and Pops was relieved to see that it was only a minor car fire. The vehicle was unoccupied, leaving Pops and the other rescue men with nothing to do for the moment except stand and watch the hose men douse the flames.

Though it was a cold night, only 28° F, these few idle moments were a welcome break. It had been a heartbreaking couple of weeks, the most difficult Pops had faced during his ten years as a Boston firefighter. Just thirteen nights earlier, a fire had broken out at the Luongo Restaurant in East Boston, a night when Pops had been off duty. The Luongo Restaurant blaze had seemed routine. The first alarm struck at 2:27 AM, with multiple alarms quickly following. Soon enough, dozens of firefighters had controlled the blaze. But just then—without warning—a wall collapsed, killing six firefighters. It was the worst loss of life since the department's inception in 1678.

There had been a massive memorial service for the men, and Pops, along with thousands of other firefighters, had donned the coarse wool of their dress-blue uniforms and lined the streets outside Holy Cross Cathedral. Pops had known the men who perished: Peter Mc-Morrow, Daniel McGuire, Malachi Reddington, John Foley, Francis Degan, and Edward Macomber. John Foley was on the verge of retirement, while Francis Degan, who was just twenty-four years old, had only recently come on the job. Like so many Boston firefighters, Francis Degan followed in the footsteps of his father, who was on Ladder 1. Edward Macomber, the father of eight, had been on the job for almost thirty years.

Pops ached for these men and their families. The Luongo Restaurant fire was a haunting reminder of how dangerous the job could be. He knew that their fate could be his on any given night—for the fundamental truth of firefighting is that the most routine fire holds within it the power to inflict grave harm.

Pops was forty-two years old at the time, a husband and father of three children, ages seventeen, thirteen, and ten. He thought not only about the dead but also about the forty-three firefighters who had been injured at Luongo's. Some would be back to work soon enough, but the word was that a dozen or more would be forced into retirement. Through the 1920s and up until 1932 when he joined the Boston Fire Department, Pops had held many jobs, yet none brought him the satisfaction of firefighting, and he couldn't imagine being forced to retire. You could be from a poor family, from immigrant stock, as so many firefighters were, and you could achieve a measure of financial stability. But for Pops there was more to it, something deeper that drew him to the work. There were other jobs that paid decently—at the gas, electric, and telephone companies, for instance—but those jobs provided a week's pay and little more. As a firefighter you had the chance to do something that mattered; something that was, in its way, noble. It was a job with a rare purity, a beautifully simple mission: *to save lives.*

Pops was born in Somerville, a densely populated immigrant area just outside Boston. His father had been a marble cutter—and a drinker. Pops was the second of five children, and family circumstances dictated that he work from a young age. When he was twelve, he came home one evening from his job as a Western Union messenger and saw a wreath on the front door of the apartment, a signal that there had been a death within. He went inside and discovered that his mother had died. Pops was soon forced to quit school entirely and work full-time, so he soon joined the New Haven Railroad as a machinist.

In the evenings, after work, Pops used to go down to the local boxing gym and work out. Though he was small, he was compactly built, and as a teenager he was one of the most skilled amateur boxers around. I remember vividly when he was in his sixties and a housefly would make it through a torn screen into his kitchen. We would fall silent and watch respectfully as Pops assumed a boxer's pose, his right hand cocked just below his chin, his left ready to jab. He would move around the kitchen, watching the fly, his concentration absolute, just as it must have been in the ring. We would watch as, suddenly, he would flash his left hand out so fast he snatched the fly out of midair. He worked his way up in the amateur ranks and eventually won a Golden Glove championship, and with it the only piece of jewelry he ever wore, a gold ring imprinted with a boxing glove.

After his mother died, Pops could see that his widowed father was not up to the task of caring for his children. The family broke up and the five siblings scattered in different directions. Pops was on his own and enlisted in the U.S. Navy at seventeen, as soon as he was eligible. It was 1917, World War I was winding down, and he never made it overseas. Eventually, he got the job he loved: as a rescue man on the Boston Fire Department.

A few minutes after ten on November 28, 1942, with the car fire extinguished, the men prepared to return to quarters. Just as they were about to do so, however, someone began shouting. Everyone turned and looked toward Broadway, where clouds of smoke were billowing above the streetlights. Engines 22 and 26 and Rescue 1 raced down Stuart Street less than a hundred yards and turned onto Broadway.

This was an area Pops knew well. He had lived for some years in an apartment on St. Botolph Street, and when he walked to work he used to follow these very streets—along Shawmut over to Broadway. Pops frequented Eddie's Lunch on Broadway. Recently, though, Eddie had gone out of business and his space had been turned into a bar, now part of the sprawling nightclub complex that Pops could see up ahead. Although he had never been inside, Pops knew it was *the* place to see and be seen in Boston, the place where the swells—political movers and shakers, entertainment industry people, a few mobsters, and anyone who wanted to be seen—went for a night on the town.

It was a raucous night in Boston, the Saturday after Thanksgiving, with throngs of revelers mixing with thousands of servicemen either on leave or about to ship out. There was an urgency in the air—people wanted to set aside thoughts of the war for a moment to enjoy themselves. Thousands more who had attended the big Boston College–Holy Cross football game that day at Fenway Park—and seen the stunning upset of national power BC—were also out for some fun. The Boston College loss forced many BC fans and team members to cancel plans for a victory celebration that night at the Cocoanut Grove. The streets were crowded with couples dressed for the evening: women with ornate hats, longish skirts, and ruby-red lipstick; cleanly barbered men in suits with wide lapels and equally wide neckties, fedoras atop their heads.

There were countless nightspots in Boston, but the jazziest, the biggest name, was the Cocoanut Grove, housed in an old cement box of a building running about a full block along Broadway. The revolving door at the main entrance led into a glitzy foyer with red carpeting and fancy draperies. Just beyond was a huge dining room with 100 tables, each with a crisp white linen tablecloth, and a dance floor surrounded by mock palm trees, giving the space a tropical feel. Adjacent to the dining room was the Caricature Bar, with stylish drawings of celebrities lining the walls and a forty-eight-foot bar top, the longest in Boston. Beyond the Caricature was the Broadway Lounge, formerly

Eddie's Lunch, where Pops used to go, a new addition to the complex. All of the club's public areas were at street level, except for a darkened bar called the Melody Lounge in the basement, thirteen steps down a narrow stairway just thirty-six inches wide.

On this particular Saturday night, people stood three and four deep at the bars. Every seat at every table was occupied. Though the legal limit for the establishment was 600, the best estimates were that 1,000 people had jammed into the club that night.

Downstairs in the Melody Lounge, a couple of minutes after 10:00 PM, about 150 people were drinking, singing, and laughing. Within the perimeter of the octagonal bar, Goody Godelle, perched on a revolving platform, played the piano and sang. The Melody Lounge had an intimate, subterranean feel. Fish netting lined the walls of the narrow stairway; the lounge itself was decorated with a dark blue satiny fabric that draped from the ceiling, and rattan-type material covered the walls.

Suddenly, bartender John Bradley looked up and saw a "flash" near the ceiling. Intent on dousing the flame, Bradley ran over with a pitcher of water while another bartender joined him with a bottle of seltzer. Along with a young busboy, they worked to pull the imitation coconut tree down, away from the fabric on the ceiling and walls. The Melody Lounge had become rather boisterous as some patrons joined the pianist in a sing-along. The place was so noisy, people were so preoccupied enjoying their cocktails and one another, that almost everybody was oblivious to what was happening. Those who did see it, perhaps affected by the liquor, found it amusing. In any event, nobody moved.

Then a shimmering blue flame formed a smooth arc on the ceiling fabric. The arc began to move—surprisingly swiftly—and as it did so, smoke and burning bits of fabric suddenly dropped onto patrons. Layers of smoke folded over one another, descending on the people in the bar. Nearly everyone in the room realized simultaneously what was happening, and when they did, there was pandemonium—crashing tables, smashing glass, and people clutching and shoving and grabbing. En masse, people sprinted out the way they had come in: up the stairs. But the fire gained strength and speed, seeming to race the throng to the stairway. People clawed, scratched, and bulled their way to the staircase, their primal instinct for survival taking over. Then the lights in the Melody Lounge went out, plunging the space into blackness. Men and women screamed, crying out as the fire caught up with those on the stairwell, showering fire down upon their skin, their faces, ears, and necks bursting into flame.

The fire and the people engaged in a desperate race for oxygen, and the only source was precisely where the panicked throng was headed: up the stairs. The fire raced the patrons, easily overtaking them and in the process destroying most of those at the bottom of the stairs or in the stairwell itself. The stairwell was acting like a funnel—a chimney of sorts—propelling the fire along. As it emerged at the top of the stairs, on the main floor of the Grove, it was no longer a flicker of blue flame, no longer an incandescent wisp, a simple arc: It had become a ball of flame, yellow and blue, speeding forward up around ceiling level. Somehow, a demonic, otherworldly force had been created. This was no ordinary fire, no benign bit of flame crackling on a piece of wood. Something incredible was happening here. "Nothing about that fire was normal," a news reporter later observed, "not its terrible speed, not its mysterious fumes, not its strange twists of fate that left some without a scratch and others to die horrible deaths."

The fire moved so fast that it had completed its destruction of the Melody Lounge, killing or injuring most of the patrons there, before anyone in the dining room upstairs was even aware there was fire in the building. The National Fire Protection Association later calculated that the fire raced 400 feet through the club in one minute.

Throughout the dining room, people thought they heard someone yelling "fight." The assumption was that a couple of drunken sailors had begun to mix it up. Though the fire was literally seconds away from destroying the dining room, there was no way to anticipate the impending doom. When the call of "Fire!" went out, some people started toward the coatroom to retrieve coats and hats. At the first stirring of the crowd, a waiter shouted: "No one leaves until they pay their bill!"

At the foyer, the fire divided itself and drove its way into the Caricature Bar and at the same time burst into the dining room, where it sped high around the room, greedily consuming oxygen. The fire devoured the flimsy fabric on the walls and ceilings, but it also seemed to burn by itself, attached to nothing at all, appearing to burn the atmosphere. Around the room, elaborate gowns burst into flame. The fire created a dense cloud of smoke that descended upon the people as it generated gases that rolled throughout the space. Suddenly the temperature shot up as an intense, searing heat settled upon hundreds of screaming people scrambling for exits amid the crash of overturned tables and chairs, breaking china, shattering glass, and screams of terror. The lights failed and the pandemonium intensified. In the dark, there was the feeling of deathly heat, the smell of smoke, of burning fabric and seared human flesh. Separated couples cried out for one another. There was the sinister sound of the fire itself, of wind and energy moving together. A double door at the far end of the dining room opened onto Shawmut Street, but it was concealed by draperies. A waiter parted the curtains to reveal the door, and a group of men pounded it open.

Rescue 1 had pulled onto the scene at the main entrance. Pops ran down to the exit on Shawmut Street and arrived as the fire was flashing out into the street and the bodies were starting to pile up. People cried out for help, while a man staggered out, took a few steps, wheeled and collapsed, dead on the pavement.

Pops went to work pulling people out.

While the Shawmut Street exit allowed for escape, it also quickly became one of the only sources of oxygen. The fire raced to the exit and began to incinerate those fighting to get out. Flames shot twenty feet into the street. The exit became jammed, blocked by stacks of bodies—people dead, dying, others still fighting for breath. Most of the dining-room patrons had rushed back to the foyer, but it was a fatal mistake. People scratched, clawed, and trampled each other in a stampede for the revolving door, but as the crowd charged forward, some fell dead or were injured within the door as it became hopelessly jammed.

Those lucky enough to have managed to escape in the early stages of the fire stood outside the revolving door, watching helplessly through the glass as scores of people burned to death before their eyes.

There was nothing that could have prepared Pops for this madness. He was a religious man, and he saw this as the Hell described in Revelations as "a lake of fire," or as written in Matthew, the unquenchable fire, "a furnace of fire [and] there shall be wailing and gnashing of teeth"—a place of perpetual torment.

At the Shawmut Street exit, superheated air sped from within the building. It collided with the oxygen outside, up around the top of the entryway, then propelled flame into the street, torchlike. Heavy smoke made it difficult for Pops to see or breathe. He ducked low, beneath the flame and smoke, and pulled bodies free from the pile.

Pops tried to force his way inside, but it was impossible. To him, this was intolerable. For a rescue man to do his job, he must be able to get inside the building, to search out the victims, to lead them or drag them or carry them to safety. That was my grandfather's job, what he had been trained to do and what he had done so well so many times. But now he literally could barely get past the threshold of the building. *Dear God*, he wondered, *what had gone on in there?*

He scanned the pile, trying to identify the living, as he worked to burrow as deeply into the doorway as possible. He reached in and pulled a body, half carrying, half dragging it to safety. He went back and grasped arms, shoulders, anything he could get hold of to pull people out of this hell. He repeatedly ducked into the doorway to grasp a person, while breathing the smoke and gases and half crouching below the flames, then dragged or carried the body back out into the narrow cobblestone street and handed the person off to a volunteer rescue worker for transport to the morgue or hospital. In the street, where he could gulp clean air before going back in again, people lay dead, others burned and screaming, still others crawling on hands and knees, trying to get away from the fire and heat. There were people whose clothes had burned off, whose hair had been burned, people crying, vomiting.

Smoke billowing into the Boston night attracted crowds from throughout the area. Even as civilians were drawn to the scene, hundreds of firefighters, police, and other rescue workers were converging on the Grove. While Pops worked to pull bodies from the pile, police and ambulance workers ferried the injured and dead in taxis, ambulances, police cars, newspaper delivery trucks—whatever was available. The narrow streets around the Grove were quickly clogged with vehicles, spectators, and volunteers offering help. Fire trucks and other emergency vehicles could get no closer than 400 to 500 feet from the fire. Newspaper and radio reporters, photographers, priests, ministers, and rabbis, along with city and state political leaders, descended upon the scene. Suddenly, the Cocoanut Grove nightclub was the epicenter of Boston. Hundreds of volunteer workers from the army, navy, coast guard, and Red Cross arrived on the scene to assist firefighters. The new arrivals helped ferry the dead and injured to Boston City Hospital or Massachusetts General Hospital. The great majority of the initial casualties were taken to City Hospital, about half a mile away.

Pops heard people shouting and screaming. "My mother and father are in there!" shouted someone. "My wife is in there!" a man cried. As he headed back in, Pops saw a priest, clad in black, kneeling on the cobblestones, bent over a body, praying. A man emerged from the building, completely ignited—a human torch, flames consuming his body. He ran, then fell to the ground, where he was surrounded by rescue workers. Another man, trying to get out through a broken window, was impaled upon the thick, jagged glass, fire all around him.

Pops noticed an arm reaching from the pile, the hand waving, a silent call for help. He reached down and grasped the hand, felt the warm burned flesh, but felt as well the small hand squeezing his hand in return. He later learned that the hand belonged to Dorothy Myles, the beautiful young nightclub singer. During the panic she had been knocked down, struck on the face by an overturned table and rendered unconscious. She awoke as people were literally running over her, stepping on her as they fled. She somehow got up and staggered toward the exit before collapsing into a pile of unconscious humanity. But now she had extended her hand, and Pops grasped it and carefully pulled her from the pile. He scooped her up in his arms and carried her into the street, where he handed her over to an ambulance worker.

As Pops worked, pushing into the entranceway where the bodies lay, he gradually inhaled so much smoke and gas that after carrying yet another body to safety, he staggered into the street and collapsed. A sailor and a cab driver loaded him into the back of a taxi and rushed him to City Hospital.

At Boston City Hospital there was a blessed coincidence: More than 100 off-duty doctors and nurses were gathered for a festive holiday party, which meant that more doctors and nurses were present at the hospital than on any other night of the year.

Pops was brought into the emergency room, where he was examined, judged noncritical, and moved over to the side of the room to await transport upstairs. He was placed in a sort of reclining seat in an area where he had a view of the emergency room entrance, the room itself, and several corridors leading away to other parts of the hospital.

A nurse told him he would soon be brought up to the ward. In the meantime, she said, she had to attend to the critically burned. Pops was in shock. He was watching a scene that seemed surreal, from some netherworld. He watched as rescue workers rushed through the doors carrying people in their arms, on stretchers, leading them by the hand. He saw bodies so badly charred that he could not tell whether they were male or female. He watched as dozens of stunned doctors and nurses moved among the bodies, conducting quick examinations of each new arrival, making instant decisions. Many patients were brought to a side of the room not far from Pops and were injected with morphine. A red M was then printed on either their foreheads or their chests. Many of those receiving shots seemed unconscious, but others were awake and in agony. Some wailed; others screamed or begged for God's mercy. Pops noticed that after a quick examination, many of the new arrivals were wheeled down a corridor leading away from the emergency room in the opposite direction of the wards. He wondered where they were going.

He watched as a patient covered with soot and dirt was cleaned by a nurse; watched as the patient's burns were scrubbed, causing him to scream in agony. He saw a man walk into the emergency room un-escorted, seeming agitated. He walked around, spoke to a nurse, then walked quickly away and suddenly fell face forward, dead. Pops had seen people die of carbon monoxide poisoning before, and he knew that the lungs filled with fluid, choking off the flow of air.

Pops watched as the victims kept coming in, wave after wave. The dimensions were impossible to grasp. As an experienced rescue man, he knew that for a half dozen badly burned people to arrive at a hospi-tal simultaneously was all but unheard of, an event that would surely tax the resources of most institutions. For dozens and then scores and finally *hundreds* of such victims to arrive—this was simply unthink-able, too nightmarish to contemplate. (It was later observed by writer Edward Keyes that "there were those who believed that no hospital anywhere had ever received so many casualties in such a short period of time.")

Pops saw sailors and soldiers carrying bodies in. He saw police and firefighters and coast guardsmen carrying bodies. He saw cab drivers and civilians in suits and ties carrying victims. He was not sure who was dead and who was alive. He watched as bodies were laid out in-side the emergency rotunda. Rows of bodies stretched from the emer-gency ward out into the courtyard across the driveway and into the street.

Pops remembered being in such a state of shock for part of the time that he felt he was watching this scene but could not hear it. Some-how, the sounds were blocked out. He could not hear the horrible screams, the crying, the begging for mercy. Nor the rush of rescue workers or the piercing sirens of ambulances and police cars. Nor the squeaking wheels of gurneys rolling across the room.

His sense of smell was assaulted by an overpowering stench, a mix-ture of burned human flesh along with the various chemicals that had been sprayed and now hung in the hospital air.

A nurse came by and examined him again. She told him he would be taken upstairs to the ward soon. He protested that he was all right and could go home. She ignored him.

He watched as more and more people were rolled down that hallway and again wondered where they were going. *Why were there so many? What was happening to them?* In his state of shock, in his haze, he was slow to realize the truth: for as a rescue man, he knew Boston City Hospital well and he knew that corridor led to a tunnel connecting the hospital to the Southern Mortuary across the street. And then he realized that all of those people being brought down that corridor—he had seen 100, if not more—were all dead.

Dear God, he thought.

He saw people coming through the doors of the emergency room crying, people who were not hurt or burned in any way. They were frantic, many of them, and Pops watched as they began walking around, looking down at the faces of each of the victims. He knew they were the families and friends and loved ones who had come to try to find their mother or son, brother or sister, wife or husband. He could not bear to watch this, for he knew that if they did not find their loved one here, they would be sent down the hallway to the tunnel. It was a blessing that Pops was in shock, because he had experienced the most nightmarish scene of his life at the Cocoanut Grove, and now he had to witness this—a scene out of Dante. He was as tough as a man could be, but this? It was too much for anyone. Soon, he was moved upstairs to the ward.

My dad—Sonny—was seventeen years old at the time. He was a six-foot-tall, 130-pound, raw navy recruit in training at Newport, Rhode Island, preparing for submarine duty in the North Pacific. Sonny heard about the fire late Saturday night on the radio, and he knew Rescue 1 would be at the fire. Sonny and Pops were stoic men, prone to neither panic nor a rush to judgment. Sonny could have sought a telephone, though his recollection is that such access was rare in the military at the time. But he said even if he had been able to use a phone, he would not have called home.

Through the years, when his father had gone off to work in the firehouse and there had been news of a terrible fire, Sonny had always operated on the same assumption—that Pops was safe. He would operate on that assumption until he heard otherwise. He could do it no other way.

Sonny went through his duties on Sunday, and by the end of the day he felt a sense of relief. He thought that if there were bad news, it would have been delivered by now. And yet he felt a nagging sense of foreboding. He did not know, of course, that his father had been hospitalized Saturday night and that he had lain in the ward throughout Sunday and would do so again on Sunday night.

But when Sonny awoke Monday, he felt a sense of urgency. He had to go home. He left Newport in such preoccupied haste that he neglected to get approval from his superior officers. At the bus station in Providence, he bought a newspaper and read the stories of the fire, trying to take it all in calmly, trying to understand it, trying to grasp the immensity of the tragedy. He noticed a list of names; some were injured, some dead, some still missing. He carefully read through the list—and there was his father's name.

Missing.

He thought about Molly, his mother, who was working as a drill press operator for Bendix Corporation, as part of the war effort. He thought about his younger sister, Audrey, who was thirteen, and of his little brother, Dan, who was just ten. He thought of his father. He could see his father's face: roundish, thinning dark hair, a hint of a smile, warmth in his eyes.

Missing.

Sonny's bus meandered north along U.S. Route 1, which became Washington Street in Boston. In late afternoon, Sonny got off the bus and walked half a dozen blocks to their five-room, red-brick house at the end of Glendower Road. Inside, he went into the first-floor bedroom. Pops was lying there looking exhausted and beat up, but very much alive.

Pops saw Sonny and smiled.

"Come to collect the insurance money?" Pops asked. Black humor was Pops's preferred method for dealing with almost any situation involving emotion. There was no hug, no "thank God you're alive," no tears of joy and relief. It was never the Kenney way. But Sonny could see that Pops was not himself. He was distracted in an odd way, and as Sonny sat with him, observing him closely, it became clear that Pops was still in shock. They spoke about the fire, and Pops told Sonny that bodies had been stacked up "shoulder high." Pops lay in the bed, shaking his head back and forth as though trying to deny the horror he had witnessed.

At one point, Pops abruptly rolled down the blanket, exposing his legs. It took Sonny a moment to understand why. Pops said nothing. He merely lay there with Sonny staring at the raw red scratches on his legs. Sonny was stunned, for he realized that these were scratches from people who had been lying in the doorway of the Cocoanut Grove, people scratching and clawing, desperate to be rescued.

2

"On Account of Injuries Suffered"

December brought a somber holiday season. There had been the Luongo Restaurant fire, the Grove, the war—it didn't seem all that festive to Pops.

During the days and weeks following the fire, the medical examiner for the Boston Fire Department, Dr. Martin H. Spellman, regularly came to the house on Glendower Road. Pops's lungs had been damaged by a toxic combination of smoke, superheated air, and gases, how deeply damaged would only be revealed later. Pops was more tired than usual and sometimes felt a persistent pain in his chest, but the only visible manifestation of his condition was a cough. It was not an ordinary cough, but rather an alarming paroxysm that set in as the normal cough subsided. Doubled over, his face bluish, it appeared that the violence of the episode might knock him unconscious, but then he would gasp for air, fight for a massive breath, somehow catch it, and eventually settle down.

While Dr. Spellman tended to Pops's physical woes, his emotional scars went untreated. Today, if firefighters are subjected to the sort of trauma Pops experienced at the Grove, there is counseling available, perhaps required. But for these men there was no post-fire trauma counseling, no psychological guidance. Pops dealt with it as best he could. For the most part, he spent his time in great stretches of silence in his bedroom or the kitchen, a mug of tea at his elbow. He seemed agitated at times, grimacing, suddenly lurching out of his kitchen chair and disappearing into the bedroom.

Most of all, Pops slowed down. In the weeks and months after the fire, it seemed as though his life shifted into a slower speed, not unlike switching a phonograph record from 78 to 33 rpm. He felt himself in slow motion, trying to think and move with care and deliberation, as though he needed to slow down to have any chance of understanding what had happened.

After his initial days of convalescence, Pops got up each morning early and dressed in dark wool pants and a blue denim work shirt, buttoned to the neck. Sometimes he donned a wool cardigan. He found things around the house to repair—a cuckoo clock, door hinges, a window sash. A naturally skilled carpenter and mechanic, he instinctively knew how things worked. He would take apart a faulty motor, quickly identify and repair the problem, then rapidly reassemble it. This orderly, logical side to his brain needed to try to understand what had happened at the Cocoanut Grove.

He forced himself to go outside, although he typically did this at night. He was not conscious of this at first, but then he realized he was uncomfortable venturing out during the day. He knew that in daylight there was a greater chance of encountering a neighbor, someone who might ask a question, want to find out what it had been like. He wanted none of that. And so, in darkness, he would saunter a few hundred yards up the street and then walk slowly back again. Of course, he made an exception for Sunday mass at Sacred Heart Church, where he found peaceful refuge. He had been raised Catholic, and his faith had always been important to him, but after the Grove it assumed a greater part in his life than ever before.

He read the newspaper when he was alone and the house was still. He was usually up before anyone, but he would not look at the newspaper until his wife had gone off to work and his children had headed to school. Then he would sit with a mug of steaming tea and read carefully, methodically. During the week after the fire, Pops read that 431 bodies had been counted thus far and 225 had still not been identified. As he worked his way through the paper, he was struck by how young they all seemed. As he read, certain words and phrases caught his eye: "father of four"; "father of twins"; "leaves mother, two sisters"; "Dorchester wife leaves five-year-old daughter"; "Boston doctor identifies brother's body"; "husband killed, wife badly hurt"; "MIT student, mother die in nightclub fire." He saw a headline: "Brighton Woman Fourth in Family to Die from Fire." The brief article recounted how Eva Healy, her husband, sister, and brother were all dead; how another brother and sister-in-law had been hurt. He scanned a lengthy list of the injured and there was his name: "KENNEY, CHARLES, Boston City Hospital."

He read that movie star Buck Jones had not wanted to be there at all, that he had been suffering from a cold and wanted to go back to the hotel and go to bed yet was invited at the last minute and did not want to disappoint his hosts. The actor perished in the fire. There were the O'Neills, young newlyweds who had gone to the Grove with their maid of honor and best man—all dead. He read about Katherine Swett, the dutiful Grove employee who refused, despite repeated pleas, to leave her cash register. She died. He read about the children from Dorchester whose parents, two grandparents, and two aunts were killed. Pops saw a photograph of a girl named Eleanor Chiampa from Newton, fifteen years old, the youngest victim of the fire. She had been at the Grove with her brother, a navy lieutenant, and his wife, who also died. There was a picture of eleven-year-old Margaret Zenkin and her twelve-year-old brother, Walter, both crying. They had lost their mother. He encountered a large photograph of a family standing at graveside during the funeral for four brothers—Henry, John, James, and Wilfred Fitzgerald of Wilmington, Massachusetts. There in the midst of the picture was their mother, slumped to one side, held up by others.

Everyone in Boston and the surrounding communities, it seemed, was touched by the fire. Tens of thousands lost a relative or friend. Thousands of others worked at the hospitals joined in the rescue effort. Hundreds of thousands of people attended funerals throughout that first week in dozens of cities and towns.

"Funeral processions wound their way through the streets of Boston and nearby cities and towns yesterday for the third successive day as sorrowing relatives and friends paid last tributes to more than a score of victims of the Cocoanut Grove disaster," the *Boston Herald* reported. "A triple funeral in Dorchester and more than ten double funerals were held throughout the day." The triple funeral was for Mr. and Mrs. John J. Murray and their daughter, whose husband's funeral had been the day before.

There were nearly 100 funerals one day, 113 the next, 52 the next—and still more than 200 to go. "Hour by hour from morning until dark, the seemingly endless chain of funeral corteges rolled slowly over city streets and country highways . . . ," the *Boston Daily Record* reported. "[T]he thousands attending last rites for their dead were from every walk of life, the rich and the poor, the proud and the humble,—but yesterday they walked a single path, the path of sorrow. There were fathers and mothers who had lost a son or daughter, husbands who had lost wives, wives who had become widows, children who grieved for parents."

Pops read about his Roslindale neighbor Francis Gatturna. Francis was a postal clerk, thirty years old, and he and his new bride, Grace, and four close friends had been in the club on the night of the fire. In the mayhem, Francis lost track of Grace. He got out. She died. All four of their friends died as well. Francis was overwhelmed by his grief. While undergoing treatment at Mass General he jumped from the window of his hospital room and died.

On Monday morning November 30, 1942, less than forty-eight hours after the fire, Boston fire commissioner William A. Reilly convened a public hearing. "I am trying to find out, if I can, first of all, where it started and who started it and why it started so fast," he said. The press covered the tense, somber hearings in minute detail, and Pops followed the reports carefully. The hearings were extensive and involved morning, afternoon, and evening sessions every day for weeks, all the way through December. The hearings revealed that many of the Cocoanut Grove doors—exits through which people should have been able to escape—had been locked from the exterior or bolted shut. Robert S. Moulton, who was the technical secretary from the National Fire Protection Association, suggested that "the chaotic condition of Boston's building laws, incompetent enforcement, political influences and careless management" all may have played a role in the disaster. He said it was clear that the Grove lacked proper exits, and that revolving doors were known to be dangerous.

Pops cringed at the testimony of his fellow firefighter Lieutenant Frank Linney. Accompanying Linney's testimony was a copy of the report he had filed after he had examined the Grove just eight days before the fire. The report read in part:

> From the fire prevention division to the fire commissioner
> Subject inspection, Cocoanut Grove, 17 Piedmont Street.
> In my opinion the condition of the premises is good.
> Sufficient number of exits
> Frank J. Linney, Lieutenant.

Linney's report had found "no inflammable decorations." He said he had held lit matches up to five or six palm trees to test them and all were flame resistant. Commissioner Reilly questioned Linney:

Q. And do you still feel in the light of what happened that the condition of the premises was good on November 20 when you inspected the premises?
A. Positively.
Q. And that there was nothing that you saw that would lead you to believe that a fire, small fire breaking out on the premises, would spread as rapidly as apparently this fire did spread?
A. No, sir. There was nothing there. If there was, I would have seen that he had a notice to abate the condition.

But there was something *wrong somewhere,* Pops thought. Linney hadn't seen it—evidently, nobody had—but there was *something* wrong.

Initially, the cause of the fire seemed straightforward. Stanley Tomaszczewski, the bar boy in the Melody Lounge, had told investigators that a patron had unscrewed a small light bulb in one of the palm trees. It rendered the area too dark, and the bartender instructed Stanley to screw the bulb back in. Stanley did so, but in the process he had to light a match so he could find the bulb. He told investigators that he dropped the match to the floor and rubbed it out with his shoe. Stanley, who managed to escape the fire through the kitchen, testified before the commission that he screwed the light bulb in "and then I turned around, got off the chair, and . . . somebody yelled to me, 'There is a fire in the palm tree.' And the fire started up so fast and came across that you couldn't do anything." Overnight, Stanley became infamous. He was presented by the Boston police and several members of the fire department brass as *the* cause. A menacing mob gathered outside his house in Dorchester. There were threats on the boy's life, threats serious enough so that he was taken to an undisclosed hotel, where he remained under police protection. Pops felt sorry for Stanley. This was a sixteen-year-old boy, a high school student, and he was being called a murderer for having ignited the "holocaust." In pictures plastered all over the newspapers, "the busboy," as he was now known, appeared young and frightened.

Maurice Levy, a student at Boston Trade School, had been in the Melody Lounge with his wife and another couple—all three had died in the fire—and he had witnessed Stanley screwing in the bulb. He testified that Stanley "couldn't find the bulb and lit a match and put the match behind the tree. That caught fire to the top of the tree and the ceiling caught. I got up from my seat and took my wife and by that time there was a mad scramble."

Jacob Goldfine, a wine steward and manager of the bars at the Grove, testified that he did not believe the palm trees would ignite so easily or quickly. "There were hundreds of people who would sit under those palms every night and smoke and light cigarettes and those things would never burn," Goldfine testified.

While some witnesses said that the fire had started in the palm tree where Stanley had tightened the bulb, others indicated it had started in the ceiling *above* the tree.

As he sat at home reading the newspapers each day, Pops was struck by how many of the witnesses remarked upon the speed of the fire. The commissioner questioned Mr. Goldfine about this:

Q. Do you think the decorations on the stairway . . . were sufficient to cause such a flame to come up the stairway?

A. It couldn't be possible the way it came up so quick. Just like somebody spilled gasoline on the building and it went up. That is how quick it went.

John J. Walsh, director of the Committee on Public Safety for the City of Boston, happened to be in the nightclub when the fire broke out. The commissioner questioned him about the timing:

Q. How much time would you say elapsed from the time that you first saw the fire to that point when the general fire was all over the room?

A. Not more than a minute to a minute and a half.

Q. It seemed as quick as that?

A. Yes, sir.

Maurice Levy testified that in order to leave the Melody Lounge, "we had to cross all the way over to the stairs. When I started I must have been about ten feet ahead of the fire and by the time I reached the stairs the fire was about ten feet ahead of me."

Pops knew Ben Ellis, a member of the fire department Auxiliary Force. Ben testified that he had "gone to every fire of any size since 1905," and he "never saw a fire in my life that gained such headway in such a short space of time." He added: "It was beyond human comprehension to see so much fire in such a short space of time."

Why? Why so fast? Pops wondered. *How could it have raged at such a speed?*

In the aftermath of the fire, a stench of corruption hung over Boston. News that exits were locked shut, that electrical work was substandard, that there were insufficient exits—all of this conspired to create a widespread sense that the corruption long endemic to Boston politics had played a role in the catastrophe. The Friday after the fire the *Herald* carried a huge front-page headline: "Novice Without License Installed Grove Wires." A twenty-six-year-old man from Brighton named Raymond Baer testified that although he did not have an electrician's license, he had installed lighting fixtures in the Broadway Lounge and in the past had altered some of the wiring in the Melody Lounge. At no time had he ever sought permits for the work.

The owner of a sign company who had done work at the Grove offered important testimony. Henry Weene testified that six weeks prior to the fire, he had been called into the Grove by owner Barney Welansky, who informed him about plans for the new Broadway Lounge. Weene said that Welansky "told me of the proposed new lighting for the new lounge. I said, 'This calls for a permit.'" Weene also told Welansky he would need a master electrician to make the installations.

Weene testified: "Mr. Welansky said that it would not be necessary because 'Mayor Tobin and I fit.'"

The newspaper noted that upon hearing Weene's accusation, the fire commissioner asked: "Now are you sure those were the words used by Mr. Welansky?"

"I am positive," Weene declared forcefully. (Months later, while testifying at Barney Welansky's trial, Weene would testify that after Welansky said "Tobin and I fit," Welansky added: "They owe me plenty.")

It was also revealed that the Grove seating capacity was listed at 460 on an application for a 1943 license that had been filed with the Boston Licensing Board, less than half the number of people estimated to have been in the club the night of the fire. Pops was not at all surprised. You couldn't live in Boston for as many years as he had and watch the city's politics without coming to believe that the system was essentially corrupt. Still, the idea that someone might have made payoffs to be able to skirt safety rules and that the result had been this catastrophe—*Jesus.*

All of this served to increase the level of anger and bitterness throughout the city. "Knocko" McCormack, a powerful South Boston political figure, lost his only daughter, Mary, in the fire. When Mayor Tobin attended the wake to pay his respects, Knocko reportedly stepped forward and punched the mayor in the face.

———

Boston had long been a city rife with corruption at many levels, even within the fire department. There were firefighters who helped themselves when fires broke out in stores, offices, and warehouses. My maternal grandfather, who lived four houses up Glendower Road from Pops, took a firm stand on the matter. Laurence Dunn Barry was twenty-five years old when he joined the Boston Fire Department in 1923, the year the last horse-drawn engines were taken out of service. He was a sturdy, muscular Irishman, reserved in manner, who believed in doing what was right, no matter what others were doing. This was the gospel he preached to his six children. Those were the days of the eighty-four-hour week on the Boston Fire Department, when firefighters were in the firehouse every morning of the year at 8:00 AM, either coming on or going off duty. They were also the days of low pay. Other firefighters claimed the long hours and low pay justified their pilfering.

Laurence Barry used to come home and tell stories of firefighters taking bottles from a liquor store fire or jewelry from a jewelry store fire, and he made it clear to his family that there was no gray area here—that the right course was the honest course.

———

Weeks after the fire, it was revealed that the financial records from the Grove, which had been removed to the police station the night of the fire, had subsequently been detoured to the law office of Barney Welansky, the result of either spectacular incompetence or corruption. The Welansky brothers had questionable histories at best. Barney had been involved with one of the most notorious organized crime leaders of the day, a man named King Solomon, who had owned the property before Barney bought it. And Jimmy Welansky had not long before been accused in a murder investigation.

In the aftermath of the tragedy came a variety of law enforcement investigations. At the end of December, ten men, including the Welansky brothers, were indicted and charged with various crimes including manslaughter. Fire Lieutenant Frank Linney was charged with being an accessory after the fact of manslaughter and willful neglect of duty, a shameful event for the Boston Fire Department. Also charged were Captain Joseph Buccigross from the police department, the Grove manager, the Boston building commissioner, and a city building inspector, all for various forms of negligence.

There was widespread belief throughout the city that corruption in the building, police, and fire departments as well as the mayor's office had led to the devastation. Some public officials, eager to deflect blame, singled out Stanley the busboy as a scapegoat. Although it worked to a certain extent—Stanley gave the public a visible target for their pain and outrage—there was a backlash. More and more people wrote to the newspapers to express anger that Stanley should be singled out. "Everyone in the city of Boston should hang his head in shame if these commissioners responsible for the Cocoanut Grove disaster are allowed to hold these responsible positions," wrote one unidentified Bostonian. "How can they call themselves men and at the same time throw the blame on a 16 year old boy?"

Sometimes at night Pops could not sleep. Some nights he would cough, the hard, wracking cough he was to possess for the rest of his life, and not wanting to awaken anyone, he would get up, dress, and go outside. Anyway, he liked the quiet of the winter nights when he could walk slowly along Glendower Road in the darkness, looking up at the stars. He was comfortable in this neighborhood of working people with its mix of one-, two-, and three-family homes. He would stroll along, past the houses packed close together, and think of the fire, of course, but he would also think about Sonny, who was in Rhode Island for naval training. He would think about the course of the war, about the Japanese and the Germans, but his mind inevitably wandered back to the Grove and the night of November 28. He could not help it, could not control it.

One night, around midnight, he was slowly sauntering along, bundled in an overcoat and hat, when he saw a young woman approaching.

"What are you doing outside so late, Mr. Kenney?" asked the girl, who was no older than eighteen. Pops was confused for a moment and forgot her name.

"It's Anne, Mr. Kenney," she said. "Anne Barry."

Oh, of course: Anne Barry who lived four houses down, whose father was also a firefighter. She was a beautiful, sweet girl just returning from her night shift as a telephone operator. Pops chatted with her for a moment and turned to go.

"I hope you're feeling better, Mr. Kenney," she said.

He stopped and turned. She was smiling, her eyes wide with concern. He could tell she meant it.

"Thank you, Anne," Pops said. "Thank you."

And he walked slowly back down Glendower.

———

By springtime, Pops was sometimes able to venture downtown on the trolley car and visit his friends at the firehouse. They would sit around over coffee talking about the war, about work, about kids, about anything other than the Cocoanut Grove. What could they say? At home, he became gradually more animated with the children and began a ritual in which everyone joined him several times a week frying homemade doughnuts.

Yet in his mind, questions lingered. Was it really the busboy's fault or was there another explanation? Above all, why did the fire move so fast? The testimony of veteran firefighter Ben Ellis echoed in Pops's head: *It was beyond human comprehension to see so much fire in such a short space of time.* How could it be, Pops wondered, that one of the most devastating fires in history stubbornly refused to reveal its secret?

Between early December 1942 and the end of January 1943, Dr. Spellman traveled from his office at 465 Commonwealth Avenue to examine Pops at home a grand total of twenty-three times—twenty-three visits in fifty-six days. From February 3 through March 31, Pops visited Dr. Spellman's office seventeen times. During the course of those forty appointments, Pops was waiting to hear one thing and one thing only—that he would soon be returning to work. But Dr. Spellman placed Pops on injured leave for an extended period to see whether his lungs would improve. Dr. Spellman waited as long as he could, hoping for a change, but by the fall of 1943 it was clear there would be no improvement. The paperwork took some time. On December 14, 1943, just over a year after the fire, Dr. Spellman wrote:

> To whom it may concern: Mr. Charles Kenney of #12 Glendower Road, Roslindale, Massachusetts, has been unable to work since November of 1942 on account of injuries suffered at the Cocoanut Grove fire in Boston and as a result of which he has been retired from the Boston Fire Department.

Pops was forty-three years old when the job he loved was taken from him. He had served on the Boston Fire Department eight days shy of ten years.

———

Sonny made a quick trip home before shipping out for the Pacific. Pops tried to assume an air of calm, but for one of the few times in his life he couldn't do it. It was late at night when Sonny arrived home. His mother, brother, and sister were asleep, but as Sonny quietly entered the house, he discovered Pops was still awake, awaiting his arrival. Pops was in bed, reading, when Sonny came in. Sonny sat on the edge of the bed and told Pops about his training, about what he had learned in preparation for becoming a submarine signalman.

They talked for a long while about the war and about Sonny's assignment. And then Pops could hold out no more—he had to tell Sonny. And so he broke the news, spoke as directly as he could. He told Sonny that he was no longer a member of the Boston Fire Department, no longer a rescue man.

3
The Aleutian Islands

Sonny was in the galley of the *S-47*, a U.S. Navy submarine, cruising the frigid
waters of the North Pacific, just south of Russia and the Sea of
Okhotsk, when his sub sighted a Japanese vessel. The skipper of the
S-47 ordered the firing of two torpedoes, which were promptly
launched. Sonny and the other crew members remained still, listening, waiting for the blast, but the torpedoes had gone off course, missing their target. The Japanese, however, had detected the torpedoes,
and made for the direction of the sub.

This was the nightmare of submariners. It was a particular fear of
men in the *S-47*, for the boat was nearly World War I vintage, a creaky
old vessel with little maneuverability and a top speed of only fourteen
knots. The captain had once observed that in the *S-47*, a routine dive
could be a perilous adventure.

Sonny was in the galley when the depth charges exploded at some
distance. Around him, the *S-47* crew was deathly still. They had shut
down anything and everything that vibrated or made noise—refrigeration units, fans, blowers. In the galley, someone near Sonny wrapped
cutlery in dish towels so it would not rattle. Sonny looked around and
realized that like him, the other men were standing stock still, utterly

silent. Sonny was a signalman, third class, wiry, with a thin face, bony cheekbones, prominent nose, and wavy black hair that came forward in a widow's peak. Though he was eighteen years old, he looked more like sixteen, and he had never been so scared in his life. He felt his heart pounding and could not help but think about the other subs that had gone out on patrol, never to return.

Sonny noticed that he and the other men in the galley had their heads cocked upward slightly, their eyes looking up as though it would help them pinpoint the location of their attackers. Sonny could feel the sub floating downward, reaching for enough depth to elude the explosives. The canisters tumbled off the Japanese ship and down into the water, exploding at different depths, rattling the *S-47*, causing Sonny to reach out and grab onto a pipe to stabilize himself. Then it seemed the next explosion wasn't quite as close, and the one after that was clearly farther away, and so the progression continued until it was clear they were safe. Soon, the *S-47* slipped quietly away.

———

Sonny had wanted to join the service on the afternoon of Sunday, December 7, 1941, when he heard about the Japanese attack on Pearl Harbor, but he had been just sixteen years old at the time. The earliest he could enlist was April 11, 1942, the day he turned seventeen. But he needed his parents' approval. He went to Pops that winter and said he wanted to go to war. Pops said he would sign the form—"as long as it's the navy"—the branch of service in which Pops had served. That had been Sonny's intention anyway, and he agreed. And so it was that on April 11, Sonny enlisted in the U.S. Navy and was soon notified he would do basic training at Newport, Rhode Island.

On the day he was to report for duty at the Fargo Building in South Boston, Sonny got up early and he and Pops headed off together, taking a local bus to Forest Hills station and then boarding the elevated railway. Sonny and Pops rode the train, crowded with men and women going to work. Sonny was headed for South Station, but Pops was getting off many stops before that at Dover Street, a short distance from the firehouse. Sonny carried a small bag that contained a change of clothes and a shaving kit. Pops was dressed in his Boston Fire Department uniform. When the train pulled into Dover Street, Pops reached out and shook Sonny's hand as a gesture of farewell. "I guess with the Irish ancestry, you have this feeling you don't display emotion so we shook hands and he said good-bye," Sonny recalled.

After training in Newport and New London, Connecticut, Sonny shipped out to Seattle, where he joined other submarine crewmen aboard the *Mormick Hawk,* a United Fruit banana boat turned troop ship. They then traveled west across the North Pacific, following the Aleutian chain of 150 islands along a route that grew increasingly frigid. This was the route, along the top of the Pacific, that the Japanese were predicted to follow if they attempted a mainland assault on the United States.

The Japanese had already tested the possibility of attacking via this route when they launched assaults on U.S. installations in the Aleutians in 1942, before Sonny arrived in the Pacific. In a series of battles, American forces—mostly bombers—had driven the Japanese west and out of the Aleutians. But there had been a blackout on the dissemination of news from the Aleutians: The brass wanted to avoid panic among civilians who feared a mainland assault by the Japanese. Yet when Sonny reached the port of Dutch Harbor in the Aleutians, he heard that in driving the Japanese out of Attu and Kiska, the United States had sustained the loss of dozens of aircraft. A measure of the environment's hostility was that nearly all had been downed not by the enemy but by raging storms.

From Seattle, the *Mormick Hawk* traveled 1,700 miles northwest to the tip of the Alaskan peninsula and put in at the Aleutian island of Unalaska. It was here, at Dutch Harbor, that the navy had established a massive installation in 1940. And here, on October 25, 1943, at Massacre Bay on the Aleutian island of Attu, Sonny was assigned to the *S-47.* The boat was one of the last S-class subs ever built, older than Sonny, in fact, having been launched from Portsmouth, New Hampshire, in 1923. Sonny joined a crew of five officers and fifty enlisted men on board what was to be his home for two years of the war in the Pacific.

When Sonny boarded at Massacre Bay, he went all the way aft to the stern with some other sailors and made his way forward, examining his new home. The boat was 260 feet long, and the interior space— the shell of the hull—was about twenty feet wide and ten feet high. The sub included six watertight compartments, any one of which could be sealed off if damaged in an attack. In the stern was the motor room, which powered the sub's propulsion shafts. Sonny moved forward to the engine room, marveling at the two massive Nelseco twin diesels on either side of the vessel, each of which ran longer than thirty feet. Then he walked into the area called the after battery, where dozens of huge batteries, five feet high and a foot and a half square, were packed in below deck, in the lower half of the boat. These batteries, along with those in the forward battery, powered the boat when it was submerged. A large control panel along one wall monitored the electrical systems. At the rear of the after battery was the galley, a compact area with a freezer, refrigerator, range, and sink that lined up along the port side. In the center were two stainless steel tables, each of which accommodated six to eight men at a time. Above the tables were bunks, barely inches above the head of someone sitting down for a meal. The after battery also contained the single shower and toilet shared by all fifty enlisted men on board.

Sonny moved forward into the control room, the central operations post for the captain and his senior officers, which contained a large, round Sperry gyroscope, the main compass for the boat. Nearby was the helm, a small gyroscopic device enabling the helmsman to steer the boat with a twist of his finger. This was one of Sonny's assignments— keeping the boat on course. A few feet away was the manual, backup steering wheel, available in the rare event the automatic steering failed. Along the wall were depth gauges and a device indicating the angle of the sub in the water. Sonny saw the two periscopes, one for normal use, the other a battle scope, smaller (about the thickness of a broomstick) and less visible on the surface.

Going on toward the bow of the boat, Sonny entered the forward battery, with its dozens of large batteries packed in below deck, as well as numerous bunks, stacked three high along the sub walls. Here also were the officers' head and shower, as well as a small stateroom for the skipper and a ward room where the five officers were served their meals. Sonny proceeded toward the bow and the forward-most compartment, the torpedo room, which was about forty feet long. He saw the four torpedo tubes, each about twenty inches in diameter, each loaded with a torpedo, with eight spares stored in racks along the walls. There were several bunks as well, for the torpedo crew. Under the torpedo room sat massive air tanks used to blow water from ballast tanks when the boat was submerged and needed to surface. (Once on the surface, these tanks were replenished by air compressors.)

Creature comforts were few aboard the sub. In all, there were about twenty-eight cramped bunks for the fifty crewmen. While an off-duty sailor slept, his counterpart worked a shift. At given intervals they swapped places. Showers were allowed every three days, except for the cook, who showered daily. The interior air grew stale with cigarette smoke and diesel fumes. During a dive of seven hours or more, the air went limp as the oxygen content declined. Inside the boat it was constantly cold and damp. The only real warmth came when a man went off-duty and zipped himself into an insulated sleeping bag.

Sonny awoke at three in the morning, feeling the submarine swaying. He slid sideways out of his bunk and stood up in the narrow steel tube that was the *S-47*. It was December 1943.

As usual, Sonny went down to the mess for coffee and then returned to his bunk to prepare for watch duty. His assignment included two shifts: from 4:00 to 8:00, both morning and evening. He dressed in dungarees and a sweatshirt, with a layer of foul weather gear consisting of heavy navy blue overalls and a matching jacket that zippered up the front. He sipped his coffee and checked the time. At close to 4:00 AM, he donned an outer layer of oilskin overalls and a hooded jacket, cinching the drawstrings tightly around his waist and his face. He made his way down the narrow walkway to the control room, where he joined two other lookouts, dressed identically.

Sonny watched the depth gauge as the sub climbed from 125 feet up through 100, through 75, and soon to periscope depth, about 57 feet. The skipper peered through the scope, then quickly clamped it shut. Everyone knew that a periscope was virtually useless in the North Pacific, where huge black walls of water washed over one another, restricting visibility to near zero.

On the order of the dive officer, Sonny climbed the iron rungs up through the narrow conning tower to the hatch as the sub ascended steadily and soon broke the surface of the water. As it did so, Sonny popped the hatch and felt the intense pressure from within the sub rushing to escape through the opening. He felt a whoosh of air so powerful it nearly launched him up out through the hole. Then he moved quickly up onto the bridge, a steel platform surrounded by a half wall and railing rising to about chest height. Sonny was quickly followed onto the bridge by the officer of the deck—an ensign, in this case—who scanned the seas, then summoned the other two lookouts to the bridge. Immediately, they would scan the area to, as Sonny put it, "make sure the area was absent people who didn't like us." The bridge itself was twelve feet or so above the deck of the control room, and no more than fifteen feet above the surface of the ocean.

The night was cloudy, an overcast sky limiting visibility. The North Pacific surged in waves that looked more like mountain peaks than water. Sonny held on as the sub rolled and creaked, riding a series of thirty- to forty-foot swells, then plunging steeply down into valleys of equal depth. It was perilous duty for Sonny and the other lookouts, who were untethered as waves washed over the bridge, threatening to propel any one of them into the frigid waters, where survival would be measured in seconds.

Sonny looked out at the blackness all around and searched for any sign of a Japanese ship. But he had already learned that the Japanese were scarce in this area and the more insistent enemy out here was nature: The North Pacific was as cruel as any stretch of ocean on earth.

He squinted as he scanned the waters, first with the naked eye and then again with binoculars. The *S-47* was approaching the western end of the Aleutian Islands and Kamchatka, Russia. The slender black boat, now in its third week of patrol, was 700 miles west of the island of Attu, the westernmost American territory in the Aleutian chain. It was a key base for U.S. control of the North Pacific, a pivotal point of defense should the Japanese ever attempt an attack on the northwestern United States.

Sonny had studied the map and knew that the Aleutian Islands formed a crescent or half-moon shape from the Alaskan Peninsula, curving southward a bit and then northward again toward Russia. The islands lay south of the Bering Sea and well northeast of Japan. From Dutch Harbor the *S-47* had traveled west past the islands of Umnak, Atka, Andreanof, Amchitka, and then turned back in a northwesterly direction to reach to Kiska and, finally, Attu. Sonny had thought that Attu seemed like the end of the earth, a desolate, moon-scaped island in the middle of nowhere. But now the *S-47* had ventured 700 miles west of the end of the earth, and as Sonny looked out they were not far from the south coast of Paramashiru. Beyond the island lay the Sea of Okhotsk, an inland Russian sea. Sonny imagined a globe and fixed his position northeast of Japan, just south of Russia—8,000 miles from Glendower Road in Roslindale. Before the navy, the farthest Sonny had ever traveled was Cape Cod.

Sonny's thoughts turned to home, as they so often did these days. He missed his family, of course, missed his little fourteen-year-old sister, Audrey, and his brother, Dan, just eleven. He missed his mother, but most of all he missed Pops, missed their quiet times together in the evening with strong mugs of sugary tea and the comfort of Irish soda bread. He missed sitting with Pops and hearing about what had happened in the firehouse—how a certain fire had behaved, how they had battled this blaze, how they had responded to an accident. He missed watching his father fix things around the house with precision and skill, something he had learned from him firsthand. Sonny's life had been well ordered. Perhaps what characterized him most as a teenager growing up was his sense of innocence and his desire to please. His natural instinct was to conform, to try to do the right thing, to be a good son. He wanted to make his parents proud of him, and he made sure that he never did anything that might discredit the family.

Though the family was hardly rich, Pops nonetheless had a good job as a firefighter throughout the Great Depression, even though he worked an eighty-four-hour week. For this job and the income it produced, the family felt profoundly blessed. It enabled them to escape the corrosive fear and apprehension that afflicted and even poisoned so many jobless families. The Depression brought a perspective on what mattered most that Sonny would value throughout his life. It was a time when life revolved around work, when work was the greatest blessing of all. The simplest pleasures were valued, for instance, the time the family spent gathered in the living room listening to a stand-up radio.

When Sonny was thirteen or fourteen, he became a fan of a number of weekly radio programs. Nearly seventy years later, he was still able to quote some of them from memory. All the radio fare was targeted for families: There was nothing broadcast that forced Pops to send little Audrey or Dan into another part of the house. The worst villain when Sonny was young was Fu Manchu in the Saturday morning serials at the movie theater. On the radio, he tried not to miss Lum and Abner and their rural adventures, and he liked Amos and Andy. And he particularly enjoyed the Fibber McGee program. Each week, Fibber, the ultimate tinkerer who could never get anything quite right, would attempt to fix or repair something. And each week, Fibber went to open the family closet and his wife, Molly, she of the Irish brogue, would shout out a warning not to open the door. Of course Fibber would do it anyway, resulting in a thunderous weekly crash of the closet's contents. One week, Fibber was planning on going into the hardware business and he boasted that he would become, as Sonny recalled, a "hardy heaver of heavy hardware high over house tops happily hopping hither and thither halfway to heaven." Even as a young teenager, Sonny loved the comedic sense of Fibber and others on the radio, and he particularly liked Fibber's creative and playful use of language. Sonny loved it when Fibber said one week that he was going into the clock repair business as "clock coaxer McGee the clever contriver of colossal chronometers and clean-cut corrector of community clocks Calcutta to Copenhagen."

Every summer, Sonny rooted for the Boston Braves—not the Red Sox—because he considered the Braves the working man's team. Church was at the center of the family universe, with at least weekly mass, regular visits to the darkened confessional, and nightly prayers. The Roman Catholic faith was so central to Sonny's life growing up that as a young teenager Sonny had aspired to become a Jesuit priest. The Society of Jesus was the intellectual elite of the church. At Boston College High School, a Catholic high school in the South End, Sonny's teachers were Jesuits. Sonny greatly admired them and thought he could become one. The idea that he could have a vocation was quite a powerful influence for a while, but as he grew into his later teen years, it faded in importance.

Sonny missed the radio programs, along with the routine and predictability of his job in the baggage department of the Greyhound terminal in Park Square. He missed the coziness of the house on Glendower. Perhaps above all, though, he missed his best pal, Swede Wilson. William Charles Wilson was aboard the USS *Ticonderoga,* an aircraft carrier somewhere in the Pacific. Just before he had shipped out of Seattle, Sonny had been thrilled to receive a letter from Swede. He thought about his pal out there somewhere on the vast Pacific, manning the deck of one of the world's great aircraft carriers. Sonny and Swede had a fantasy that at some point during the war, they would put into the same port somewhere in the Pacific—they both hoped it would be Hawaii—and be able to spend some time together.

Since age twelve, Sonny and Swede had been inseparable. They were both members of the Seminoles, a group of boys their age who hung out at the corner of Hillview and Crandall Streets, a few blocks from Roslindale Square. The group included a dozen boys from the neighborhood: Joe Devlin, Billy McKay, Nicky Kelly, Teddy Dineen,

Billy Pruyn, Jock and Bobby Coakley, Henry Parmieri, and Arthur (Buddy) Oberaker. The boys would horse around together, often going down to a vacant lot and playing pickup games of baseball or football. There was nothing formal about the club, it was just a group of boys who decided to name themselves. Someone had the idea one day to buy club sweaters, so to raise the money they convinced the milkman whose route covered their neighborhood to let some of them ride with him on Saturdays when he did his collections. The boys rode along, selling raffle tickets to the dairy customers. After a few weeks they had raised enough to raffle off a cash prize and buy the sweaters. They traveled several miles out to West Roxbury, to Armstrong Knitting Mills and ordered heavy wool sweaters, royal blue with an Old English S about eight inches high on the front. Sonny and Swede and the rest of the boys wore the sweaters with pride. Sonny loved the sweater because it was a symbol that he belonged, that he was part of something special, part of a group of great boys who were smart and industrious and admired throughout the neighborhood.

Sonny liked everybody in the group, but he and Swede had a special bond. Pops used to say that if you see one, you see the other because they were inseparable and never grew tired of being together. They hung out at the ball field, rode bikes, went for ice cream on summer evenings. On special occasions they would head down to Roslindale Square and bowl a few strings, waiting patiently after rolling a frame for the ball boy to reset the pins. Sonny was not much of an athlete, but Swede was a gifted baseball and football player. Sonny was rail thin, but Swede was barrel chested, with muscular arms and legs. He was sandy haired, broad shouldered, and handsome in a rugged way. Swede was like a bull with the football, impossible to bring down unless he was gang tackled, and then he would still battle two, three, four tacklers, dragging them along the dusty field.

Swede's father had one of the best jobs around—chief chemist for the City of Boston. But during the Depression, Mayor James Michael Curley fired Swede's father and replaced him with a patronage hire, a devastating blow to the Wilson family. To support the seven children, Swede's mother, a registered nurse, went to work at the Peter Bent

Brigham Hospital. And when he was not much past twelve years old, Swede got a job at the First National food store on Poplar Street, just around the corner from where the Seminoles hung out. Customers would phone in their orders and Swede would bag them, load them into a pushcart, and wheel them to the customer's home. As he grew a bit older, Swede worked every afternoon after school, as well as all day Saturday. If Sonny was off from the Greyhound station, he would spend Saturday helping Swede with his deliveries. And every Saturday, when his work was done, Swede would take his pay and go through the store buying groceries for his family.

Sonny looked forward to the end of the war when he and Swede planned to get back together, don their sweaters, and maybe go out for a bite or go bowling—or just hang out at the corner of Hillview and Crandall.

While Sonny was in the Aleutians, letters from home helped. Pops wrote every week, although sometimes the mail took three to four weeks or longer to travel from Roslindale to the fleet post office in San Francisco and then up and across the North Pacific to Massacre Bay or Attu. Sonny relished news of home, morsels that reminded him of family, friends and neighbors, and a semblance of normal life. He also received letters from his mother and notes or cards from his sister, Audrey, and from a couple of girls he had known in high school. Shortly before shipping out, on January 28, 1943, Sonny wrote home from New London, a major U.S. sub base.

Dear Mom,

Didn't do a thing today except scrub paintwork all morning and shovel snow in the afternoon in [a] . . . blizzard. I am not tired (I am trying to convince myself) and I think I will go to the show tonight.

I have learned today that I am appointed section leader over 12 mad electricians. A section leader is a guy who has no authority and who gets hell . . . if all the guys aren't at muster, plus that you get called everything by the kids.

The weather is [here Sonny wrote the word CENSORED] and we shoveled it all afternoon. Since I've come down here I have lost a few pounds, I think. They have *real* work details and there isn't any goldbricking. . . .

The electricians said they couldn't have a crumby looking section leader so I shaved just now (3 days and I had a cute mustache) but I feel nice and clean. I use Noxema by the case.

It's a nice clean life down here and I feel better than I ever have before. I will dash off another epistle tomorrow.

Love

P.S. Will you please get me a money-belt. I will pay you when my ship comes in.

In the North Pacific, Sonny wrote at least weekly and sometimes more often. Officers on board the *S-47* were diligent about going through the boat each week and reminding the men to write home. Sonny did not need the prodding, but he appreciated the fact that the officers cared about their staying connected with parents and friends. During downtime he sometimes curled up in a bunk and scratched out a letter to his parents. He was prevented from writing anything about his location or mission and therefore stuck to fairly mundane topics, such as how good the food was and how bad the weather was. He would note that they were seeing good movies on shore between patrols, but he skipped writing about playing poker (where he nearly always won money) or drinking beer in Massacre Bay or Attu between patrols. Every letter he wrote home was read by a censor and bore a censor's stamp of approval in the upper right-hand corner.

A few days after Christmas in 1943, when Sonny had just completed his first war patrol, he sent home a V-mail card. These were brief missives on something like an index card and were commonly used by servicemen.

Dear Folks,

Just a line to let you know I am still kicking. Got four letters and the S.S. Pierce package you sent for Christmas. The package was swell but the letters were all more than a month old. Also got Aud's

Christmas card and it seemed as though I detected lipstick on the envelope. What goes on there?

This Christmas was different from the others but I was thinking of you just about the time you sat down at the table. We had turkey and all the trimmings and it was very good but it was different than being home . . .

Love to all

Soon after Sonny came on watch, a storm moved in. Sonny's three layers of gear afforded little protection against an icy rain that first came down in sheets and then rode a fierce wind, driving it sideways, pelting him in the face and upper body. The winds on recent nights had been reaching velocities of sixty and seventy miles an hour, and it became nearly impossible to look in the direction of the storm.

Sonny carried a pair of 750 Bausch and Lomb binoculars, amazing instruments that allowed striking magnification from great distances. But in the Aleutians, with the black water washing over the sub, with relentless battering from storms and little visibility to begin with, the binoculars were of marginal value. Nonetheless, Sonny clutched them close and spent much of his shift working to keep them from getting soaked. While he was being battered by the weather, Sonny looked forward to the ritual he followed after each watch. His ice-encrusted clothing would be stripped off him in the control room, then draped across the engines for drying. He would go to the mess for a steaming half mug of black coffee and then proceed to the torpedo room, with its fifty-gallon stainless-steel tank of torpedo alcohol. The tank was padlocked by the officers, but the enlisted men had found a small spigot underneath that enabled them to access the alcohol. Sonny would step up to the tank and a torpedo man would open the spigot, providing a generous shot of torpedo alcohol mixed with the black coffee. Sonny would take this elixir back to his bunk, drink it down, and go to sleep.

During the early days of the patrol, the rough seas had tossed the *S-47* around, creating havoc within the sub, throwing men from their bunks, sending equipment crashing across cabins. Not only was the weather on the surface of the North Pacific some of the most hostile anywhere, but the jagged ocean floor below created an ongoing state of turbulence. On good nights the seas were twenty feet high, on bad nights three times that. From the first few moments of a watch period, Sonny would be soaked through and freezing. The stated mission was to spot enemy ships, but the real struggle was to survive the elements. To remain upright on the bridge, to keep from getting knocked into the sea—these were Sonny's goals.

When the sub was submerged, it ran on electrical power, but at night, on the surface, it ran on diesel fuel. Diesel engines required that air be sucked in through the hatch, which meant the hatch had to be open and water would pour down the conning tower and slosh across the control room, where a sump pump ran continuously while the boat was surfaced.

Sonny liked it best when the submarine was submerged. He loved the idea of running quietly 100 feet beneath the ferocious surface of the ocean, out of harm's way. Down under the ocean there was a sense of camaraderie among the submariners, a special breed within the navy. For many navy men, the mere thought of being submerged in a tightly confined space was enough to clutch them with a claustrophobic terror. In contrast, men like Sonny were comforted by it. There was plenty of coffee, and Sonny thought the food was the best he had ever had. The cook on the *S-47* was also a talented baker, and Sonny had his fill of fresh bread and pastries.

Sonny was drawn, more than anything, to the notion of being part of the war effort, to being part of this great cause for freedom. He would do whatever it took, play whatever role he was ordered to play for his country. It felt good and honest and right to do so. He knew the danger was great. He knew that a single depth charge from a Japanese warship could blast a hole in the *S-47*, breaking it apart and sending the boat and its crew to the bottom of the ocean. But he was part of a noble cause and that was its own reward.

On the bridge, Sonny could see the storm weaken, and shortly, the rain and winds lessened. Visibility improved. Sonny was awed watching the power and immensity of the ocean: the massive waves, the sheer, unmitigated power of the surging water. He was respectful of it, but, in the face of it, calm and unafraid.

Looking eastward, Sonny could make out the faintest hint of light in the sky. And then it seemed only minutes as the horizon grew brighter—even on days when both ocean and sky were a blended slate gray. It was thrilling to see. He was cold and wet, chilled to the bone and eager to go below for warmth, yet he savored this moment when the darkened sky would brighten ever so gradually, until suddenly, there was the dawn. Somewhere inside Sonny was the soul of a philosopher, and it was at moments such as these that he felt an instinctive excitement about life and its renewal.

It was much too dangerous for a sub to remain on the surface during daylight, and, at dawn, the order came to dive. The switch was made from diesel to electrical power, and the other watchmen climbed below. As the boat began to slide under the surface, Sonny was the last man on the bridge. He liked to take a quick look around at the surging water as the boat sank beneath his feet before jumping into the conning tower, pulling down on the hatch and spinning it hard to secure it in the seconds before the Pacific Ocean washed over the boat.

4

"Of Unknown Origin"

P ops sat on a waterfront dock in Boston Harbor, night watchman for a coal company, gazing out across the Atlantic at the rising sun. One moment it was dark, and the next there was a hint of light, then shafts of brightness across the water and, finally, there was sun on the eastern horizon.

These fall days of 1943 were difficult for Pops. He worried about Sonny at war and he struggled with his ever-present thoughts about the Cocoanut Grove. As the months passed, Pops saw that people were putting the catastrophe behind them and shifting their focus to the war. He realized it was an entirely rational and appropriate progression, yet he was unsettled by it in a way he didn't quite understand. After a few months during which the Grove dominated the Boston newspapers, coverage rapidly dwindled. There was nothing new to say about it, and after all, the world was at war. But the Grove was not so much forgotten as put aside. Pops noticed everyone getting on with their lives, as he was trying to do, but the truth was that thousands of people had been profoundly and permanently affected by the fire. Beyond the 492 dead, hundreds had been injured, with many disfigured, some grotesquely so. Others were disabled, prevented from ever working again. Countless relatives and friends of those injured and killed, as well as hundreds if not thousands of firefighters, police officers, doctors, nurses, and others had been traumatized by the event.

One evening around this time, Pops received a telephone call from a nurse at Boston City Hospital inviting him to visit one of the people he had rescued, a young singer named Dotty Myles. The nurse explained that Dotty and her mother had done some research and figured out that Pops was the man who had saved her. Dotty had been through a difficult time, the nurse explained, but she was progressing. The nurse told Pops that Dotty's mother from New York had moved up to Boston and was her daughter's constant companion.

When Pops arrived at the hospital, a nurse explained that Dotty had been burned over 40 percent of her body and had already undergone several surgeries, with more to come. Pops was led into a spotless room with a steel-frame bed and two chairs. Dotty was sitting in one and her mother was standing nearby. When the nurse introduced Pops, Dotty's mother came forward, looked into his eyes and embraced him. Dotty could not touch Pops, of course, but she thanked him as well "from the bottom of my heart."

He looked at Dotty but tried not to stare. Before the fire, Dotty had been a milky-skinned beauty with thick, wavy dark hair, high cheekbones, romantic eyes, and a pretty smile. But now, Pops could see that the skin on her face was tight and dry, cracked in places, splotched red. A webbing of reddish veins was visible from her cheek midway down her neck.

"Nobody really thought I would make it," she said in a clear, sweet voice. She paused and smiled. "But I did. And I am going to perform again," she said, leveling her eyes at his. "I want you to know that." She told him that after he had pulled her out of the pile and carried her across the street to hand her to another rescue person, she was placed in the back of a police wagon with a collection of dead bodies. She told Pops that a policeman gave her his raincoat—all she had on were panties and a shredded jacket. She paused for a moment as though reflecting upon that night and what had happened. And then she began talking in a way that made it clear that she wanted him to know the details of the life he had saved. Pops sat up straight in the chair, holding his hat in his hand, listening intently. She spoke in a matter-of-fact way with a composure that impressed him. Her real name, she said, was Dorothy Metzger and she had been born on West 101st Street near Broadway in New York City. She had been drawn to Broadway, both figuratively and literally. At age eight, she sang on the "Horn and Hardart Kiddies Hour," an event sponsored by the famed Automat. She began voice training at age nine and started tap dancing lessons as well. At twelve, she competed in a prestigious competition at Carnegie Hall and won the Lily Pons Gold Medal. That same year, at the Education League competition, she was selected as the "best junior voice."

She was not bragging, but rather informing, wanting Pops to know all of this. She sang on CBS and NBC radio, and by the time she was in her midteens, Dotty was invited to sing in nightclubs in Syracuse, Key West, and Boston. At age seventeen came the opportunity of a lifetime: She was invited to audition for the Jimmy Dorsey Band, one of the most popular in the country. She wanted to be at her very best for the audition, sing as she never had before, and she sought a nightclub appearance that would prepare her for the big moment. She would have auditioned for Dorsey in late November or the first week in December. An opportunity for the ideal preparation was presented to her: She was invited to perform throughout much of November at the Cocoanut Grove. Dotty opened there on the eighth, a Sunday night.

A hush fell over the hospital room. Dotty's mother sat silently, her hands folded on her lap. Dotty sat for a long, reflective moment and Pops thought she was finished, but she continued, recounting the details of the night of the fire. Dotty arrived at the Grove at 9:15 PM to prepare for the 10:00 PM show. She changed into her stage dress and went into the sitting area of the ladies' lounge, located opposite the front revolving door to the club. At one point, she glanced through the open door to the foyer to the club and saw musicians walking by with their instruments. A few minutes before 10:00, a small man

Dotty recognized appeared in the doorway to the women's lounge. He seemed quite drunk when he looked in and just said, "Fire." He did not shout it, and there was no urgency to his voice. The girls sitting with Dotty thought it was a sick joke. Dotty walked through the foyer and had started in the direction of the stairway down to the Melody Lounge when "a blinding flash" knocked her down.

In fall 1943, fifteen days shy of the first anniversary of the fire, Massachusetts fire marshal Stephen Garrity issued his final report on the Cocoanut Grove. For Pops and many others, the report served to deepen the mystery surrounding the fire's origin and method of acceleration.

"After exhaustive study and careful consideration of all the evidence and after many personal inspections of the premises, I am unable to find precisely and exactly the immediate cause of this fire," Garrity wrote in his report to Governor Leverett Saltonstall. Garrity issued one important finding. He explicitly ruled out the possibility that the busboy, Stanley Tomaszczewski, had caused the fire, stating in his report, "It is clear to me that [Stanley] did not ignite the palm tree in the Melody Lounge and thereby cause the fire. [He] . . . was not the person who set the fire." Garrity's pronouncement notwithstanding, there remained thousands of people who held firmly to the view that Stanley had, in fact, been the cause. The initial wave of publicity surrounding the busboy and the lit match had been so overpowering that it had served to demonize him in the public eye, and for many people nothing the state fire marshal said was going to change their view.

The official Boston Fire Department finding echoed the state report. The fire commissioner wrote that "the fire will be entered in the records of this department as being of unknown origin."

It seemed incredible at the time, yet of the ten men who had been indicted on various corruption charges in connection with the fire, all but one were exonerated. The sole exception was Barney Welansky, the principal owner, who was convicted of involuntary manslaughter for the unsafe conditions within the club. Welansky was ill with cancer when he was sent to prison and died not long thereafter.

Pops found all of this barely comprehensible. Four hundred and ninety-two people killed in minutes—in a building with horrendous conditions—and one man alone was held responsible under the law? After the reports were final and Welansky had been sent to prison, there lingered in Boston a festering sense that political corruption lay at the foundation of the fire. There had been threats on the life of the chief investigator for the state fire marshal's office, and threats as well on the lives of the fire marshal and the state attorney general. In fact, police were needed to protect the six-year-old son of the chief investigator. Yet when the reports were released and most of the men indicted walked free, the public reacted with a shrug of the shoulders. There was deep and profound anger among some of course, but for many others there was a sense of resignation that the system was rotten and nothing would change that.

Pops was left wondering how it was possible that the cause of such a catastrophe could remain a mystery. He was so logical, so talented mechanically, that he felt a compulsion to understand the how and why of things. He wanted to know what had caused this fire that had so completely and forever changed so many lives. But it seemed unlikely anyone would ever know for sure.

Pops turned forty-three the summer after the fire and was back to working where he had in the 1920s—the Massachusetts Transit Authority power station on East First Street in South Boston. This massive facility was perched on the edge of the harbor, a cavernous industrial building running a full city block. Pops was a machinist skilled in the inner workings of boilers, generators, and turbines, and he was also a trained welder. Pops sometimes watched as a cargo ship from the Midwest or Southeast docked in the deepwater anchorage just outside the power station and unloaded hundreds of tons of black coal. Large coal cars lumbered along an overhead tramway, carrying the coal to the boilers, releasing billowing clouds of coal dust that swirled inside the building and darkened the space, dimming visibility and settling upon everything and everyone. But it was a good steady job and Pops was always pleased, riding the trolley home to Roslindale, that he had had a hand in generating the electricity that brought all of these good people to and from work each day.

When Pops was not working, he would wash up and escort his wife, Molly, to the Fidelia Club, where they socialized with friends. Fidelia, a social club for blue-collar clientele, was housed in a two-story wood-frame building on Rockland Street, in the West Roxbury neighborhood of Boston. As the war progressed, clearly moving in favor of the Allied forces, the music at Fidelia grew a bit louder and the drinks flowed more freely. Sometimes on weeknights a crowd gathered for bingo. On weekends there was a three- or four-piece band—maybe a pianist accompanied by sax, trumpet, and drums. Favorites from Glen Miller and the Dorsey bands prevailed as patrons enjoyed fifteen-cent glasses of beer and twenty-cent highballs. Customers dressed presentably, but hardly fashionably. These were the working people: men who needed more than a few minutes to scrub clean before going out for the evening, women who worked in factories supporting war production.

In letters home, Sonny mentioned that he looked forward to being able to accompany his parents to Fidelia for the evening. Pops knew many of the returning vets would spend their time with pals or sweethearts, and surely Sonny would do some of that as well, hanging out with Swede Wilson and the gang. But Pops knew his boy and he knew Sonny would be comforted by the presence of his family. Pops could not help but love that about Sonny.

In the winter of 1945, the *S-47* cruised south from the Aleutians across the Pacific, to Hawaii for maintenance, and then proceeded to New Guinea and Australia for training missions. In summer 1945, the *S-47* returned to the United States and was cruising toward San Francisco Bay when word came of the war's end. The *S-47* was moored with other subs on Angel Island, not far from Alcatraz, then proceeded to a shipyard near Oakland for decommissioning, a process that involved removing, categorizing, and storing all of the ship's gear. Sonny was in charge of optical equipment, including sextants, binoculars, Polaris rings, and two chronometers.

The *S-47* was officially decommissioned on October 26, 1945, two years to the day after Sonny had signed onto the crew. The captain presided over the dockside ceremony, with all fifty enlisted men and five officers topside. For the first time since its launch twenty-two years earlier, the boat was crewless within. Captain Alan Bergner was a big man, stoic yet professional. Sonny could see he was affected by the reality of the moment. Standing amidships, the captain read the formal decommissioning order in a somber voice. The order's stilted, formal language officially sent the boat into retirement. The *S-47* had been from the Atlantic to the Pacific, from the most hostile northern reaches of the Pacific to the beauty and tranquillity of the South Pacific. The captain called for the removal of the boat's commissioning pennant, a two-colored steamer about three feet long that flew from a flagstaff on the after end of the bridge and signaled that the boat was officially commissioned. And then came the order to lower the colors for the final time. There was hesitation, then the flag was lowered. Never again would the *S-47* sail under the colors of the United States, and Sonny was struck by the finality of it. These men had gone to war together and now, for the most part, they would never see one another again.

With the close of the decommissioning ceremony, Sonny was assigned to a sub that sailed to the East Coast via the Panama Canal.

From Portsmouth Naval Base in New Hampshire, Sonny rode a bus into Boston and on December 6, 1945, he reported to the Fargo Building in South Boston, where he was discharged from the navy—three years, three months, and twenty days after joining (and still not old enough to drink or vote). The circle was complete, for this was where Sonny had started his naval career. When Sonny had boarded the *S-47* he had been a signalman third class. During his time in the Aleutians, he made signalman second class, and it was at this rank that he was officially and honorably discharged. He stood outside the Fargo Building wearing his winter dress blues. He had arrived on the East Coast without a coat or jacket and had managed to scrounge a peajacket at the Fargo Building. As he started to walk toward South Station, he was struck with the oddest feeling: Though he was deeply happy to be going home, to have the war behind him, he suddenly felt as though his connection to something special had been severed. He stood on the sidewalk in South Boston, a few blocks from the harbor, and turned and gazed out at the ocean. He missed it already. He missed the space, the rhythms, the grandeur and vastness of it; he missed the constant reminder of a power in the universe greater than man. And he missed the brotherhood, the camaraderie among his fellow submariners. This had become precious to him. He had been part of something important, part of a noble cause. He would miss that feeling. He lingered a moment, then turned his collar up against the wintry breeze, tossed his seabag over his shoulder, and headed for home.

It should have been the most joyous homecoming, but when Sonny walked in the door at Glendower Road and embraced his parents, his father took him aside and gave him the terrible news.

"Sonny," Pops said softly. "Swede was killed on the deck of the *Ticonderoga*. A kamikaze."

Sonny was thunderstruck. His dearest friend in the world was gone. He went outside to the tiny backyard and in the cold, dark December night, sobbed as he never had before in his life. He remembered Swede so clearly—could see him in their boyhood days, could see Swede bulling his way across the vacant lot, the football tucked securely under his arm. He could see Swede's blocky frame and crooked smile. He could see him in his Seminoles sweater, the one they all wore so proudly. He could see Swede on Saturdays, pushing the grocery cart along Poplar Street, making his deliveries, cashing his check, buying food for his family. Throughout the war Sonny and Swede had exchanged letters, both looking forward to the day they would be back in Roslindale hanging out together.

The news changed everything about the homecoming. It made Sonny want to stick close to home and be near his family. There were evenings when Sonny went out with his mother and father to the Fidelia Club to have dinner or listen to music. Other nights he went down to the local pub with some of his friends. But mostly Sonny was comfortable at home. He and Pops would sit around late in the evening after the others had gone to bed and talk.

Pops asked about his plans and Sonny said he intended to take a little time off, then go back to his job at Greyhound. He thought he would enroll at Boston College on the GI Bill. He was thinking about studying English and maybe becoming a teacher. Pops nodded, smiling, taking it all in. "After the war I was just so darned glad to be alive," Sonny recalled. "All I wanted from life was some peace and quiet, a white picket fence, a nice wife and some kids."

They got to talking about the Grove one night, and Sonny said he couldn't believe that the conclusion was "of unknown origin." Pops shook his head. It had been three years now, and it seemed they didn't know anything more about how it started or what caused its speed than they did the night of the fire. It seemed an unfathomable mystery, and from what Pops heard, nobody around the department thought that it would be solved. And no one was even working on it anymore. Its time had passed. The war was over and everyone was looking to the future. There had been enough tragedy and death for one country to handle.

A few weeks after Christmas, in early January 1946, Sonny returned to work at Greyhound. Under federal law, designed to protect the jobs of veterans, Greyhound was required to give Sonny his old job back if he reapplied within ninety days of leaving the service. When he had left Greyhound for the navy, he had been a "baggage smasher," and it was to the baggage room he assumed he would return. But Greyhound was short staffed, so Sonny was tossed into a variety of positions from dispatcher to reservations and, later, ticket agent.

Sonny signed on for the night shift, working from 11:00 PM to 7:00 AM five days a week, enabling him to go to Boston College full time. He enrolled at BC in February 1946, excited about the prospect of furthering his education. He had been blessed with a curious, analytical mind, and he passed the simple entrance examination with ease.

Sonny's biggest challenge was logistical, shuttling between work, classes, and home. The nights were bustling, usually until around 2:00 AM, when a pleasant quiet began to settle upon the station. This gave Sonny a three-hour window for studying, since the next buses were not due until 5:00 AM. Sonny found that the quiet of the baggage room in the early morning hours was a fine place to get schoolwork done. He did not find his schedule burdensome in any way. In fact, he thought it a blessing to be able to hold down a full-time job and be a full-time student. He was cheerful and productive both at Greyhound and at BC, and he never complained. He had grown up in a home and a culture where work was the greatest of virtues, where there was dignity in all work. He had always known that his father was in the workforce at age twelve and had barely taken a vacation since then. In Sonny's world, work was what you did.

It was all worth it, and something very good was happening at Boston College. He was taking challenging classes and meeting professors who were opening up the world of ideas to him. Sonny was particularly drawn to his religion class, taught by a charismatic Jesuit named Russell M. Sullivan. Father Sullivan had been captured by the Japanese during the war and interred in a prison camp in the Philippines, along with Philippine president Manuel Quezon. Although much older than his students, he could relate to them as veterans, as a man who had just shared the war experience. As a theologian, Father Sullivan was a powerful intellect and compelling teacher. It was not as though there was a vast spectrum of course offerings in the Religion Department; this was, after all, Boston in the 1940s, as closed an Irish Catholic society as there was anywhere in America. The BC theology faculty, for example, was populated by a dozen or so Jesuits, including

Fathers O'Brien, Flaherty, McCarthy, Murphy, Doherty, Shea, Burke, Casey, and, of course, Sullivan. The department could hardly have been more Irish had it been recruited in the streets of Dublin.

The course offerings suggest the intensely—and unquestioningly—Catholic nature of the college: The Divinity of Christ, The Church of Christ, Existence and Essence of God, God the Creator, God the Redeemer, God the Redemption; The Sacraments I and the Sacraments II. No world religions, comparative religion, or questioning. There was God, there was church doctrine, and there was a quiz on Friday. As much as Sonny got into the early English literature—from Beowulf to Milton—he was most comfortable with the religion classes. Perhaps because he had been brought up so strictly Catholic, he was comfortable with the concepts and enjoyed digging down beneath the surface and getting at some of the ideas behind Catholic doctrine. In his first semester, except for a C in math, he performed honors work, acing both religion and English.

That fall, Sonny seemed to open up a bit more socially, as well. He had noticed a girl down the block on Glendower Road and thought she was quite attractive. It was Anne Barry, the sweet telephone operator who had expressed concern over Pops late one night on her way home from work. Anne dressed stylishly and had a warm and pretty smile, and her father was also a rescue man.

Under the GI Bill, each student received a free ticket to each BC home football game. A classmate of Sonny's mentioned he would be away for the weekend and offered his ticket to Sonny. The next morning, Sonny timed his walk to school to coincide with Anne Barry's return home from the overnight shift at the telephone company. They stopped and chatted for a moment. They had never talked much, but they had always been neighborly. Sonny didn't know whether she had a boyfriend, so he was a bit nervous.

"I was wondering if you would like to go to the football game against Villanova Saturday," he said. Her eyes brightened. "I would love to," she said. And so they did, taking the trolley into town and then another trolley out to BC. After the game, Sonny took Anne for cocktails to the lounge in the venerable old Hotel Vendome on Commonwealth Avenue in the Back Bay.

———

"There's a department exam coming up," Pops casually mentioned to Sonny one evening that fall. They were sitting in the kitchen, each with a mug of tea.

"For what?" Sonny asked.

"The fire department," Pops said.

"Oh," Sonny said, shrugging it off.

Pops sat a moment. "Tough test," Pops said.

Sonny had been gaining confidence at BC. In his second year, he was becoming an ever stronger student and enjoying the feeling of success.

"Anybody could pass that," Sonny said dismissively, a hint of condescension in his voice.

Pops bristled.

"I'm not so sure about that," Pops said.

Sonny laughed derisively. "I mean, it's a pretty menial job, how tough could the test be?"

Pops was quiet a moment. When he had taken the test, there had been thousands of applicants. Having done well enough to earn a position was a point of great pride with him.

"It'll be competitive," said Pops, hurt but not showing it. "Lots of vets will take it. Most won't make it." This was not like Sonny; not the reserved, quiet, deferential young man Pops knew. Where had this cockiness come from? Perhaps it was surviving the war. Perhaps it was the Jesuits—a bit of their arrogance rubbing off on Sonny. He was a college man now, an intellectual.

Pops looked Sonny directly in the eye, locking on his gaze. Pops was unsmiling when he said: "You couldn't do as well as you think you could."

In the wake of the announcement that there would be a test to select a new class of Boston firefighters, the department was flooded with applicants. The test was set for that fall, with results to be announced in the winter of 1947. Sonny had never quite been challenged by his father before, certainly not like this. He had made the mistake of arrogantly demeaning the job his father had loved, so now he had to prove that he was as smart as he said he was. He had to take up the challenge. Besides, Sonny really did believe the test would be easy. It was based on information contained in a single publication— the so-called Red Book, published by Massachusetts Civil Service and jammed with technical information about firefighting. Sonny picked up a copy a few weeks before the exam and worked his way methodically through the book. He was well prepared, and after taking the test, he knew he had achieved a strong score.

In the months following the test, Sonny ran into more and more vets who talked about how desirable the firefighting job would be. For one thing, the city was about to make a dramatic change and reduce the workweek from eighty-four to forty-eight hours. For another, the job carried good benefits, decent pay, and, perhaps most important, it was secure. After the Depression and World War II, there were an awful lot of people drawn to the notion of security. Sonny began questioning whether he really wanted to be a teacher. He figured he would be twenty-five at least before receiving his bachelor's degree and then maybe twenty-seven before getting his master's. That was a lot of overnights at the Greyhound terminal.

5
No Such Thing As Routine

Although it was one of the most perilous jobs in the world, Sonny had not given much thought to the danger of possibly working as a firefighter. He had grown up knowing firsthand how hazardous it was, of course. He knew all about the Luongo Restaurant fire and had seen what his own father had been through at the Grove.

He was reminded of the danger anew in the fall of 1946, just as he was contemplating whether to join the department. On the night of October 22, fire broke out in the basement of Kakas Brothers furriers on Chauncy Street. Patrick J. Cady of Engine 39 and Warren E. Barnard of Rescue 1 led a group of half a dozen firefighters into the basement. Also in the lead group was Elmer Porter of Rescue 1, who had been on duty with Pops on the night of the Grove. The men descended into the dense black smoke of the basement, intent on quickly subduing the small fire. The firefighters who remained outside had no sense of imminent doom. A couple of minutes passed, then a few more. The men in the second group of firefighters made their way down to the basement, but as they descended, the lead man stumbled. He looked down and saw Cady, Barnard, and the others lying face down in pools of water. The injured men were rushed to

Boston City Hospital, where it became clear that deadly fumes had permeated the air and their masks had failed.

At the hospital, several men were revived, but Patrick Cady and Warren Barnard were pronounced dead. A third firefighter survived but suffered oxygen deprivation to the brain and remained mentally handicapped for the rest of his life. Pat Cady was twenty-eight years old, an army veteran, recipient of the Purple Heart. He had been on the job less than a year. His wife was pregnant with their first child. Warren Barnard, also twenty-eight, lived with his wife and two young sons and, like Pops, had been a member of Rescue 1. An investigation suggested that fumes from hydrochloric acid had combined with the smoke, overcoming the men and killing them.

Were men attracted to the job in spite of or because of the danger? In a way, the idea of battling such a powerful force as fire held a certain allure for men like Sonny, particularly war veterans. Sonny had seen the power of water in the North Pacific and now, if he joined the BFD, he would witness the power of another of the elemental forces. Sonny realized fire had the power to destroy as nothing else quite could. The enormity of fire's power was somehow magnetic for Sonny. He knew that in religion, myth, and legend, fire was the ultimate horror, for the worst possible fate in the afterlife was eternal damnation in the flames of hell. He knew that some of the most horrible moments in history involved fire—including February 1945, when British and American planes had bombed the German city of Dresden, raining incendiary bombs and creating a firestorm that resulted in the city's complete destruction and the deaths of tens of thousands. He was vaguely aware of the Great Chicago Fire, in which 300 people died, 17,000 buildings were destroyed, and 90,000 people were left homeless. Most important, he knew how truly dangerous fire in Boston could be, with the city's creaky old buildings where rapid burning and collapses were common. But he was in no way deterred by this and was perhaps in some way drawn to it.

Fire department lore—outlined in an entry on the BFD Web site— explained why firefighters' uniforms displayed the symbol of the Maltese cross. The story involved the Knights of St. John, a holy and loyal band of warriors who fought in the Crusades and lived for centuries on the Mediterranean island of Malta. In the sixteenth century, the Knights of Malta fought a raging battle against the Saracens (the term then used to broadly define Arabs or Muslims). During intense fighting, the Saracens launched canisters containing naphtha, a highly flammable liquid, splattering the knights. The Saracens then hurled large torches at the knights, setting hundreds ablaze. Many suffered horrific deaths, while others were injured and disfigured. The Boston Fire Department Web site notes that "Some knights rode to the rescue of the burning victims, and when the battle was over, these rescuers—the first firefighters—were honored for bravery and presented with a Maltese cross, a sign of valor. Thus was the Maltese cross adopted by firefighters everywhere as their symbol—representing a fireman's commitment to do whatever is necessary, including risking his life, to accomplish his mission."

At the time Sonny was contemplating joining the department, the incidence of destructive fires in the United States had reached an alarming rate—so alarming that President Harry Truman convened the National Conference on Fire Prevention of May 1947. "The serious losses in life and property resulting annually from fires cause me deep concern," the president said, appearing in person at the conference, which drew hundreds of experts from throughout the country. "I am sure that such unnecessary waste can be reduced. The substantial progress made in the science of fire prevention and fire protection in this country during the past forty years convinces me that the means are available for limiting this unnecessary destruction." Prior to the opening of the conference, the administration issued a statement providing a framework for the meeting, which indicated that from the mid-1930s through the mid-1940s, an average of 10,000 people died in fires annually. Statistics for part of 1946 showed that if the trend continued, it would be "the most disastrous [year] in our history with respect to fire losses. . . ."

As Sonny debated what to do, however, it was not the danger of the work that concerned him. He had already cooled on the idea of becoming a teacher, but there was still, somewhere in his mind, the thought that the job of a firefighter was somehow menial. This was not a thought he wanted to admit, not one of which he was particularly proud, but it was there nonetheless.

In making up his mind about whether to join the department, Sonny consulted one person in addition to Pops—Father Russell Sullivan, his religion professor at Boston College. Sonny sought out Father Sullivan in the Gothic stone residence building where many of the Jesuits on the BC faculty lived. Father Sullivan welcomed Sonny warmly, and they sat in a private, paneled library, a hushed setting where a candid conversation could take place. Sonny talked about the fire department, about the opportunity it presented in terms of job security and money. He expressed concern about the time it would take to become a teacher. He spoke of the conflict he felt about leaving school. Father Sullivan listened intently. It may well have been that the priest could see that Sonny had essentially made up his mind and wanted support and approval, wanted to be comfortable with his decision. Father Sullivan told Sonny that at that moment he was ranked number one in his class, wonderful news that infused Sonny with pride. It would be easy, considering this, to imagine Father Sullivan urging him to stay on track toward his degree, but Father Sullivan— for whatever reason—did the opposite. Perhaps the priest was as much a product of the Depression mentality as Sonny and Pops; perhaps he recognized the desirability of a secure, steady job with decent pay and benefits. Father Sullivan told Sonny about another student he had taught, calling him "the most brilliant student I ever had." That student, Father Sullivan said, "is pushing a broom as a janitor on the Boston Elevated Railway. And he is very happy with what he does. No matter what you do," the priest said to Sonny, "do it well and be happy doing it." This approach, he said, will please both you and God.

The drill tower of the Boston Fire Department was a striking yet incongruous building at 60 Bristol Street in the city's South End. The tower, constructed in 1891 of soft yellow brick, is a replica of the bell tower of the Palazzo Vecchio in Florence, Italy. The tower stands 156 feet high, and every twelve feet or so, ascending up the side, there was a window with a narrow ledge.

On January 21, 1948, Sonny and about 100 other newly minted recruits gathered in the chilly air to begin a one-month training period. Their essential mission would be to learn to respond to fires quickly, get as close to the source of the fire as possible, and extinguish it while at the same time rescuing anyone at risk. An essential skill for firefighters was an ability to identify the appropriate equipment for any given situation. Thus, much of the training involved learning to identify and use a wide variety of equipment, from different-sized hoses and brass nozzles to masks and other protective breathing apparatus. Sonny learned the basics of raising aerial and ground ladders and scaling those ladders in full equipment. In particular, he liked the Halligan tool, a three-foot steel bar with a right angle at one end and a wedge shaped device at the other. It was essential for gaining entry to a building and could be used to jam into a door frame to pry open a door, or to smash windows, or for whatever else was necessary.

Sonny learned that what appeared to be chaos at a fire scene was actually the result of a well-planned strategy and basic rules about assignments among firefighters. Engine companies typically operated with two trucks—a hose wagon and a pump. Responding to an alarm, the hose wagon headed directly for the scene of the fire, stopping first at the nearest hydrant—sometimes 100 feet from the fire, sometimes 100 yards. During this stop, the man on the back of the wagon stepped off and wrapped the end of a hose around the hydrant. The wagon then continued to the fire, while a line of hose unfolded onto the street behind it. The engine company pulled up to the scene but avoided parking directly in front of the main entrance to the building—a space reserved for the ladder truck. After the hose wagon came to a stop, the pump pulled up and hooked a four-inch line onto the hydrant. The pump then hard-suctioned the water out of the ground through this line, feeding it out the other side of the hydrant into the line that the hose wagon had laid down on the pavement. At the fire scene, the lead hoseman connected a nozzle to the hose and headed for the front door of the building.

At the same time the engine company was beginning its work, the ladder company pulled up directly in front of the building. The rule was clear: If there was smoke showing—from anywhere in the building—the driver on the ladder truck would be responsible for throwing the "stick" to the roof. This meant swinging the 100-foot aerial ladder into position to get to the roof, a task requiring a series of rapid, deft moves by the ladder truck driver and tillerman, whose seat was atop the aerial ladder. As soon as the truck came to a halt, the tillerman disconnected the tiller wheel, set it aside, then pulled a catch on the side; the tiller seat would swing back and out over the side of truck, making room to raise the aerial ladder. The driver of the truck would do this by hopping onto the turntable and swinging the ladder into position. The tillerman then headed up over the stick with an ax or Halligan tool to ventilate the roof. This was a crucial move in any fire, because unless the roof was ventilated, the fire within a building could grow diffuse and unpredictable, lurching in one direction or another. The theory was that with ventilation, a sort of chimney effect was created, drawing the fire up to a particular spot, lending a greater level of predictability to its behavior and making it more manageable for firefighters. With proper ventilation, the base of the fire would remain contained and the engine company would be able to get water on it more quickly and effectively. While this was happening, a side man on the ladder company would make for the front door, sure to beat the hose man there, and he would open the main entrance—often with an ax or a Halligan tool.

Sonny liked the order of it, the simple logic of the approach. It seemed so chaotic when you watched with an untrained eye, but once he learned the basics, he found it to be a pleasing performance piece where every man knew his role. When the companies got to a building fire before it was out of control, it was amazing to watch how swiftly and efficiently they would gain the upper hand and put the fire out.

Sonny realized during training that fighting fire required a precise plan, not unlike a military battle. He became more aware of the danger posed by fire—of its fierceness as an opponent—and he realized that the term fire*fighter* was particularly apt; it was a fight. The idea was to get to the fire as rapidly as possible so that it had minimal time to develop, and then to kill it before it could get out of control.

During training, Sonny learned the basics about fire as an element. As he already well knew from the Cocoanut Grove, fire was capable of moving at astonishing speeds. In less than a minute, a seemingly innocuous fire could get out of control. He learned about the intensity of fire's heat and was taught that the reason firefighters often crawled through smoky rooms was that temperature at floor level might be 100° F, while at ceiling level it could be three times that or even higher. Sonny was taught something else he already knew too well—that inhaling superheated air could scorch the lungs, burning the lining and in many cases killing or disabling the person. During training there was talk of the deadly toxins produced by fire, of the dense smoke, of the need to wear a protective mask. He learned that most people who die in fires are killed by breathing smoke and toxic gases.

But the most physical and dangerous part of the training was done on the tower with a pompier (French for "fireman") ladder, also known as a scaling ladder. These were ingenious devices about twelve feet long, slim and relatively lightweight. The ladder consisted of a single beam a few inches wide with rungs extending to either side of the beam. At the top of the ladder was a large hook so that a firefighter could stand on a windowsill and reach up to the window above, hook the ladder onto the sill, and then ascend the ladder.

The training period was highlighted by two drills that all of the trainees conducted with pompier ladders. The first was a group exercise known as "chain pomps" (short for "chain pompier"), in which the men formed a kind of chain going up the side of the drill tower. In this drill, a man reached up to the second-floor window, placed the hook of his ladder on the sill, and climbed the ladder. He then sat off to the side on the windowsill while the next man climbed the first man's ladder, then used his own ladder to get to the third floor. The process was repeated until there was a trainee on each windowsill, going up eight stories. On the order of the drill instructor, the men stood, faced the window, and attached their safety belts to a small hook in the wall. They then all leaned back, raising their hands in the air, supported only by the safety belt, a demonstration of a man's trust in his equipment. Historically, some trainees had found this so terrifying that they were unable to do it. But this was a group that for the most part had been to war. Sonny and many of the other men had faced conditions more hazardous than leaning backward while snugly tethered to a building.

The final part of training involved what was called the "single pomp" (single pompier) challenge. Sonny stood at the base of the tower with his ladder and reached up, hooking it securely onto the windowsill. He climbed the rungs, careful to balance his weight so the ladder would not sway too much to one side or the other. When he reached the second floor, he sat on the sill, carefully reached down and lifted his ladder, then reached up and extended it to the third-floor windowsill. Sonny realized any slip would be disastrous. He scaled the fourth and then the fifth floors. When he reached the sixth, he looked down and was surprised by how small the men gazing up appeared. He had never much liked heights, and he experienced a sudden moment of anxiety. But he brushed it aside and reached his ladder up to the seventh floor, climbed to the sill, pulled up the ladder, and climbed to the eighth. He stood up, careful not to look down until he was facing the building and had hooked his safety belt onto the neck of the pompier ladder. At that moment he smiled to himself, extended his hands straight up in the air, and leaned as far back as the tether would permit.

Sonny was assigned to Ladder Company 30 in Egleston Square, a section of Boston's Roxbury neighborhood. Sonny's new firehouse was home to both Ladder 30 and Engine Company 42 on Washington Street in Egleston Square, a lively commercial district with a large Metropolitan Transit Authority (MTA) station for both street trolleys and the elevated railway. On one side of the firehouse was a popular movie theater, and on the other, the JA Café, a bar and nightclub. There were a few shops and two popular bars just across from the firehouse, the Plainsman and the Quarter Deck. Legend held that the bar next door to the firehouse was owned by a man who had been mixed up in the infamous Brinks robbery in Boston in January 1948.

When Sonny arrived at Ladder 30 he quickly felt at home. The company included a couple of friends he had known from high school and the neighborhood, as well as half a dozen old-timers who had been on the job with Pops.

One of the first things Sonny did was learn the telegraphy system for the department. This was a time well before radio communication on fire departments, and a company at a fire would call in a second alarm using Morse code, which Sonny had mastered in the navy. Inside each fire alarm box throughout the city of Boston was a telegraph key that could be used to communicate directly with fire headquarters. Sonny took the telegrapher's test and passed easily, increasing his value to the ladder company.

Sonny was fortunate to be among the first firefighters working the new forty-eight-hour week. Typically, he worked two night tours per week, from 6:00 PM until 8:00 AM, and two day tours, from 8:00 AM until 6:00 PM. During his initial days at Egleston Square, Sonny learned the basics. During downtimes, the officers had the men drive the ladder company up to Franklin Park, not far from the firehouse, allowing each man to learn how to drive the tiller position, a tricky maneuver that some men took to more easily than others since it required steering in the opposite direction the truck was turning. Sonny was fortunate to have a progressive young lieutenant leading his group. Although some officers favored specialization, Lieutenant Walter Maraghy believed every man in the unit should become expert in every position. Thus, during downtime, he drilled the men on various tasks so that everyone learned to drive the truck, steer the tiller, operate the stick, and so on.

Sonny was particularly fond of the tiller position. He liked the view it gave of everything up ahead and also liked that he would race up over the stick to be the first man ventilating the roof. During off hours, they also practiced driving the ladder truck out of the firehouse and backing it in. This was no easy task at the Egleston Square house, for it faced Washington Street at an odd and rather awkward angle. Making matters worse was that the city's elevated railway ran along Washington Street on tracks twenty-five feet above the roadway. The tracks ran so close to the firehouse that from the bunk room you could nearly reach out and touch them. As Sonny quickly discovered, the incessant screeching of elevated railway cars made getting any rest in the bunk room nearly impossible.

The first working fire, that is, a fire at which all hands responding are working at once, came soon after Sonny was appointed. A box was struck for Highland and Millmont Streets in Roxbury. When Ladder 30 pulled in, there was fire showing and thick smoke billowing from a three-story residence. Engine 42 got a line in through the front door, and the lieutenant ordered Sonny up to the second floor. Sonny went in the main door and up the stairs, but before he had even reached the second floor, the smoke was so thick and black he could see nothing. Remembering that day, he said, "I didn't know smoke could be that thick." He heard the voices of men on his crew. "Come over here and open this wall," the lieutenant said to him. Sonny couldn't see the lieutenant, let alone the wall. But he felt his way along and when he found the wall, he promptly swung his ax. The problem was that one of the men from Engine 42 was standing behind him, and Sonny caught him in the helmet with the butt end of the ax. Fortunately, he was okay. Sonny was soon out of the building, but he saw two men from the rescue company—known in fire department shorthand as simply "the Rescue"—taken out, overcome by smoke.

Because so many of the men in the firehouse were returning veterans, most were in their early and mid-twenties. The men got to know each other on the job, of course, but they also enjoyed spending time with one another socializing after work. They often went to one of the pubs in Egleston Square for a few beers and conversation. The Haffenreffer beer company was not far away, and whenever there was any sort of fire in the brewery—which was not infrequent—Teddy Haffenreffer would send a few barrels of beer over to the firefighters for an off-duty party. This bonding and sense that they were all in it together was the bedrock of the department.

Sonny had not been on the job long when he was faced with his first bad accident. A trolley car was careening down Seaver Street toward the Egleston Square MTA station clearly out of control. The tracks came down Seaver and then turned sharply right into the terminal building, but when the trolley reached the turn it was going too fast to hold the tracks and derailed, tilting to one side and smashing into the overhang of the terminal building, partially decapitating the top half of the trolley. It clipped one of the steel girders that supported the elevated railway, launching the motorman forward out of his seat, flinging him onto the pavement in front of the trolley, where he was then run over by its massive steel wheels.

Ladder 30 and Engine 42 responded in under thirty seconds. In those days—long before the existence of EMTs or paramedics—the fire department handled all such calls. Sonny and his company responded to calls for people threatening suicide, car wrecks, and all sorts of industrial accidents, from butchers getting their hands caught in a meat grinder to printers getting limbs dragged into massive presses.

During the MTA accident, Sonny and the other men climbed through the wreckage and began carrying injured passengers out to the street. Sonny then crawled under the wreckage and came upon the motorman, whose legs had been severed in the accident. The man was in shock, bleeding profusely from both severed limbs. This was a tragedy of course, but it was also a test for Sonny. Not everyone could handle this type of situation. Many people, in fact, were made physically sick by the sight of such gore and trauma, but Sonny was steady. He stayed with the motorman for the few moments it took for the Rescue to arrive. The rescue men then stabilized the driver and quickly got him to the hospital, and he survived. Sonny was impressed with the work of the men from the Rescue. They were quick, quiet, and incredibly efficient. He thought about his father and his father-in-law having performed similar rescues.

The next morning, Sonny woke to see a large newspaper picture of himself in full gear working at the accident. He was amazed by this minor bit of celebrity, and just about everyone he saw for a week or more mentioned it to him. It felt good. His picture was in the paper for doing a special job, a job where you face danger and help people. That felt good; actually, it felt great.

Sonny loved his job and found that just about everybody else he encountered at the department did, as well. It was something he'd probably known instinctively from his father, but learning it firsthand was a wondrous discovery. Was this the case with other jobs? Certainly not many. As much as he loved his job, however, he felt a desire to continue his education. He was so committed to the idea that he methodically went through the firehouse, talking to a number of the married men and offering to swap his day shifts for their nights. Swapping was common and permitted, but rarely did anyone try to swap out of days and into nights. Sonny was offering to give up *all* his day shifts in return for *all* night shifts to be able to continue his studies at Boston College. And his plan was working beautifully: Everyone he asked was more than delighted to swap. Sonny had it all lined up so that he would work nights and be free weekdays to attend classes. He went to the lieutenant of his company to explain what he had done, and the lieutenant thought it was fine. Sonny then went to the captain of the house and explained how he had lined up a new schedule so that he could go to school during the day shifts. Sonny said that he had the support of the lieutenant as well. But the captain, a bullheaded man named Packy Burke, killed the idea.

"I can't swallow that," he said. "I've got fifteen other veterans." Sonny pleaded with him to let him proceed. The captain flatly refused. "If I let you do it, then I'd have to let everybody do it," he said.

It was a remarkably stupid statement because there was no one else in the house who *wanted* to do it. Sonny was not prone to anger. Like Pops, he was usually calm and reserved, but he was furious about the captain crushing his plan. My God—he wanted to better himself by earning a degree. Shouldn't that be encouraged? Maybe the captain didn't want anybody in the house who was different, who was ambitious about anything outside the department. Maybe he was envious of someone who had an opportunity, and the ability, to go to college. Maybe it was just the ugly underbelly of the culture: that dark side of smallness and envy, that sneering determination to make sure no one else got ahead. There was no question that in ethnic Boston there was a tendency to smallness and parochialism. Perhaps that was it—a man suspicious of ambition, mistrustful of an intellectual pursuit. In retrospect, it was one of those defining moments in Sonny's life, one of those crossroads where the road not taken is forever lost. Had he been able to go to BC and earn his degree, who knows how his life might have been different? Would he have left the department to go into some sort of white-collar profession, doing something less dangerous and better paying? Would his new profession have imbued him with the sense of confidence and self-esteem he would later lose?

He was so angry that he felt he could no longer work in a firehouse under the command of Captain Burke. The day after his plan was crushed, Sonny went to his lieutenant and requested permission to speak with the district chief. He specifically waited until District Chief Redshirt McCarthy was on duty, because McCarthy and Pops were friends. Sonny went to McCarthy and asked permission to go to the personnel department downtown to request a transfer. As Sonny knew he would, McCarthy said yes. Sonny went downtown to fire headquarters on Bristol Street and spoke with the deputy chief in charge of personnel. It so happened that his desk was right next to the desk of the chief of the department, Black Jack McDonough, who overheard the conversation. McDonough had been at the Cocoanut Grove and knew Pops. McDonough asked Sonny whether there was anything he could do to help. Sonny asked whether he would overrule the captain and permit him to continue with his plan to go to BC. Chief McDonough said he would not overrule a captain making rules within his own firehouse, but if Sonny wanted to leave the house and transfer elsewhere, he would help him. He asked where Sonny wanted to go and Sonny said he wanted to go to Engine 6, a company being newly formed and stationed downtown.

"All filled," McDonough said. Then he thought about it for a moment and said to Sonny: "How about the Rescue? Your old man was a rescue man. There's an opening on Rescue 3."

Sonny was astonished. His ambition since joining the department was to eventually make it onto a rescue company. Rescue 3 was housed in Bowdoin Square, the biggest and best firehouse in the city, a house with more action than any other. "That would be great," Sonny managed. And it was done.

Anne Barry, shapely and vivacious, was one of the prettiest girls in the neighborhood. She loved to laugh and was easy for Sonny to be around. Whereas Sonny was somewhat reserved and shy, Anne was outgoing and at ease in almost any setting. Sonny was not the most organized person in the world, but Anne was solid and dependable, her feet planted firmly on the ground. She and Sonny went to parties or the movies and, over time, grew increasingly comfortable with one another. After they had been together for about a year, in fact, Sonny realized he could not imagine his life without her.

On October 8, 1949, after two years of dating, Sonny and Anne were married at Sacred Heart Church in Roslindale. After a honeymoon trip to Niagara Falls, the newlyweds moved into a one-bedroom apartment at 155 Poplar Street, just a block off Roslindale Square. The apartment was in a three-story brick building, and by no means fancy, it was clean and in a lovely residential area. This location was quite familiar to Sonny, as it was barely a block from the store where Swede Wilson had worked and a couple of blocks away from the Seminoles' hangout.

Sonny was warmly welcomed into Anne's family by the Barrys. On the Kenney side, however, came an unpleasant undercurrent from Sonny's mother, Molly, about the marriage. Molly tended toward a sour disposition in general, but there was no mistaking that she thought Anne not quite up to the standard she expected for Sonny. Happily, Anne was entirely ignorant of her mother-in-law's feelings toward her. In the early days of the marriage, Anne continued working as an operator at New England Telephone Company, while Sonny worked in the firehouse. Two months into their marriage, in December 1949, Anne learned that she was pregnant.

The Bowdoin Square firehouse was constructed in the late 1920s, located at the foot of Beacon Hill, just a couple of blocks from the State House with its resplendent golden dome, and a few blocks from Haymarket, the city's central marketplace. It was a mere half mile from the waterfront and a quarter mile from Boston Common. In building the Bowdoin Square firehouse, the leaders of the department wanted to create a unique place that would house more fire companies and more men by far than any other firehouse in Boston, and more than most in the world. It was so massive it became known as the Big House. Most firehouses had two or perhaps three bays for apparatus, but the Bowdoin Square house had seven, all facing out onto a broad expanse of Cambridge Street. Inside Bowdoin Square there were no internal columns—just a vast open space covering the better part of a city block.

The Big House was more than five times the size of Egleston Square firehouse. At Bowdoin Square there were two ladder companies, three engine companies, the district fire chief, Rescue 3, two specialty companies—Tower 1 and the Lighting Plant—fourteen company officers, eighty firefighters, and two chief officers. Tower 1 looked like a ladder truck, but its ladder carried a huge pipe up to the summit, where a water cannon could be fired at burning buildings from a distance of 100 or more feet away. And the Lighting Plant was a truck with enormously powerful portable lights that were fueled by its own internal generator and used to illuminate a large area during nighttime fires.

Bowdoin Square was the Times Square of firehouses, with companies responding to fires and accidents in the hub of the city throughout the day and night. Sonny felt as though he had just gone from Double A ball to the big leagues. Companies from the Big House covered fires and accidents from the tenements of the West End, one of Boston's ethnic cauldrons, to the waterfront docks; from the meatpacking district to the leather district near South Station; from Brahmin Beacon Hill to Irish South Boston. The firehouse itself was populated by men who very much wanted to be there. They craved the action and were willing to take on the challenge of one of the busiest and toughest firehouses anywhere—and a number of the men, like Sonny, were sons of firefighters.

The house was right in the center of Bowdoin Square, with a number of burlesque houses and a dozen or more bars nearby. It was a hub of activity for the neighborhood, with people coming and going throughout the day and well into the night. At the firehouse, many of the men enjoyed gambling and poker games were a regular activity. When the local bookie came by each evening, there was an announcement over the house PA system that "the numerologist is in quarters." Arthur Fiedler, the conductor of the Boston Pops orchestra, was a "spark" (a civilian passionate about firefighting) and a frequent visitor to the Big House, where he would hang around for hours and chase fires with the men.

One of the most unusual aspects of the Big House was that there were two men, "Santo" and "the Engineer," who were not members of the fire department but who lived at the firehouse. No one seemed to know how they had come to take up residence, and no one ever seemed to ask about it. Sonny, like the other men, simply accepted the fact that Santo and the Engineer lived there. Although the Engineer actually slept in a hotel behind the firehouse, he spent all his time and kept his things in the firehouse. The Engineer was a blind man named Joseph Cosgrove, and word was that he had lost his sight in an industrial accident. Santo was a small, squat man with somewhat limited mental abilities. He worked at National Casket Company in Cambridge and would rise each morning in the firehouse and walk to work, returning each evening to hang out with the men and often, quite cheerfully, run errands such as going out for coffee or sandwiches. The firefighters treated him like one of the family. Sonny enjoyed the camaraderie, and he liked the oddity of a place that welcomed men as different as Santo and the Engineer.

Sonny reveled in the work. Some days were quiet, of course, but typically the pace was intense, with fires in tenements, downtown hotels, office buildings, waterfront docks, and warehouses, and an astonishing variety of accidents with trucks, cars, trains, and construction equipment. When a major alarm came in calling for every unit in the house to move, it was an event of almost magisterial power to Sonny. Dozens of men would slide the brass poles and within seconds be in their boots, coats, and helmets, all as the house alarm blared. The ladder and engine companies would mount up and roar out the door, followed by Rescue 3, Tower 1, and the Lighting Plant and led by the district chief in his shiny red car with his driver careening through the streets.

"It was a thing of beauty," Sonny would say with a broad smile. "A real thing of beauty."

Sonny was quietly proud of his standing as a member of the elite rescue squad. It was akin to being a submarine sailor within the navy—a member of a special team, a smaller force within the larger organization. As a firefighter, Sonny was called upon to perform a wide variety of tasks, all of which he embraced with energy and determination. He was proficient at ladder work, at going up over the stick to ventilate a rooftop. He was comfortable with engine work, with lines and nozzles and hydrants. He possessed a keen understanding of the responsibilities of engine and ladder companies and, when called upon, could perform any task required at a fire.

Joining the Rescue meant Sonny added to his abilities, and as he worked to learn the skills and equipment essential to a rescue man, he also learned about the job's heritage. Rescue companies as such had not existed as a specialty within fire departments until early in the twentieth century, when a number of catastrophes in New York City changed that. A fire at the Triangle Shirtwaist Company in 1911 proved an important impetus for the creation of a specialized rescue company. Seven hundred young immigrant women were working in the company's Manhattan clothing factory when fire broke out. Mayhem ensued, with scores of young women falling to their deaths on overcrowded fire escapes. The interior stairwell doors had been locked, trapping hundreds of women and preventing firefighters from getting to them. In all, 146 workers died in the fire.

Ten months later, in January 1912, another tragic event struck Manhattan when the Equitable Building caught fire and partially collapsed. According to an account written by New York City rescue man Paul Hashagen, a businessman named William Giblin, along with a clerk from his company and a watchman, were trapped in Giblin's basement office. Two-inch-thick steel bars protected his sidewalk-level windows from burglars, and with the collapse those same bars locked Giblin and the other two men in a confined space. With burning debris and massive amounts of water falling from above, a New York firefighter struggled to free the men. The firefighter, lying face down, began the painstaking process of trying to cut through the bars with hacksaw blades, which he was forced to change fifteen times in under two hours. His actions were heroic, but his equipment was woefully inadequate to the task. During the slow process, the clerk died. It took more than two and a half hours to free Giblin and the other man, and it was clear that improved equipment and a rapid rescue would have saved all three.

In the wake of these fires, New York officials sought a way to insure in the future that faster, more expert rescues could be accomplished. They realized that specially trained rescue men—supplied with the proper tools (including cutting torches and other devices to free trapped victims)—could save lives. Thus, Rescue 1 went into service in New York in 1915, and the modern rescue company was born. Boston officials took note of the New York innovation and followed suit in 1917, establishing a rescue company in Fort Hill Square.

There are some in fire service who consider it the job of rescue men to rescue firefighters trapped or injured fighting a fire. The expression has long been that when a civilian needs help, he calls a firefighter; when a firefighter needs help, he calls a rescue man.

After his first year on the Rescue, Sonny began to feel like a true veteran. He had been to hundreds of fires and accidents, and he felt as though he had learned how best to handle each type of situation. He felt as he had during the war—as though he was part of a select fraternity, a group of good men united in a worthy cause. It was a wonderful feeling that nourished and sustained Sonny for years, just as it had Pops.

Sonny's appreciation for Bowdoin Square grew as he became acquainted with another firefighter who would become one of his closest friends. Nelson Pittman was an inch or two over six feet tall, thin, with a gangly appearance. His brown hair was thinning, hairline receding. Nelson had two distinct facial features. One was a wide mouth that seemed to stretch most of the way across his face and a nose that was Durantesque—oversized, crooked, and the first thing you noticed about him. Nelson was an uncomplicated man who had transferred into Bowdoin Square from Readville, an outlying Boston neighborhood and one of the sleepiest firehouses in the city. Like everybody else assigned to the Big House, Nelson craved action. Prior to joining the fire department, Nelson had been an iron worker. In many ways, he reminded Sonny of Swede Wilson—a dependable straight arrow. It was a tribute to Sonny, in a way, that his closest friends in life were not trimmers or wiseguys with angles and schemes, but simple, honorable men. Soon after Nelson arrived, he and Sonny became partners on the Rescue and, ultimately, good friends.

On September 23, 1950, far from Bowdoin Square, a small fire broke out in the basement or sub-basement of the Eagle Mattress factory in the Brighton neighborhood of Boston. Lieutenant Roy Burrill and Private William Robert Benson descended into the sub-basement to douse the fire, but they did not emerge. Other firefighters went down looking for them and discovered both men face down in a pool of water. The men had died of carbon monoxide poisoning and smoke inhalation in a fire that did a grand total of $100 damage to the factory. Lieutenant Burrill was thirty-eight years old and had been a firefighter since 1940. Like Sonny, firefighter Benson was twenty-five years old

and was also a navy veteran. He had come on the job the year before
Sonny. Benson was survived by his parents and siblings, including a
brother who was also a Boston firefighter. Lieutenant Burrill was survived by his wife and two children. Sonny had gotten to know Burrill
during his time on the job. He was a pleasant guy and Sonny liked
him. Burrill was one of the few black firefighters on the department.

At Bowdoin Square, as was the case in firehouses across the city,
there was a subdued period of grief and reflection. The men would sit
in the kitchen over coffee and quietly discuss what had happened, try
to understand what had gone wrong. Had their masks come loose
when they jumped into the sub-basement? Had the masks simply
failed? The sobering reality was that it had been a nothing fire, a single
alarm that should have been routine. But that was the problem—
there was no such thing as routine. You never knew what you would
face when you went out that door. And you never knew who would
be next.

6

The "Ideal Life"

In April 1955, when Sonny turned thirty, he felt as though everything in his life had fallen into place. He and Anne now had three boys—me, Michael, and Tom, with a fourth (Patrick) on the way. Only eleven months apart, Michael and I were "Irish twins." With the children, a two-family home on Gurnsey Street in Roslindale, and a job he loved, Sonny felt he was blessed with the "ideal life."

So much had changed during Sonny's lifetime. There had been many years growing up when there had been want and unemployment and so much insecurity across the country during the Great Depression. Then there had been World War II and the terrible price so many families had paid. But the Depression and the war were over and Sonny marveled at the sense of security that settled upon the land. He felt a sense of supreme confidence that he would work his entire career on the Boston Fire Department until he and Anne could live out a peaceful, happy retirement—maybe on Cape Cod or somewhere else near the ocean.

Sonny truly appreciated his many blessings. On weekends, sometimes Pops came over, and they would sit out on the back porch of the house on Gurnsey Street—a brown stucco with five-room apartments on the first and second floors—and drink a can of beer and talk about the kids or the fire department. Pops was delighted with what Sonny had achieved, and Sonny derived real satisfaction from his father's pride and pleasure, for Sonny knew what Pops had been through in his life. Now Pops was part of Sonny's family, part of a warm, loving clan. Pops could dote on his grandchildren, who loved to frolic with him. And Pops was proud of Sonny, watching his devotion to his boys—to us. And we looked up to Sonny as sons do, believing our father was the biggest and strongest and greatest. No one could tell a story like Sonny, and each night he was home from the firehouse we would plead with him to tell us a Smokey and Joe story.

Smokey and Joe were veteran firefighters, actually characters of Sonny's imagination, who faced the most daunting fires and rescues and always summoned the courage and skill to save the day. At night, after Patrick was born and Pat and Tom were in one room and Mike and I in the other, Sonny used to wait until all of the lights upstairs were off, and then he would sit in the hallway between the two rooms and spin out a magical yarn. A hush would fall over our bedrooms as we lay snug in our beds, listening to Sonny's soothing voice in the dark.

"One night very late—after midnight when the city was asleep—fire broke out in a warehouse on the waterfront," Sonny began, his voice soft. Then he continued:

Smokey and Joe responded with the rescue company and found a small fire that looked like it would be controlled very easily. On the waterfront that night, there was a full moon and the yellow light of the moon reflected off the water.

"Let's go," Joe said, leading the way into the warehouse as he always led the way. Joe was always itching to get into a fire, and Smokey knew it was his job to be the careful one. That's why everybody thought they were such a good team—because they were so different.

Smokey and Joe wanted to make sure there were no people inside, and they also wanted to get as close to the source of the fire as possible to put it out. They knew that the danger was in letting a small fire get up a head of steam. They knew from experience how quickly a fire could get out of control.

They had gone a long way into the warehouse and were about to turn and head back outside, when all of a sudden black smoke began filling the place. The tar from the timbers on the wharf created a thick smoke—so thick that you could see almost nothing.

It took only a split second, but suddenly Smokey and Joe were separated. That was the way in fires—inside a fire—because unless you've been in there, it was impossible to know how fast conditions could change. Smokey and Joe knew and had experienced it many times, but still it was a frightening experience to be disoriented inside a burning building.

Joe found himself moving along a narrow area that seemed like a maze. He felt his way along as the smoke thickened around him and he could feel the intensity of the heat. He turned and began moving in a different direction and then changed directions again, trying to move away from the heat source. He soon realized he was lost—the worst feeling for a firefighter. He did not panic—Smokey and Joe never panicked. But he was close to it. He was worried that he might not get out; might not be able to find his way.

Joe kept searching and searching trying to find some sign that would guide him. And then he prayed. With the smoke getting thicker and the fire getting hotter, Joe asked for God's help.

And it was then that he felt a hand on his shoulder—it was a firm, steady hand and before he turned around he knew it was the hand of his trusty partner Smokey. When Joe turned, Smokey nodded for Joe to follow and Joe did so, and Smokey moved through the burning structure, and soon they were outside in the sweet night air and there was the harbor and the moonlight. There were squads of firefighters on the exterior quickly bringing the fire under control so Smokey and Joe weren't needed just then. Smokey could see Joe's hands trembling, so Smokey fished a pack of Luckies out of his shirt pocket and handed one to Joe and lit one up for himself. They stood watching the fire as they smoked, but neither said anything for a while. Joe thought about what happened and he realized for the hundredth time maybe that Smokey always knew where he was in a fire. Smokey always knew where everybody was. How many times had Smokey found guys who were in trouble and led them to safety as though it was nothing at all? He couldn't even count the times. There was something inside Smokey—some inner system that allowed him to keep track of everyone. Kind of a sixth sense.

"So, listen," Joe started to say, but Smokey patted him on the shoulder and got back to work.

It was not until some years later that I realized there was a pattern in all the Smokey and Joe stories. They were stories of small moments, yet moments infused with drama. They were not stories of heroic rescues, not the hyperbolic once-in-a-lifetime events; these stories were more prosaic. In telling us about Smokey and Joe, Sonny was telling us about how it really was, about his life as a firefighter. And I realized that most of the stories were about danger posed to firefighters, not civilians. Firefighters were, after all, the ones who raced *into* burning buildings. Civilians had sense enough to get out, but it was a firefighter's job to get inside there and rescue people or find the source of the blaze and extinguish it.

I came to realize that Sonny was represented by the character Smokey—that Sonny was the responsible one, the one with a knack, a genius, even, of keeping track of everybody at a fire and knowing when someone was in trouble. How many times had Sonny found a stray firefighter and led him to safety? How many times had Sonny quietly been responsible for preventing someone from getting hurt? Saved a life? There was a modesty about Sonny, a humbleness that was revealed in the Smokey and Joe stories during those hushed nights at home. He was telling us stories that thrilled us—but he was also telling us about himself.

The culture of second jobs pervaded the fire department. Off duty, firefighters worked as carpenters, painters, roofers, window washers, bricklayers, plumbers, electricians, funeral directors, bartenders. There was even a firefighter who was a podiatrist—or claimed to be (Sonny took me to this man's home in Mattapan where, in his cellar, he performed minor foot surgery on me). Sonny and his firefighter pal Nelson Pittman found work on large industrial jobs, painting warehouses or other commercial structures. This involved operating the staging, which was sometimes seven and eight stories above the street. Sonny and Nelson worked for Louie Millburn every weekday they were not on duty in the firehouse. The practical result of this was that Sonny and Nelson were together six or seven days a week and at least a couple of nights, as well.

There were times Louie sent them out to Worcester or even Springfield on a job. One summer, Sonny and Nelson used their vacation time to paint an eight-story cold-storage building in Springfield. The deal was that they would work a nine-hour day but get paid for ten. In addition, as was usually the case, they were paid a premium of an extra twenty-five cents an hour for any work over the second floor. Louie put them up in the Charles Hotel in Springfield. This was a novelty, because neither Sonny nor Nelson were accustomed to comfortable hotel living. When Sonny returned from Springfield, he handed Anne a fat roll of cash.

In 1956, Patrick, the fourth Kenney boy, was born, joining me, Michael, and Tom. By this point, Sonny and Anne had put aside enough money so that they were ready to buy a single-family home. Their savings, combined with a small profit on the sale of the Gurnsey Street house, enabled them to buy a brand-new home on a quiet, dead-end street in the West Roxbury neighborhood of Boston. Heading away from the central city, West Roxbury was a sprawling residential area just beyond Roslindale. The neighborhood, part of the building boom of the 1950s, was becoming a haven for Boston police, firefighters, and other city workers, as well as employees of the telephone, gas, and electric companies. It was a pleasant, safe community with spacious ball fields and affordable real estate. The neighborhood was mostly single-family homes, a few rather grand and expensive, but most of modest size with small yards. The properties were well kept, and there was a one-story commercial district running about half a mile along Centre Street, with a selection of bakeries, convenience stores, pubs, a jeweler, and other businesses.

Sonny and Anne bought a three-bedroom colonial with a half acre of land at 27 Wedgemere Road, a short, dead-end street about two-thirds of a mile from St. Theresa's Church. Ours—barn red with black shutters—was the last house on the road. It was a simple house, but perfect for our family at the time. There was a small front yard, but the side yard was big enough to throw a baseball back and forth. Beyond the open grassy area was a stand of trees, hardwoods mostly.

Approaching the house from Wedgemere, there was a driveway on the right, and just past it, the side entrance, the door we always used. Through this door was our modest-sized kitchen, with an imitation walnut table against the rear windows looking out on the backyard. Next to the kitchen was the dining room, and at the front of the house, the living room. Upstairs were a full bathroom and three bedrooms: a large one at the back of the house, a good-sized master bedroom to the side, and a very small bedroom at the front. When we first moved in with two parents and four boys, the place was ideal—two people to each bedroom. But with the later addition of two more boys, the space seemed to shrink dramatically.

This was where our lives unfolded for the better part of the next three decades, where the story of the Kenney family was staged. Over time, the fresh new look gave way to chips, scratches, the wear of age, the result of six boys growing up and using the house as a playground—a place to play football, hockey, basketball, a place to wrestle and chase one another.

When we first moved in, there were only two other houses on the street, and both were occupied by firefighters. West Roxbury was a world of municipal workers, of Irish and Italian Americans, large families and perhaps above all, Catholicism. St. Theresa's Church and the parish school were at the center of the community. Catholic families sending their children to Boston public schools rather than St. Theresa's were considered a bit odd. St. Theresa's sprawling complex of church and school lay at the epicenter of life. On Sunday mornings, there were five or six masses, and most were filled to capacity. Mothers were active in parish women's group such as the Theresians, men in the Knights of Columbus. The priests who said our masses, heard confessions on Saturday afternoons, and administered the sacraments were men of unquestioned authority and vaunted standing in the community. They represented God on earth. The nuns who taught at St. Theresa's School—a brand-new tan-brick box of a building containing twenty-four classrooms and a cafeteria—were deemed saintly and revered throughout the community. The nuns were Sisters of Saint Joseph, an order founded centuries earlier in France. They wore elaborate black head-to-ankle habits with curved, heavily starched white bibs above their breasts. Their heads were covered with a tightly fitting starched white cap, draped over the sides in black, and they all had large rosaries around their waists, dangling down the sides of their long habits. Winning favor with the nuns was a competitive activity. Many children in primary grades would arrive early at school to line up outside the convent, hoping to be chosen by one of the nuns to carry her heavy black briefcase the 100 or so feet from the convent to the school and then perhaps all the way inside to her classroom.

The children in grades one through eight wore identical uniforms—maroon jumpers and white blouses with Peter Pan collars for the girls, dark slacks with a white dress shirt and maroon tie with the school logo ("STS") on it for the boys. Every classroom was identical: Desks were arranged in five rows of ten, with fifty children per classroom, a 50 to 1 student–teacher ratio. Children were seated in alphabetical order. There was no talking at any time except recess. Children were permitted to leave their desks to go to another class, lunch, the bathroom, recess, or one of the frequent air-raid drills staged to prepare for a Russian ICBM assault.

In the small society of West Roxbury, there was rarely a thought about the world beyond, unless it concerned a relative in the old country or the Red Menace. Everybody was Irish or Italian, except for the odd Lithuanian here and there—an object of curiosity and sometimes ridicule. There were no people of any color except white, and few non-Christians. There was nobody with an accent, unless it was an Irish brogue—and then there was reverence.

Our family's universe was a few square miles that included church and school, a couple of ball fields, a skating pond in winter, and our friends, who typically lived a few houses or streets away.

As much as we were all defined by the church, Sonny was also defined by the Boston Fire Department: In the department he found his identity, his definition of himself, his confidence, self-esteem, and passion. The firehouse was Sonny's home away from home. He felt a sense of comfort there, a sense of family and security that was rare in any job. He would arrive for work—whether a night or day shift—and invariably hang around the firehouse kitchen, where his friends and co-workers had coffee and cigarettes and checked in with one another. The men exchanged stories and updates about their kids and wives, about outside jobs, about their lives. After catching up for a while, they typically checked their equipment, particularly their masks. Sonny and the other rescue men habitually ran a quick inventory of the rescue wagon's equipment to make sure all was in working order. Everyone pitched in to keep the firehouse clean. Some men swept up, while others polished brass, washed windows, scrubbed the bathrooms. At mealtime they often pooled their money to buy groceries, preparing meals in the kitchen. There were dinners of franks and baked beans, spaghetti and meatballs, steak tips, and salads.

There was a collegiality that characterized life in the firehouse—a bond, a closeness derived from their interdependence. It was the rare profession where each man depended for his safety and survival on every other man and everyone recognized that reality as the foundation of their commitment to the job. Anyone who didn't accept that basic tenet washed out of the job quickly. This fundamental belief in the cooperative commitment of each man—the rock-solid knowledge that they were there for each other no matter what—was akin to religious doctrine for these men. The bond was evident not only in a burning building but in the firehouse kitchen as well, where the connectedness, and the contentedness each man brought to the work, was so evident.

It was not the least surprising that Sonny's closest friends and neighbors were firefighters and that the culture permeated our lives, our home. The only two permanent fixtures atop our kitchen table were a large red fire-department alarm box that Pops had turned into a lamp, and a multichannel public safety scanner tuned to the Boston Fire Department. When a box was struck—when the beep-beep-beep signals were sent out—a hush would fall over the kitchen as Sonny cocked his head, the better to hear the box number. No one dared move or make a sound when the signal was coming through. We sat in silence as we listened to a single tap, then two, then five, then one. "Box 1251," Sonny would announce. "Richmond and Commercial Streets." This would happen repeatedly throughout the evening, with Sonny offering to give anyone who wanted to listen a detailed description of the box location and the surrounding area, and speculation about the type of fire. He would explain whether it was a commercial or residential area with wood-frame buildings or brick. He would note whether there was a school or hospital nearby and would often recall from personal experience a fire he had been to in that area.

Each Sunday morning, our family headed down to St. Theresa's for the family mass at 9:00 AM, and if we were well behaved, there would be doughnuts afterward.

"Shoulders back," Sonny would say as we popped out of the Ford station wagon in the church parking lot. "Stand up straight and shoulders back." We would stand up straight, try to thrust our shoulders back, and pause briefly at the entrance to the church as Sonny would drop his Lucky Strike butt to the pavement and grind it under the sole of his shoe.

And so the snapshot of the "ideal" life had a pretty, freckle-faced wife standing smiling with her four boys, all of whom were standing straight, shoulders back, in front of a nice new colonial on a quiet, leafy street. In a collage, there would be a fire department logo, a church steeple, a friend or two.

Once a year or so, hundreds of Boston firefighters donned their dress blues and boarded the train for New York City for the ostensible purpose of attending a communion breakfast. This was a trip Sonny thoroughly enjoyed. It was an opportunity to travel—which he rarely got—and a chance to get away from the routine and a house full of often overly energetic little boys. In 1959, Sonny rode the train down the coast from Boston into New York's Pennsylvania Station. He arrived Friday afternoon, and with the communion breakfast scheduled for Sunday morning after mass, there was plenty of time to socialize and enjoy himself. The men from Boston divided up into scores of groups and moved from one pub to another, mostly in Manhattan but also in several of the boroughs. Sonny visited a few firehouses and talked with some of the men. He walked through Manhattan, gazing up at the skyscrapers, thinking how difficult it would be to fight a blaze in the upper floors of the Empire State Building, for example.

Before heading to New York, Sonny had heard that Dotty Myles was performing in a place called the New Studio Club in Mount Vernon, New York, a town about fifteen miles outside the city. Sonny had not seen Dotty in almost a decade, although he had received regular information about her from his mother. Molly and Dotty's mother had stayed in touch through cards and letters after Dotty's surgeries were completed in Boston and Dotty and her mother had returned to New York. Sonny knew that Dotty had made progress medically— that the reconstructive surgery had restored some of her lost beauty. Sonny had also heard from his mother that while in Boston, Dotty had secretly married a technician from one of the radio stations where she had been singing. Sonny had also heard that the marriage was brief, yet after returning to New York, Dotty had given birth to a daughter. Early Saturday evening, Sonny found his way to the New

Studio Club, a swanky spot with upholstered banquettes and small tables. He arrived around six o'clock and found the place nearly empty, but there, sitting at the end of the bar, was Dotty. Sonny went over to her and was struck by how different she looked than the last time he had seen her. Had he not been aware of her scars and burns, Sonny would never have guessed Dotty had been in a fire. Her skin looked fairly smooth, almost normal, and she struck him as quite sophisticated and beautiful. She looked striking in an evening gown.

Dotty was thrilled to see him. She insisted he sit down and join her for a drink. She asked all about what he had been doing, wanted to hear about his wife and sons, and where he was living, and the job—everything. She probed about Pops and Molly, and asked about Sonny's little sister, Audrey, and brother, Dan. Sonny asked about her career, and she told him she'd been performing at various clubs in and around New York. As they sat there chatting in the early evening, Sonny was surprised at how much Dotty was drinking. It was hours before she was supposed to perform. Dotty told him she had recently cracked up her car driving home from the club late one night. There was a dinner that night as part of the firefighters' trip, so after an hour or so, Sonny bid Dotty good-bye and headed back into New York. It was the last time he ever saw Dotty Myles.

It was March 7, 1959. The late afternoon was raw and cold, the sky gunmetal gray, when Sonny left Wedgemere Road and drove to Roslindale to see his mother. Sonny had a gift for her—she turned fifty-eight that day—and he stopped off briefly to deliver it and wish her happy birthday. Then he headed to the firehouse.

When Sonny arrived, he ran into Bill Shea, who was assigned to Ladder 24. The Massachusetts General Hospital was just a quarter mile down Cambridge Street from Bowdoin Square, and Ladder 24 was kept in the general vicinity in case of an emergency at the hospital. Bill Shea was relatively new on the job, and decades later he would vividly recall how he looked up to more experienced firefighters like Sonny. Bill thought of Sonny and the other men assigned to the Rescue as "the real jakes," and Bill marveled at the number of runs the Rescue would make. Bill felt a bit of envy as well, wanting to be like the rescue men, whom he considered to be the "big shots" in the house. He had watched as the Rescue roared out the door day and night, sometimes continuously, responding to the worst fires and accidents all across the city. Bill aspired to be like the rescue men—to be one of them, in fact. Sonny liked Bill and thought he was an excellent ladder man. Bill was always upbeat and positive, and Sonny enjoyed being around him.

It was a quiet evening. The engine and ladder companies sat idle throughout much of the night. The Lighting Plant and Tower 1 were quiet as well. Sonny headed up to the bunk room well before midnight and went to sleep. He had brought a crabmeat salad sandwich from home, one of his favorites, which he planned to eat later. Sonny woke about 3:30 AM. Hungry, he headed down to the kitchen for hot cocoa and his sandwich. From where he sat in the kitchen, toward the rear of the house, Sonny could hear the man on the patrol desk at the front of the building. It was nearly 4:00 AM when he heard a long ring on the patrol desk phone, indicating a call coming in from Boston Fire Alarm, the nerve center of the city's alarm system. It signaled that at least some of the companies in the house were about to move. The man on desk patrol answered the phone, listened for a brief moment, then hit a switch illuminating every light in the house. A split second later, he hit the house alarm, summoning the men. As they slid the poles and threw on their gear, Sonny jumped up from the table, leaving his crabmeat and cocoa behind, and ran for Rescue 3.

Cornhill Street, which ran through the heart of the city, had witnessed some of the fiercest fires in Boston history. In 1711, fire broke out on Cornhill and eventually destroyed more than 100 stores, homes, and warehouses. At the time, the city was so densely packed with wooden structures that a significant fire could threaten multiple blocks. Fires in this area in the early days of Boston were such a problem that the Massachusetts legislature insisted that all new construction rely on stone or brick, not wood, but the expense of those materials rendered the law unenforceable. Cornhill was the site of another disastrous fire in 1760, when more than 300 commercial and residential buildings were destroyed. Remarkably, no one was killed. After this epic event, the city was divided into fire districts. Among the men in charge of the districts were John Hancock and Samuel Adams. Abolitionist William Lloyd Garrison published his famous newspaper, *The Liberator,* out of offices on Cornhill Street, starting in the 1830s.

One of the most devastating fires in Boston's history had started only a few blocks from Cornhill Street. The Great Fire of 1872—nearly seventy years to the day before the Cocoanut Grove—burned more than sixty acres of the city and in the process destroyed an astounding 776 structures. Seventeen hundred firefighters from as far away as New Haven and Providence battled the blaze. In an eerie parallel to the Cocoanut Grove fire, the official department investigation concluded that "no answer could be made," concerning the cause of the fire.

Box 1262, the source of the alarm, was in a dense downtown area of the city, an area requiring a significant response to any sizable fire. While sirens wailed and trucks roared from the bays at Bowdoin Square, down on Hanover Street in the North End, Engine 8 and Ladder 1 were on the move, as was Engine 10 from Mount Vernon Street on the other side of Beacon Hill. When a box was struck in this area, three engine and two ladder companies would converge from different houses in a kind of pincers movement. Also responding from Bowdoin Square was the district fire chief to direct operations at the scene.

Rescue 3 pulled out of the house, with Sonny, Nelson, and Tom Callahan in the back, and turned right on Cambridge Street, then proceeded three blocks and took a sharp left onto Cornhill Street, which ran from Cambridge back to Haymarket. This location was only a matter of a few blocks from Boston Common. On a run such as this, Sonny had learned, you could never be sure what was out there. It could be anything from nothing to a three-alarm inferno.

The Rescue arrived thirty seconds or so after the engine and ladder companies from Bowdoin Square, and when Sonny pulled in, he could see smoke showing from the second floor of a six-story office building that faced Cornhill Street and backed up to Brattle Street. Someone from Ladder 24 was opening the front door with his ax, gaining rapid entry. As this happened, the tillerman was headed up over the stick to ventilate the roof. Other men from the ladder company were throwing ground ladders to the third floor. Simultaneously, Salvi Castranova from the engine company was entering the front door with a booster line, intent on finding the source of the fire.

Sonny and fellow rescue man Tom Callahan followed Salvi inside and up the stairs to the second floor. The fire was intense enough so that Salvi called for a bigger hose line. Often in these old buildings there was some elderly gent who worked as a night watchman, and Sonny wanted to make sure they conducted a thorough search just in case. There had been countless instances where the Rescue had responded to a warehouse or office building fire and found an old-timer sprawled unconscious, overcome by smoke. The rescue man's rule was always to assume that someone was in the building. Sonny and Tommy quickly searched the first floor, then moved to the second, searched there, then moved up. The smoke on three was heavy enough for both Sonny and Tommy to don their masks.

Theoretically, the path of the fire would be directed by the tillerman and others now on the roof hacking open a ventilation hole, which would draw the fire upward in a predictable path, and predictability was crucial to the safety of the men inside the building.

In the street, the men of Ladder 24 were throwing ground ladders and the aerial against the building. Marty Nee was about to ascend a ground ladder to the third floor when Bill Shea said, "I've got my mask on, I'll go." When he reached the top of the ladder at a third-floor window, Bill did something he had done only once before in his time as a ladder man—he dogged the ladder, that is, he chained the ladder to the windowsill, securing it with a spike pounded into the wooden sill. Dogging a ladder was theoretically standard practice, but it was routinely ignored by many ladder men rushing to enter a building. Why Bill Shea did it this night and not hundreds of others, he's not sure.

Inside, Bill encountered dense smoke and limited visibility. Across the room he saw two wheat lights, or safety lights, coming through the smoke: It was Sonny and Tom Callahan. Sonny and Tom went from the hallway into a conference room and encountered Bill Shea. As Bill approached, he looked over Sonny's shoulder and shouted, "Jesus!" with a look of alarm spreading across his face. Sonny and Tom turned and saw a massive fireball roaring down the third-floor hallway. Tommy Callahan slammed the conference room door shut and dropped his Halligan against the door to brace it, but the fire blew the door open. Somewhere in the back of his mind Sonny thought, *This doesn't make sense—the fire should be moving* up *not across; it should follow a funnel of oxygen drafting from the roof.* The conference room walls were solid until about two feet below the ceiling, where there were glass panels. The fire shattered the glass panels and lunged into the room over the top of the walls, and Sonny saw streaks of flame flash across the top of the partition over their heads. He reached up to pull his helmet tighter, and his hands were burned by the superheated air. He could feel the flames burning the part of his face near his ears, an area exposed by his mask.

"This is it," Sonny said. "Let's go."

The three men made for the window that Bill Shea had used to enter the building. They looked down and saw a massive sheet of flame shooting out of the building from the second floor. It was thirty feet down to the street, but getting there meant having to pass through a sheet of flame so thick and intense it looked like an extension of the building, an abutment of sorts.

The ladder Bill Shea had used to get into the building was set outside the window, which had been blown apart by the fire. But the ladder was securely in place because Bill had dogged it. Tommy Callahan went first, spreading his legs as though on a seesaw, jumping onto the ladder, and grasping the beams with his hands as he slid all the way down in a couple of seconds, flashing through the sheet of flame, his rubber coat burning as he descended.

Sonny went next. He quickly decided to step out as far away from the building as he could to possibly get beyond the most intense flames. As he jumped from the windowsill toward the ladder, his foot landed on the second rung of the ladder and in the intense heat of the flame, the rung gave way. Bill Shea watched from above as Sonny disappeared into the flames and smoke. Sonny pitched forward past the ladder, falling headfirst toward the street, his momentum carrying him through a full somersault as he plunged downward, feeling parts of his body burning. Other firefighters saw this and thought, "Jesus, God, he's dead." And if he had landed on his head, he would surely have been killed or brain damaged or paralyzed. But as he fell, the large square battery of his safety light—his wheat light—shifted on his belt from the side to the square of his back as he landed in the street. He lay on the ground and watched as Bill Shea came out of the building, aflame. Once Shea slid down the ladder, men immediately doused him with water.

Bill Kelleher, Sonny's next-door neighbor on Wedgemere Road, was riding Ladder 30, heading downtown from Egleston Square. As he rode into town, Bill could see flames from the Cornhill Street fire against the night sky.

7

"My Son Is an Honorable Boy"

Tom was a gangly five-year-old, tall for his age and bony thin. The third son, he possessed Sonny's narrow face and jet-black hair. Though quiet and reserved, Tom was keenly observant. When Sonny came home from working in the firehouse, Tom used to follow him around the house, studying the distinctive way Sonny packed up his dirty work clothes after a fire. Sonny took off his dungarees and tied off the bottom of each leg, then stuffed his underwear, socks, and sweatshirts into the legs; sometimes the dungarees would get so full that it looked like the bottom half of a person.

Tom would watch as Sonny tossed the dungarees down the cellar stairs, where Anne would pick them up and launder them. But what Tom noticed most was the intense smell of smoke coming from Sonny's clothes. After a fire, Sonny always showered at the firehouse and put on fresh pants and shirt, but the smoke permeated his work clothes, clinging to the fabric long afterward. Tom, always curious about the fire that had produced the smell, would ask Sonny about it and listen intently as Sonny explained what had happened.

Tom was fascinated by Sonny's stories, and while the other boys focused on sports, Tom's focus was on the fire department and its shiny red engines, its ladder trucks, its treasure boxes of tools that Sonny showed him. Somehow, at age five, Tom could see his future. He knew then that he wanted to be like his dad and his grandfathers: He wanted to be a fireman.

We four boys were all watching cartoons early one Sunday morning, clustered together in the living room in front of the small box with its black-and-white picture tube, watching maybe the *Little Rascals* or *Superman* or even the *Lone Ranger*. I was eight, Mike was seven, Tom, five, and Pat, four. Patrick—the free spirit—was naked, but the rest of us had on pajamas. It was not much past 7:00 AM when we heard a knock at the front door, and there stood the commissioner of the Boston Fire Department, Timothy O'Connor, dressed in a magnificent black uniform, with white shirt and gold trim on his hat and coat. He stood there with his driver, and beyond them, parked in front of the house, was a big shiny red car with BFD 1 on the side, the commissioner's car in all its magnificence. We gathered around the door as I opened it and greeted him. He smiled and spoke to us in a friendly way. We were thunderstruck when he handed each one of us a brand-new silver dollar. He asked me to go and get our mother, and I ran upstairs and woke her up, telling her who was here. When she came rushing down the stairs, still throwing her robe on, I could see that she was pale and frightened. She sent us all upstairs so she could talk with the commissioner in private.

———

Sonny lay on the frigid pavement, pain shooting up his lower back, pain clawing at the burning skin on his hands and the sides of his face. He was conscious, though barely. He tried to call to someone that Bill Shea was coming down. He half saw Shea come down over the ladder, in flames, and saw someone from the engine company hitting Shea immediately with a powerful stream of water to kill the flames. And then Sonny was carried off by two men and loaded into the back of a paddy wagon. They rushed him to Massachusetts General Hospital, half a mile down Cambridge Street toward the Charles River. He was wheeled into the hospital emergency room at approximately 4:30 AM on March 8, 1959, and he blacked out almost immediately. He was placed on the danger list, and his condition was serious enough that in the ER, Sonny received the last rites of the Catholic Church twice—once from a local priest and again from the BFD chaplain.

Sonny had sustained second- and third-degree burns on his hands and the sides of his face, particularly along the patch of skin below his sideburns. Much worse, however, was the damage to his lower back, where he had suffered compression fractures to all five lumbar vertebrae. It was extremely painful, and no one knew what the precise impact would be on his mobility and quality of life.

The medical staff put tubes down Sonny's nose and throat, and he lay unconscious for several days. Anne, at the hospital on Sunday morning, was shocked by his gray pallor and unresponsiveness. His hands were heavily bandaged in bright white wraps, as were the sides of his face and his ear. He awoke in a large, airy ward. Bill Shea and Tom Callahan were in beds nearby, both, like Sonny, heavily wrapped in white gauze around their hands and faces. Since they could not use their hands, all three men were spoon fed by nurses.

In the weeks after the fire, the three men talked quietly about what had happened. Sonny had no doubt that if they had stayed in the building another few seconds, they would have burned to death. Although they had all suffered serious injuries bailing out in the way they had, they had also saved their own lives.

As Sonny lay in bed trying to regain some strength, he wondered why the fire behaved as it had. He had had a number of firefighters visit from Bowdoin Square, of course, and had learned that several men from the ladder company had gotten to the roof and ventilated it. That meant the fire should have been moving up, not across. Still, he knew it was never entirely predictable. Yet Sonny could not help but feel there had been some breach in the building somewhere that had caused a draft that drew the fire across rather than up. As he thought about it, he realized it was the sort of mystery his father had so often spoken of concerning the Cocoanut Grove. He started wondering what had caused the Grove fire to move so swiftly. He found it amazing and bothersome that now, after seventeen years, no one had solved the mystery about that fire. But as he lay there at Mass General, he also realized that scores of victims from the Grove had been taken to this very hospital, and might even have lain in this very ward. He also knew that the techniques being used to treat him had been pioneered at this hospital on burn victims from the Grove.

A few weeks after they were admitted to the hospital, Sonny, Bill Shea, and Tom Callahan were wheeled down to an operating room, where skin was grafted from other parts of their bodies and moved to cover burned areas on their hands, faces, and ears. Sonny lay on a gurney in the hallway waiting while Bill Shea remained in surgery for four hours; then Tom Callahan went in for three hours. Finally, it was Sonny's turn. Several hours after the operation, he woke up in recovery, his hands rewrapped, with skin grafts from his legs on his hands.

Pops came in and sat on the edge of the bed, and they talked about the Cornhill Street fire. Sonny explained precisely what had happened, and Pops, like Sonny, found it a bit mystifying. "Why would that have happened?" Pops wondered aloud. But Sonny had no explanation.

After a couple of weeks in the hospital, Sonny was talking with one of the doctors about his recovery. He raised the issue of when he would be going back to work. The doctor dismissed the idea out of hand.

"You're not going back to work," he told Sonny. *Not on the fire department; not with a broken back.*

Sonny was shocked. He did not know what to say. He found himself literally speechless. *My God,* he thought. *What is he talking about? How can that be?* Sonny was weeks shy of his thirty-fourth birthday. He had a career on the Boston Fire Department that ought to last another thirty years. What was the doctor talking about?

———

After more than a month in the hospital, Sonny was released. He was given a treatment plan that called for three sessions of physical therapy per week for approximately one year, and was to undergo monthly examinations by the Boston Fire Department physician. As time went by, it gradually sank in that Sonny really would not be going back to work on the fire department. He hadn't really believed the doctor, and the notion was so shocking that it was difficult to absorb. Firefighting was not merely a job, it was Sonny's identity: It was his definition of who he was. He felt fortunate to be alive, not to have been paralyzed in the fall, but as the year of physical therapy progressed, he felt increasingly uncertain and disoriented. What was happening to him? What would happen with his life? What would he do?

On June 1, 1960—fifteen months after the fire on Cornhill Street—it became official: Sonny was formally pensioned from the Boston Fire Department. His name was moved from the roster of active firefighters to the rolls of retirees. On the list of retirees, his name was next to his father's.

The Eighty-First Annual Concert and Ball of the Boston Fire Department was held at the Boston Garden on the evening of April 25, 1960. It was a hugely popular event, and only the largest gathering place in town could handle the crowd—firefighters and their wives, along with politicians and thousands of others wishing to pay tribute to the city's fire service. Sonny saw that the program contained a page with the headline: "Firefighting Is a Hazardous Profession." Beneath the headline were six photographs that formed a "word-picture story of a fire: 4:22 AM—Sunday—March 8, 1959—Box 1262—4 alarms." The first picture was of heavy fire showing, then an overwhelming mass of flame shooting out of the building and over the street. Then there was a photograph of Tommy Callahan, Bill Shea, and Sonny himself, lying in their Mass General Hospital beds, heavily bandaged, Sonny with tubes running through his nose. The caption read: "These men were severely burned and barely escaped with their lives from the third floor over the ladder pictured below." A photo of the ladder—bent and broken—was captioned: "Burned rungs are mute evidence of heat and flames from which men escaped."

Weeks later, the guys at Bowdoin Square cleared the apparatus out of a couple of bays and got other companies to cover for them. On a steamy summer night in 1960, Sonny went downtown believing he was headed to dinner and a movie with Anne and two friends, but there was a last-minute detour into Bowdoin Square. When Sonny walked into the firehouse, the men were there to greet him, applauding him as he walked in the door, a bit stunned by it all: A surprise retirement party.

There was Nelson Pittman and Harold Matulitis and Dan Moynihan and Marty Pierce. There was Sonny's captain, George Comfrey, and his lieutenant, Tom Feeney. Bill Shea and Tom Callahan, both of whom were back on the job, were there as well. And, of course, there was Pops, smiling broadly. Wooden folding tables had been set out in the bay reserved for the rescue company, and there was food and plenty of beer. Marty Pierce, who would go on to become the secretary of the International Association of Firefighters, and whose son would one day become the fire commissioner in Boston, was the master of ceremonies. He stood and spoke of Sonny and his career in nearly reverential tones. Nelson got up and spoke briefly, though he was painfully shy. But this was about his partner, the man he had worked with side by side, with whom he had entrusted his life on many occasions. Bill Shea and Tom Callahan spoke, as did others. Sonny sat at the center of the head table, flanked by Marty Pierce on one side and Pops on the other. The black-and-white photographs from that evening are a fascinating study, for they show something other than a raucous bunch of firemen swilling beer on a night off. Rather, each photo reveals men with serious expressions. There are few smiles, though there were some good laughs that night. The photographs capture the essence of the evening: a serious time with somber moments, a send-off of a friend and colleague, a forced retirement, a painful passage, a moment of sadness for these men.

Nobody knew it at the time, but it would not be long before this grand building would be retired as well. The Bowdoin Square firehouse was in operation from 1930 until 1962, when the building was razed in the name of urban renewal. Sonny was one of the 280 men who served there during that period. Of those, six died in the line of duty and dozens were permanently injured. The Big House produced great firemen and strong leaders. Back in 1942, when a small group of men sought to unionize the department, twelve of the sixteen men signing the original union charter were from Bowdoin Square. More than fifty years after he had started there, Sonny said that he was never in his life happier than when he was on Rescue 3.

The evening was a blur. So many men said so many nice, flattering things, things that meant everything to Sonny. They said he had been "a good jake," that he had always been there when another man needed him. They presented him with a beautiful Wittenauer watch and a set of cuff links and a tie clasp adorned with rescue wagons.

It was happening again. Fourteen years earlier, he stood alone outside the Fargo Building on a wintry December day when he mustered out of the navy. He had felt an acute sense of loss back then, and he felt it now, even more sharply than before. He felt the loss of the connection to these men, felt the loss of the bond, the brotherhood. No more would he come into the beautiful building—a building he had come to love—and spend the night with his friends. No more racing to the pole, to the jarring sound of the house gong, and careening out the door in the rescue wagon. Toasts were offered, glasses raised in tribute to Sonny, and he was deeply moved by it all. It was not that it meant something to him. It meant *everything*—the respect and affection of these great men. He was losing something that felt like part of his soul, something that was from the core of who he was. He was thirty-four years old, and he had been blessed with a life he had considered "ideal." He thanked God that he was alive and that he was not paralyzed, and he thanked God for what he had in life—for his wife and his boys. But underneath it all, he suffered. He had lost his best friend in the war, lost his affiliation with the U.S. Navy, lost an opportunity to go to Boston College, and now this. And he realized, as he sat there next to his father, that what had happened to the father was now happening to the son.

The personnel people had been nice down at headquarters, explaining his retirement pay and benefits. He would receive 72 percent of his previous year's pay, which had been $5,500, in an annual pension payment, and as a disabled firefighter this would not be subject to income tax. In addition, he would receive an annual allowance of $312 for each dependent child under eighteen years of age (this would not cover subsequent children).

One evening that summer, Sonny was sitting out on a lawn chair in the front yard reading the paper. In the soft warmth of dusk, he was enjoying a cigarette and a beer when he saw old John Hernan strolling down Wedgemere Road. John was a Welshman with a thick accent who had worked on Ladder 8 in Fort Hill Square. John lived a few blocks from Sonny and had been at the Cornhill Street fire, in fact. John was a gruff character, short and stocky with a particular eccentricity: He almost never spoke. It was not that he disliked anyone in particular, it was just that he simply did not speak unless he absolutely had to and then it was in monosyllables. But he had always been a very good and reliable firefighter and was thus widely respected within the department. Sonny saw that John was out for a stroll with his nephew, young Father Burke. Sonny set his paper aside and went over to greet John, unsure if John would even say anything. But this was a dead-end street and our house was at the end. John Hernan had come down Wedgemere Road for a reason.

When John and Father Burke stopped, Sonny and the priest fell into talking and when there was a lull in the conversation, John Hernan looked into Sonny's eyes and said, "It's a damned shame what that dumb bastard did." John spoke of the second-floor bursting into flame underneath Sonny, Bill Shea, and Tommy Callahan. And it had happened because a firefighter on the back of the building—on the Brattle Street side where John Hernan had been—had shattered a plate-glass window on the second floor, creating a cross draft that had fueled the fire. It had been a mistake, and it had caused the blowout that injured Sonny and the other two men.

Sonny stood, his heart beating, waiting to see whether John would identify the man—and he did. He spoke the man's name to Sonny, and now Sonny knew what had happened and he knew who had caused it. Sonny knew the man and liked him, and he knew the man was a good firefighter. But he had made a bad mistake. Then Sonny did what he thought was the right thing: He tucked the man's name away in the back of his head and never revealed it to anyone.

———

Sonny was walking in the neighborhood one day when he passed by a home for the elderly and ran into a couple of guys he knew who worked for a fire equipment company. Their assignment had been to go through the building and provide a fresh charge to all of the extinguishers to make sure they would work in an emergency. What they had done instead, however, was go through the building, rip the old cardboard tags off the extinguishers, and replace them with new, updated tags, making it appear that the extinguishers had been recharged that day, though they had not. The two men laughed about it to Sonny. "Couldn't be easier," they said. "Rip the old tags off, put the new ones on and we're done."

Sonny was stunned. The facility housed 100 elderly residents. If there were a fire and if the extinguishers failed, it would be a catastrophe. *Jesus,* Sonny thought, *that's insane; it's dangerous, and it's just plain wrong.*

As he walked home thinking about what the men had done, Sonny had the answer to what he would do for a living: He would start a company that would sell and service fire prevention equipment. Sonny called Pops and told him the news. "A *business,*" Pops said. "We don't know anything about business." But Sonny said, "We know fire, and we can figure out the rest. We'll be honest. We'll do the best job. Our stuff will work perfectly. We'll make sure of it." Sonny selected a name rich with irony for both Pops and himself: He called the company Firecontrol.

Sonny went to work studying the fire and building codes until he knew them cold. He studied an array of fire-prevention equipment—extinguishers, sprinkler systems, and the like—until he knew it all. He delved into the study of fire, the analysis of its nature and properties. He studied how various fires were most effectively controlled and extinguished. He found a tiny office—about eight by eighteen feet—for $10 a month just off Washington Street near the Forest Hills transit station in Jamaica Plain. Sonny set up a desk and chair in the tiny office, and all alone, he was ready to begin. Sonny was alone in the early stories of fire control, for Pops had traveled to California to spend an extended period of time with Sonny's sister, Audrey, who was going through the breakup of her marriage.

His first step was to contact the Walter Kidde Company in New Jersey, the largest manufacturer of fire extinguishers in the country. He learned that if he sold and serviced Walter Kidde Company extinguishers, the company would supply him with postcards he could send out to prospects, offering a free fire-protection survey. Sonny filled out one card after another. He would open the Yellow Pages on the desk and move through it category by category. He sent postcards to restaurants, factories, laundries—any sort of company that required fire-protection equipment. He mailed out up to 200 cards per week and found that the response ranged from 2 to 3 percent. As the returns came back, the cards indicated that some prospects wanted a free fire-protection survey, whereas others specified that they needed extinguishers recharged. Sonny realized he needed a way to go out and pick up the extinguishers in order to transport them back to his shop to be recharged. He heard of an old panel truck for sale that had been used by a billboard advertising company to carry tanks of paste used to put up huge outdoor sheets of advertising on billboards.

From such a modest beginning, Firecontrol grew steadily throughout the 1960s. After only a few months, Sonny had enough business to hire his pal from Engine 8, Don Flynn. Don would go out in the old paste truck and pick up used extinguishers and bring them back to the shop, where he, Sonny, and Pops would recharge them and get them quickly back into action. Sonny and Pops prided themselves on the quick turnaround. Pops liked to say that the extinguishers were not doing anybody any good sitting in the Firecontrol offices, so as soon as the used ones arrived, they worked feverishly to get them recharged and back out the door. It was not long before Firecontrol had outgrown its space and moved into larger quarters. Sonny hired a couple of additional salesmen, both of whom worked on commission. By this time, he had three trucks out each morning with men going out to recharge extinguishers throughout eastern Massachusetts.

Sonny spent an increasing amount of time going out on the road trying to land large accounts. Typically, when he was working in the shop, Sonny wore coveralls with a Firecontrol logo on the chest. These were uniforms he had made up that were worn by all the servicemen. But for the sort of sales work Sonny was doing on the road, he donned a coat and tie. During the early and mid-1960s, Sonny won business from the Howard Johnson's restaurant chain, the Sheraton Boston and Ritz Hotels, Durgin Park and Dini's Restaurants, the Red Coach Grille, American Telephone and Telegraph, New England Telephone, the U.S. Post Office, the Boston public schools, and Kentucky Fried Chicken of Massachusetts. Firecontrol had become a nice little company.

Sonny did so well one year selling Walter Kidde products that he was rewarded with a weekend trip to New York with hotel, dinner, and a Broadway show—*Hello Dolly* with Carol Channing—all included. One summer evening in the mid-1960s, Sonny and Anne had just returned from a Walter Kidde Company awards dinner. He had been given a brand new shiny brass fire extinguisher as a sales award. He hoisted it up over the kitchen table, turned it upside down, and out tumbled 500 weighty silver dollars. My brothers and I gathered in the kitchen to see the bounty. Our mother sat at one end of the table, beaming. Sonny sat by the open window, smoke from his Lucky Strike drifting out into the summer night. He had worn a tie and jacket to the dinner, but he had unbuttoned the top button and tugged the tie down a few notches. There was a smile of satisfaction on his face as he sat there sipping a drink and listening to our mother tell us all about the award dinner—how there had been a lot of men competing, with smaller prizes given out before the grand prize; how Sonny didn't expect to win it and when they called his name from the stage, he hesitated at first, uncertain whether to believe it. She described him going up to receive the extinguisher—a thing of beauty in itself—and then felt how heavy it was and looked inside to find the money. She told about the MC announcing the total award and everyone clapping and coming over to pat our father on the back and congratulate him.

As a teenager I was mesmerized by all this, by the beautiful, polished extinguisher, by the enormous pile of huge coins on our kitchen table, and I loved my mother's description of the scene at the hotel ballroom. I pictured it in my mind, my parents sitting at a table, my father maybe secretly hoping he would be chosen, though not really believing it. I imagined him being called to the podium amid the ovation, and I wanted desperately to know what that felt like. I wanted to see it, though I knew I had already missed it. I wondered how he had done it. How had he gone out into the world and sold those extinguishers and those sprinkler systems? What did he say to people? What kind of questions did they ask? How was he successful at it? I wondered all of these things and as I did, I realized that I did not know how the world worked, at least not the adult world and certainly not the world of business. But my father knew! And the proof was right there—spread across the kitchen table. As I studied my Dad's face that night, I saw an expression of contentment and happiness that for me, defined him during that period. He was a man with a quiet confidence, a man who had faced adversity and changed his life, and now he had been successful. He had done something special, and I felt like he was a very great man.

The truth was, though, that Sonny had no formal training, and over time it became clear that for all his success in landing new accounts, rarely did revenues exceed expenses by more than a few thousand dollars a year. Firecontrol was a business, but it was also a sort of fraternal organization. Sonny hired only firefighters to work as servicemen, and each workday started over coffee with the firefighters talking about the events of the day or night before in the firehouse. Sonny knew all the men personally, having worked with some of them at Bowdoin Square and even at Egleston Square. Hiring these men—and they were all first-rate firefighters—was a way for Sonny to remain connected to the department, to its culture. Sonny did not mind at all that the company was not profitable. He made a little bit of money from a salary he paid himself (never more than $9,000 a year). He knew, as he put it, that "I was a firefighter who went into business and not a businessman." Each year at tax time, Sonny's accountant characterized the business the same way: "marginal."

But it hardly mattered, for Sonny enjoyed it, particularly the association with his firefighter employees. He loved working with Pops, too, and, in time, a couple of my brothers would join him as well. But best of all, Sonny felt he was doing something positive and constructive. He and Pops were preventing fires, protecting people from their horror.

Sonny had always been more comfortable belonging than not: as a member of the Seminoles, then in the navy, then as a member of the Boston Fire Department. In the early 1960s, he attempted to recapture some of that connection by joining the new Massachusetts chapter of the Submarine Veterans of WW II. Sonny was invited to a meeting down at the South Boston army base, and though the numbers of members in Boston were relatively small, he was delighted to be part of a group of the naval elite. The group would meet to plan a memorial and discuss other ways of commemorating the submarine service. But they would also spend considerable time socializing together, hanging around the Quonset huts at the army base, drinking and telling war stories. At these sessions Sonny would look around at the other men and feel a sense of comfort: *These are men who have been through what I have been through,* he would think. In time, he became state commander of the Massachusetts chapter of submarine vets. He proudly dressed up in a jacket and tie and went off each month to preside over meetings, and then went on to the army base for an evening of drinking with his brothers in arms.

Working at Firecontrol also gave Sonny something he had never before enjoyed—a predictable schedule with plenty of time for his growing family. In 1962, John became the fifth Kenney brother and two years later, Timothy was born, the sixth and last. By the time Tim arrived, I was fourteen and Mike was thirteen, Tom was eleven, and Pat, nine.

Mike, Tom, Pat and I were all enrolled in St. Theresa's school, and we were united in our growing dislike of the place. The sisters of St. Joseph evinced a marked preference for girls over boys and seemed to like only boys who were neat and tidy. There was a severity to the nuns that made many days at school unpleasant. It was an atmosphere in which penmanship was prized over just about all else, and any sort of non-conformity was actively discouraged. Yet our parents—like nearly all the other families at the time—considered it the highest possible honor to be enrolled in this Catholic school with these devoted nuns teaching their children. The nuns were goddesses—selfless, dedicated, devoted to Christ and teaching children. The nuns could do no wrong in the minds of most parents.

As an eighth-grader in 1964—my final year at St. Theresa's—I disliked everything about school. My handwriting was dreadful, and I was thus required to revise my "Palmer paper" dozens of times until, finally, my penmanship exercise was accepted by the nun, though she made it clear it remained substandard.

A defining moment for me came early in the eighth-grade year during a test of some kind. I was seated at my desk, dressed in the uniform of dark gray slacks, white shirt, and maroon school tie, when Sister Cornelius, a grim red-faced woman, charged forward and ordered me out of my seat. During the hush of the test, she ushered me into the hallway and waved her finger at me.

"You were cheating, weren't you, Mr. Kenney?" she said, lips thin and tight, eyes full of fury.

"No, Sister, I was not," I said.

"Don't you lie to me, mister! I saw you looking at Edward Spellman's paper!"

What she actually had seen was me daydreaming from crushing boredom during the test, and it may well have been that during my daydreaming, I was vaguely gazing in the direction of Edward Spellman. But the truth was that I was not cheating on the test.

"You were cheating, weren't you?"

"No, Sister," I said. She glared at me and then grasped me by the ear and half dragged me along the long, spotless hallway, down two flights of stairs and through the corridor leading to the front of the building where the principal, ancient Sister Maruna, had her office. Sister Cornelius sat me down in the principal's outer office and went in and told Sister Maruna that I had cheated. She wanted my parents called at once and summoned to the convent for a conference that night. Sister Maruna placed the call to my mother, who was naturally distraught at this news. When I arrived home from school that afternoon, my mother was visibly upset. I had never before been accused of cheating, and she could not understand why I would do it now. I told her I had not cheated. She pressed me. I said I had not cheated. She did not know what to think.

When my father got home from work, he sent the other boys upstairs and took me into the living room. He was wearing green work pants and a matching green work shirt. He sat on one end of the sofa and I on the other. He leaned to the side, half facing me, a Lucky cupped in his hand, held to the side.

"I want the truth," he said to me in a quiet voice.

I knew that if I had cheated and admitted having done so that I would be smashed across the face, probably with a lightning-fast backhand, possibly with an open palm. Either way it would be fast and hurt like hell. But I had always been truthful with my father. When I had done things I shouldn't and he had asked me about them, I had always confessed. He had always asked me, whatever the deed, to be honest with him so that he could trust me. Trust is everything, he would tell me.

"No, Dad," I said, looking him straight in the eye, "I did not cheat on the test."

He stared at me a long moment, searching my eyes. "I'm going to ask you again," he said. "I want to be sure. Did you cheat on the test? Tell me the truth."

"Dad, I did not cheat on the test. That is the truth," I said.

He hesitated a moment, then nodded.

Supper, at 5:30 PM, was a subdued affair. When it was over, Sonny and I headed out into the night. We rode in silence the short distance down to the convent, set at the end of a dead-end street adjacent to the school. I had never been there at night, and actually, I had never been inside the convent. We rang the bell. Sister Maruna opened the door and, unsmiling, led us to a small room halfway down the hallway. There stood Sister Cornelius, who greeted my father coolly and me not at all.

The room was narrow, a place for quiet parent conferences. Within the closed quarters of the room was the overwhelming smell of starch from the nuns' habits. They sat down in two small chairs, and my father and I took that as a cue to sit opposite them. Above their heads, a crucifix hung on the wall. Sister Maruna was a diminutive woman, elderly, or so it seemed to me at the time, with a shriveled face and pinched manner. She spoke in a hushed tone about the importance of honesty.

"We take these cases very seriously," she said, barely above a whisper. She paused, looking at my father, then turned to the strapping Sister Cornelius, more red-faced now than she had been that afternoon when originally accusing me.

"Sister," Sister Maruna said, turning the proceeding over to my teacher.

Sister Cornelius was shrewd. She spoke in a tone of utter reasonableness. "Children make mistakes," she said. "Children do things they should not do. We understand that. No one is perfect. That's why we have confession for the children every Saturday afternoon in the chapel."

"Nonetheless," Sister Cornelius proceeded, her tone suddenly sterner, "even when mistakes are made, children must own up to them. Children must be honest." She glanced at me, yet only briefly, and returned her attention to my father.

"Charles cheated on a test today," she said. "When caught in the act and confronted, he denied that he had cheated." She again glanced briefly in my direction.

"This will not be tolerated." She turned to sister Maruna, who nodded.

There was a brittle silence, silence and the smell of the starched habits. My father sat in his green work pants and shirt and said nothing. He glanced down at the floor and then looked from one nun to the other. Then, to my surprise, he turned to me.

"I'm going to ask you again whether you cheated on the test," he said. "All I want is the truth." I stared at him, his eyes steady, his face calm, strong. "Did you cheat on the test?"

I hesitated because I was struck by this feeling: The event had somehow turned militant and felt almost as though it was a challenging of unchallengeable authority.

"No," I said, my mouth cottony. "I did not cheat on the test."

My father's eyes lingered on me an extra beat, and he nodded, then turned back to the nuns. But he did not say anything. He merely looked at them and waited. They were clearly flustered by this, taken aback that he had actually asked me my version.

"I saw Charles Kenney look at Edward Spellman's paper," Sister Cornelius said forcefully. "I saw him with these eyes that God gave me. There is no doubt."

She looked at me, and I can't be sure, but I think my father caught the look of contempt or hatred or whatever it was in her eyes.

"He cheated on the test and he is lying about it!" She said this as though trumpeting the news.

My father paused a moment. Then again he turned to me. "Excuse us, will you," he said to me. "I'm going to speak privately with the sisters."

My father addressed Sister Maruna: "Could he wait in the next room, Sister?"

"Of course, Mr. Kenney," she said, leading me out, a few short steps down the hallway and into a similar room next door. Instead of chairs, though, there was an upright piano and bench. I sat down on the bench opposite a framed picture of Jesus and listened—the doors to both rooms were open and I could hear clearly.

"This must be severely dealt with, Mr. Kenney," I heard Sister Cornelius say. "Your son is compounding his sin by continuing to lie about his actions."

". . . this kind of misunderstanding," I heard my father say. "I spoke to my son earlier today. I asked him directly whether he had cheated, and he said that he had not. I asked him again, and again he said he had not. My son has always been truthful with me, and I believe he is being truthful now."

"I don't think you understand, Mr. Kenney," Sister Cornelius said in her pedantic fashion. "I *saw* your son cheating. I *saw* him with my *God-given eyes.*"

There was a pause. "Sister, I'm sure that's what it must have looked like, but maybe he was looking in a certain direction, Sister, but not at the other boy's test paper. Isn't that possible?"

"I saw him," she said.

"I am sure you believed that what you saw was my son cheating, Sister," my father said, his tone calm. "But standing in the front of the classroom—you were standing up front, Sister?"

"I was."

"Standing in front with fifty children I would guess it would be possible that he was looking in a certain direction and it appeared he was looking at the other boy's paper but was actually staring off into space or looking beyond the other boy. My son has been known to get bored in school and stare off into space. I think it's the type of situation where a misunderstanding is possible. I see it as a misunderstanding—unfortunate, but these things happen. I hope we can move on from here."

It was so shocking to me. I had never experienced anything like this in my life. In the culture of West Roxbury at the time, it is unlikely that Sister Cornelius had *ever* been challenged before—and she knew only one way to deal with it.

"*There is no misunderstanding,*" she said, her voice louder, harsher. "I saw what I saw with my own God-given eyes and *I saw your son cheating*, Mr. Kenney."

It felt as though her words had a physical dimension, as though they echoed around the hallways of the convent. In their wake there was only silence, and I thought for a crushing instance that my father might give in. That's what parents always did, because they felt intimidated. No one ever stood up to the nuns or priests.

But then I heard his quiet, firm voice. "My son and I are going to go home now," he said, speaking slowly, enunciating each word carefully. "I don't want to hear any more about this accusation you have made. There has been a misunderstanding, a mistake. Call it whatever you want to call it, but you are mistaken, Sister. My son did not cheat. My son may not be perfect, he may have the worst penmanship in the class, as you have said before, and he may not pay attention in class very often. But I want you to know something about my son that you obviously do not know even though he has been at your school now for eight years. He is not perfect, but my son is an honorable boy."

I could hear the shuffling of feet and the rustling of my father's jacket. He had risen, signaling an end to the meeting. As soon as we were out the convent door, my father paused on the sidewalk to light up a Lucky. He took a long drag and let the smoke settle in his lungs, then slowly exhaled. It was dark and the night was cool, the street deadly quiet. We got into the car and headed home. I looked over at my father, who was staring straight ahead at the road, and I did not know what to say. I wanted to grasp him in my arms and hug him and thank him—but in our family we did not do such things.

"You heard all that?" he asked, as he drove.

"Yes," I said.

He nodded.

The drive was only a few minutes long, and we were about to turn into Wedgemere.

"Dad, thanks," I said.

He turned and looked at me but he didn't say a word. He just nodded.

8

"Sister Hit Me"

Anne Barry had grown up in Charlestown, just down Bunker Hill Street from where Sonny and his family had lived. Not long after the Kenneys moved from Charlestown to Roslindale, the Barrys did, too, again winding up on the same street, this time only a few houses apart. Anne was the second of six children, four boys and two girls. Though Anne had five siblings, they all joked that they were the sibling to an only child, for her brother Thomas entered the priesthood and thus gained a vaunted status within the family for the remainder of his life. Father Tom was ordained a Franciscan priest in Washington, D.C., in 1957, one of the biggest occasions in family history. He went off and did missionary work in Paraguay for many years before settling into parish work in Miami.

Anne was small, just five feet, two inches, but she possessed a curvy figure, thick auburn hair, full lips, and a pretty smile. She was calm and well adjusted, considering some of the eccentricities of her relatives. Anne's Aunt Mamie responded to thunder and lightening by shutting herself in a closet. Anne's mother, Elizabeth, was sweet and loving but often flighty and unfocused. Anne's aunts, Frances and Anne, re-mained single all their lives and shared a home with their brothers George and Billy, who never married either. Frances and Anne were sociable and would often come to our house on Wedgemere Road for holidays. George and Billy, though, were reclusive, Billy particularly so. George would come by on Christmas Eve to drop off $2 bills for the children, but he would never actually enter the house. He would drive down Wedgemere Road, come to the front door, stand on the steps out front in an overcoat and fedora, crack a few jokes, hand over the $2 bills, and be gone. His brother Billy never visited our house. Billy, in fact, rarely left the home they all shared in Roslindale except to go to work. Whenever our mother would take us over to Roslindale to visit her aunts, we would see the man in the living room who never spoke. My brother Tom, for many years, believed Billy incapable of speaking, though that was not the case. (Billy died in his eighties. I never heard him utter a single word.)

Remarkably, while growing up, Anne managed to escape all the nuttiness around her. She liked calm, normalcy, and peace, and she hated it when her sons fought, which we often did. When we went too far, she would cry and report us to Sonny, who would take out his wrath with hard slaps or painful backhanders across the face. But all her sons developed an intense desire to please her. All of us felt the same way—making her happy made us happy. She was so warm and loving, so forgiving and understanding, that being in her presence made us all feel good. No matter what was happening at school or with sports, whether things were going well or poorly outside the house, at home she made us feel special and loved unconditionally— which was not easy, with six boys competing for attention.

As we got older and our schedules changed—sporting events at different times, different work schedules—Anne often cooked a full meal for just one of us at around 4:00 or 4:30 PM, then did it again for the rest of the family an hour later. If you happened to be the one whose work or sports schedule required eating earlier, she would sit and chat, engaging in conversation about whatever it was you were interested in. She was perfectly happy to simply be in the presence of her sons.

At home, Sonny relied upon Anne for everything domestic, from laundry to food shopping, from cleaning to preparing every meal. She was forty years old when she gave birth to Timothy, her last son, on June 18, 1964, making her the mother of a newborn as well as five boys ranging in age from fourteen to two. She had kept the name Jane at the ready during her final two pregnancies, but Jane turned out to be John, and then Tim. The saving grace was having enough older boys to help with the little ones. Even with that help, though, she worked hard from the moment she awoke in the early morning until she finally fell asleep at night. She took on an enormous workload each day—preparing meals for six children and her husband, doing loads of laundry that were continuous, food shopping, and cleaning the house.

Anne was more lenient than Sonny, not nearly as strict, and at times she protected us from his wrath. One night when he was sixteen, Patrick was out drinking beer and got so drunk he had to be dragged home by his friends. The following morning when he awoke, she was standing over him scowling.

"Don't ever let it happen again," was all she said. She never told Sonny.

Before Christmas one year, Anne took a part-time job evenings at the Chestnut Hill branch of Filene's, a venerable Boston department store. She loved getting out of the house and into the world for a few hours each night. When the Christmas season passed, the manager at Filene's told her she had done a great job and that they wanted her to stay on. She was thrilled with the affirmation, and she continued to work part-time some evenings and weekends. She frequently came home from work with stories about women she had waited on. She marveled at their willingness to pay full price—something she never did. She would talk about a woman who couldn't decide between two items and bought both. Or another customer who had paid $300 for a dress. Or another who couldn't decide among three items and bought them all. These women shopped and spent money with such ease, without thinking twice about the cost, as though this was how life should be.

It was not long after Sonny was pensioned from the department that a book entitled *Holocaust,* by Paul Benzaquin, a longtime newspaper reporter in Boston, was published about the Cocoanut Grove fire. Sonny read the book and was mesmerized. It had been eighteen years since the fire, which felt like ancient history to Sonny. He had learned after years at Bowdoin Square that there were several old-timers there who had been at the Grove but had never spoken about it. Sonny had had many conversations with Pops about it through the years, but even Pops now rarely spoke of it. It was as though the fire had disappeared in some massive black hole of history, covered up by the war and the unwillingness to relive the horror. Sonny read with astonishment that there had been a BFD inspector in the club only weeks before the fire and he had pronounced the club safe. He could not believe it.

The book came as a sort of revelation to Sonny. He had either never known or had forgotten much of the information. The Benzaquin book told the story of various club employees, of some of the chorus girls, of Buck Jones the actor. Sonny thought Benzaquin created a vivid depiction of the events, and it left him wondering, as Pops had done now for eighteen years, what could possibly have caused the fire to race out of control with such ferocity and speed. Sonny felt bad about this aspect of it because he could recall certain conversations with his father: Pops had talked about this very question, but Sonny had never paid enough attention to it, never seeing it as the critical question Pops considered it. But now Sonny finally saw it. By reading Benzaquin's description of the mayhem and the massive loss of life in a matter of just minutes, Sonny felt as though he was experiencing it for the first time. It seemed incredible to him that his own father had been part of it, not only that he had been there—present at the greatest fire in the city's history and one of the defining fires in world history—but that he had rescued countless people and been injured in the process.

The only aspect of the book that left Sonny dissatisfied involved the BFD. Sonny thought the department perspective was not fully represented, and that was too bad. He would like to read a book that offered that perspective. There were no interviews of any depth with firefighters, and Sonny would love to read those.

———

Summers were glorious. In the evening, the older boys would play baseball down at Billings or Baker Fields. The Little League program in West Roxbury was filled with talented ballplayers and committed coaches. During afternoon practices, we were drilled on the fundamentals over and over again. Dozens of parents and siblings would gather around the park at Baker Field for games. My brother Mike and I were members of the Braves and wore our major league uniforms with pride. As a third basemen, it was important for me to develop quick reflexes and sure-handedness. I had an insatiable appetite for practicing, and Sonny was there with me just about every evening. There was a grassy lot next to our house, plenty of room in which to throw and catch. When Sonny got home from work, usually clad in his dark green overalls, I would be waiting with my glove, a ball, and his first-basemen's mitt. This was an old mitt we had found, with dried-out leather, discarded at a ball field, missing the stitching that held the leather together over flimsy padding. Sonny examined it and saw the possibilities. We salved it with linseed oil to bring the leather back to life and Sonny used a lengthy piece of rawhide to painstakingly stitch the glove back together, forming a beautiful pocket. When he arrived home, Sonny would barely have time to say hello before I hurried him out to the yard. From the raw cold of April through the sultry heat of August, Sonny was out there with me, night after night. We would start off with a relaxed game of catch, just tossing it back and forth with an easy motion to loosen up. We'd begin by standing no more than twenty-five or thirty feet apart, lobbing the ball in a languid manner. As we warmed up, I would move back, stretching the distance between us, and we would throw the ball with increasing velocity. At some point, Sonny would call out to me: "Ready?"

I would bend my knees, lean forward, placing my glove and throwing hand down near the ground, an infielder's ready position. And with that Sonny would throw ground balls, hard at first, then harder and harder still. He would throw smooth rollers and choppy bad bounces. He would mix in line drives and intentional short-hops that had to be attacked. The drills would go on for an hour, and then two, and sometimes longer. "Set your feet before you throw," he would say over and over. "Never throw off balance." He threw grounders to my left, to my right, some nearly out of reach, which would force me to dive, stretching out as far as I could, trying to snag the ball in my webbing. The practice sessions started when I was about seven years old and lasted through age twelve. Over time, Sonny threw tens of thousands of grounders to me and to my brother Mike, as well. As I got older, I would come up with the ball, set my feet, and sometimes gun the throw back to him so hard he would have to take a break, removing the mitt and rubbing his hand. In these instances he would stand there smiling, not pleased with the pain but happy I was capable of throwing hard enough to sting his palm. In the spring there was drizzle, on summer nights, mosquitoes. But Sonny didn't mind.

Sometimes on weekends we would all pile into the station wagon and make the drive down to Nantasket Beach in Hull, a few miles south of Boston. Anne packed sandwiches, and we would swim and play on the beach. Every time we went to Nantasket, we would plead with our parents to take us across the street to Paragon Park, an amusement park with a giant roller coaster and dozens of other rides and attractions. But the cost, with so many boys, was prohibitive and we went only rarely.

By the early 1960s, summers also became a time when the older boys worked as caddies at Charles River Country Club in Newton, a suburb of Boston. Michael and I, starting at age eleven, would get a ride from our mother early in the morning and wait with the other caddies, hoping to get a loop for the day. Eighteen holes with a single bag meant $3 or $4. The very first day I went, in the fall of 1961, I caddied eighteen holes in the morning, earning $3, and an additional nine holes in the afternoon, earning $2. I had never earned so much money before, and I could hardly believe my good fortune. I took the five single dollar bills into the golf shop and asked to trade in the ones for a $5 bill. When I returned home, thumbing a ride so that my mother wouldn't have to come and pick me up, I walked down Wedgemere Road and she was outside in the yard. I didn't say anything. Instead, I pulled the folded $5 bill from my pocket and showed it to her, and she said, "Oh, my God! I don't believe it!"

I was fascinated with the lives of the men for whom I caddied. They were cheerful for the most part, and kind. They would pull into the club parking lot in their Cadillacs and Buicks, their Pontiacs and Oldsmobiles, huge cars, shiny and new. A few of the members drove the ultimate—a Lincoln Continental. The older caddies would tell us what various men did for a living, where they lived and how big their houses were.

"A single-family with ten rooms *and* he has a fuckin' pool!"

The idea of twelve rooms would be challenged. "Bullshit," someone would say.

The sage older boy would shake his head: "I shit you not, my friend."

In our house there were technically six rooms, although the living room and dining rooms kind of connected. There was one full bath and three bedrooms for the eight of us. My parents had their own room, of course, while Mike and I shared a smaller room, a space about eight by ten feet. Tom, Pat, John, and Tim shared a larger room with two bunk beds.

I began to see—riding through Newton going to and from the golf course past the elaborate and stately homes—that there was another way to live. I saw the clothes the members wore. I saw their new golf bags from Burton, their new sets of Haig Ultra irons, their Hogan woods with leather head covers. I saw their sterling-silver money clips. They would play golf and sit in the grill room enjoying a leisurely lunch. A group of them would remain in the grill drinking for a while after lunch until late afternoon or early evening, when they would come downstairs—ruddy faced—and play six holes, betting heavily.

Some of them would play a fair amount in spring and fall and all but disappear for the summer. I learned they relocated their families to second homes on Cape Cod, wives and children living at the beach for the summer. I learned, over time, that many if not most of these men were college graduates. Some had gone to law school, a few to business school. They were smart, sharp, but in so many other ways, they were just like me. They were sons of firefighters and cops, products of blue-collar families from various city neighborhoods. Many were of Irish descent—all were Roman Catholic, consistent with the segregation of Greater Boston country clubs by religion. I got the thought in my head that they started out just like me, and once I seized upon it, I embraced it with a sense of joy and wonder. I told no one about this notion because it seemed too fanciful; it seemed to be reaching too far. But I believed it. They were just like me, I convinced myself—and I wanted to be just like them. And none of them were Boston firefighters.

My younger brothers Tom and Patrick were a different story, though. As the 1960s progressed, it became clear that their interests were focused almost exclusively on firefighting. When Tom was just eleven years old, he would hop on his bike and pedal a mile up Centre Street to the firehouse, where Engine 30 and Ladder 25 were stationed. He told them his father had been a rescue man and they would ask his name. When Tom told them, the men would invariably nod, at the very least knowing the name but in many instances smiling and saying: "I know your father," or "Your father is a friend of mine." And they would often say what a "good jake" he had been or what a fine guy he was. Tom would be thrilled by this, deeply proud that his father was so well known and respected within the department. Tom found that some of the old-timers knew Pops as well, and that was a real treat.

Tom was inquisitive and a good listener. When he asked a question he was spongelike in absorbing the answer. As time passed, Tom felt increasingly comfortable at the firehouse as he got to know more and more of the men, most of whom were quite friendly. Some of the guys, seeing Tom's keen desire to learn, would select a piece of equipment off the truck and let Tom handle it, explaining what it was used for and how it worked. Over time, Tom learned the details of scores of pieces of equipment and their uses—and he was barely twelve years old. Tom also made a point at home of listening to the BFD radio and learning the boxes. It was not too many years before Tom had nearly as encyclopedic knowledge of the box numbers as Sonny. When a box would sound over the kitchen radio, Sonny would sometimes sit back and listen as Tom leaned forward, focusing on the number of taps. Then Tom would think a moment and announce the location. He was right nearly every time.

During the summer, Tom headed up to the firehouse most evenings after supper. During the school year, he typically went after school and then again on weekends. Tom had become a "spark," a person fascinated by fires and firefighting. There were hundreds of sparks throughout Boston, men who felt a kinship with the fire department and who were drawn to fires and the men who fought them. The most active sparks would hang around a particular firehouse, get to know the men, and accompany them to fires, usually observing at the scene but occasionally pitching in to help with the work.

On Wedgemere Road, Tom would often encounter our neighbors, firefighters Bill Kelleher and a father and son, Ray Frazel Sr. and Jr. Tom used to stop and chat with them, asking about fires they had been to and fires in their districts that Tom had heard about in the firehouse. Sometimes Tom would hear a box struck over the kitchen radio and recognize it as a location in West Roxbury. He would jump on his bike and race to the site to watch the firefighters in action. He observed every detail, and when there was something he didn't know about or understand, he would make a mental note and later quiz Sonny about it and often Pops as well. Anytime we were riding anywhere in the family car and Tom spotted a fire engine, siren wailing, en route to a fire, he would implore our parents to follow it so that we could watch the men. Whenever we happened by the scene of a fire, he insisted we stop to watch. His fascination might have been considered an obsession in another family, but both his grandfathers had been firefighters, as had his father; his neighbors were firefighters and several of his friends' fathers were firefighters. He was immersed within the culture from birth.

After a year or two, when Tom would go up to the West Roxbury firehouse, he was welcomed by just about everyone. He was free to hang around the ground floor of the house pretty much whenever he wanted. Sometimes, when the companies would go out on a run, Tom would go into the alarm desk to see which box had been struck. If it was close enough, he would ride there on his bike and take it all in.

As Tom got older, he switched from the West Roxbury firehouse to Rescue 1, which was located at 123 Oliver Street in the downtown business district, just a couple of blocks from the waterfront. He would go in with Nelson Pittman on a Sunday morning and ride with the Rescue all day long. "If you went in on a Sunday morning, you could stay there the whole day and just hang out," Tom recalled. "Every time the Rescue got a run, you'd get in the back. And of course, the thing with the Rescue was it wasn't like an engine or a truck where they had only outside spots and guys hanging on. On the Rescue you could ride inside, so it was much safer and the officer was in a better position to let you ride than on an engine or a truck because you're inside of a vehicle."

Whenever Nelson dropped by our house, Tom would make it a point to sit nearby and listen to Nelson and Sonny exchange stories about the fire department. Sometimes Pops would be there, too, and that would be even better. And one day Tom knew, without any doubt at all, not simply that he wanted to be a fireman but that he *needed* to be a fireman. "I knew it all along," he said. "It was the only thing I wanted, the only thing for me. I wanted to be exactly like those guys. It was something that just said 'that's what I have to do.'"

But there were constant reminders of the job's dangers. There were newspaper articles declaring that mining and firefighting had been judged the most hazardous occupations in the country, and there were many days when the papers carried stories of injuries and deaths. With thousands of wood-frame buildings, Boston was a particularly dangerous place for firefighters, for the danger in fires was not so much that men would be overtaken by flames and burned to death. The greater danger was working inside a building where fire corroded the structural integrity causing a collapse.

On the night of October 1, 1964, fire broke out in a large former toy factory on Trumbull Street in the South End. Companies responded shortly after 12:30 AM, and only minutes later there was a terrible rumble and a portion of a brick wall collapsed, burying firefighters beneath a massive pile of rubble. Men began frantically digging through concrete and bricks with their bare hands in a desperate rescue attempt. Assistant Chief of Department John E. Clougherty arrived on the scene to direct operations just after a number of men were removed from the rubble and rushed to Boston City Hospital, Clougherty's son Robert among them. The Cloughertys were members of one of Boston's most distinguished multigenerational firefighting families, and Assistant Chief Clougherty focused on his duties until the time came when he knew he had to go to Boston City Hospital to see his son. At the scene of the fire, he said, "They did not tell me, but from the way they were talking I had a good idea of his condition."

At the hospital, Chief Clougherty was informed that five firefighters had died: Lieutenant John McCorkle, age fifty-three; Lieutenant John Geswell, age forty; Private Francis Murphy, forty-two; and Private James B. Sheedy, thirty-eight. Andrew Sheehan, a twenty-seven-year-old spark, was also killed. Clougherty was informed that his son had also died.

"My boy, my boy! Oh, my God," he murmured. Robert Clougherty, age thirty-one, had been crushed under the rubble. The newspapers noted that it was the worst loss of life among firefighters since November 15, 1942, and the Luongo Restaurant fire.

As teenagers, both Tom and Pat went to work part-time at Firecontrol, initially working with Pops in the back of the shop recharging extinguishers. Both boys marveled at the intensity of Pops's work ethic as well as at his pure skill. Pops was gifted with his hands, and they watched and learned as he fixed even the most difficult problems with an extinguisher. Pops pushed the boys and himself to produce. If the service trucks rolled in on a Friday with thirty empty extinguishers, it was a point of pride with Pops to send thirty refilled, ready-to-go extinguishers back out the door Monday morning, even if it meant working late Friday and all day Saturday.

Both Tom and Pat could see that Pops loved Firecontrol, working around the other men and being with his son and grandsons. Pops would get irritated when he would hear that the other boys didn't want to work there and were interested in other things. Pops felt the family should be committed to the business—*all* the boys.

When he was old enough to drive, Tom moved from the back shop with Pops to working a truck on the road. He went out, just as the other service men did, and picked up extinguishers to be recharged and brought them back to the shop. In other instances, Tom did some recharging on site. It was a lot of responsibility for a teenager, but his preparation with Pops and Sonny enabled him to handle it well.

Patrick, who was two years younger than Tom, was shorter, with a muscular build. He was more voluble than Tom, eager to offer his own opinion on a variety of matters, unafraid to challenge an opinion or argue a point, even when he was quite young. But Pat was virtually identical to Tom in his desire to be around the firehouse. From age twelve all the way through high school, Patrick both worked part-time at Firecontrol and spent much of his remaining free time in the fire-house as a spark. Pat picked up where Tom left off at the West Roxbury firehouse. Pat had heard all his life about the virtue of working in a busy downtown firehouse, and he came to believe—from Sonny, Pops, and others—that that was the pinnacle in the Boston Fire Department. Life at Engine 30, Ladder 25 in West Roxbury was quiet, with one of the lowest run totals of any house in the city. One day, Pat was talking with a young firefighter there, Bob Staunton, and Pat, in his typical blunt fashion, asked Staunton, "Why does a young guy like you want to be out here in a house like this?" Staunton was taken aback, but then laughed heartily at this young boy's earnest directness.

When Patrick was thirteen or fourteen years old, he had a special treat: Nelson took him into the firehouse for the night to ride in the back of the Rescue. After that it was "all firefighting all the time" for Pat. One evening while Pat was in the kitchen at Wedgemere Road monitoring the BFD radio, he heard about a working fire at Lincoln and Beach Streets in Chinatown. He knew the Rescue would respond, and he also knew from the location that it would take many hours to subdue the fire. Patrick ran out the door and up the street, caught a bus to Forest Hills and rode the subway into Chinatown. He ran into Nelson Pittman at the fire and when it was over, Nelson invited Pat to return to quarters with the Rescue. At the time, the Rescue was housed near Chinatown on Oliver Street. Pat called home and received permission to stay the night in the firehouse. The rest of the night was mostly quiet until about 4:00 AM when the Rescue was called back to the scene of the Chinatown fire. This was an ominous sign. A man from Engine 26 was missing, a young firefighter named Patrick Kelly. A search of the fire scene was conducted and, soon enough, his body was discovered at the bottom of an elevator shaft. It appeared he had fallen five floors from the roof. Patrick was working with the rescue men, and he assisted in putting a ladder down the shaft from the first floor. It was a terrible, somber moment as Pat watched the men gather up one of their own, place him into a thick canvas body bag commonly used at the time, and carry him from the scene.

Patrick, along with the other men, rode back to the firehouse in stunned silence. The men milled around the equipment when they returned, no one certain what to do. Patrick wanted to give them space, so he went to the back of the house and into the kitchen, which he thought was empty. But there, seated at the table all alone, was the legendary Leo Stapleton, then deputy chief of the department, soon to be commissioner. Patrick apologized for the intrusion and made to leave, but the chief invited him to sit down. Chief Stapleton spoke in a calm tone tinged with sadness. It seemed important to him to comfort Patrick, to make sure Pat was okay. They talked about firefighting in general for fifteen minutes or so, and then Chief Stapleton got up, said a warm good-bye, and left.

More than ever, Patrick yearned to be part of this amazing brotherhood. He loved that when the trucks rolled out the door, the engine and ladder company units were tight and cohesive, that men relied upon one another in dark, smoke-filled rooms, that everyone had to perform or there was a risk someone might not survive. He had heard it called a fraternity, a brotherhood—whatever it was, Patrick wanted to *belong*. And he would belong, there could be no question of that. Before the start of a shift, Nelson would check out the equipment on the Rescue, teaching Patrick. It was not long before Patrick was intimately familiar with the acetylene oxygen cutting torch (which sliced through metal), the grip hoist (for winching various items), the Voleski bar cutter, and the Porter-Ferguson hydraulic tool (a precursor to today's jaws of life).

Patrick was paid the highest possible compliment by Joe McCauley, who drove the Rescue. He called Patrick "a natural firefighter." He was treated like a member of the family because he *was* a member of the family, a member of the fraternity by virtue of his lineage and his love for the job.

When Patrick was in the eighth grade, just before starting high school, he hopped the subway and rode into the State House, just as Sonny had done a couple of decades earlier, and went into the secretary of state's office to pick up a copy of the Red Book. Pat began reading it on the train home, and he kept reading it in his spare time until he had read every word with care. And then he went back to the beginning and worked his way through it again and again. By the time Patrick completed high school, he had been more attentive to the Red Book than his studies. But he knew it cold and when his time came to take the Civil Service test based on the Red Book, he knew he would ace the test.

As Patrick grew older, it reached the point where he had his own fire coat and helmet at Engine 24, Ladder 23 in Roxbury. He had become one of the guys in every way except officially, and that would come in a few years when he took the test. The reality was that he was so good that the lieutenants and captains entrusted him with every assignment except driving the truck. He would even be allowed some nights to go up over the stick and ventilate a roof.

On the night of January 29, 1966, news came of a horrific explosion in downtown Boston. A gas leak had triggered a massive blast at the ten-story Paramount Hotel on Boylston Street. The explosion set the hotel ablaze, damaged fourteen nearby buildings, shattered windows for blocks, sent huge chunks of cement and granite curbstones airborne, and ripped a massive chasm into the sidewalk and street in front of the hotel. A woman walking along Tremont Street at the time said she thought an atom bomb had exploded. The blast sent a huge block of cement into the air, crashing down onto a car, flattening it to its wheels. One of the newspaper reporters wrote that "hell burst forth" in the form of the explosion. The ground-floor bar and coffee shop in the hotel were lifted into the air by the blast and then sent crashing into a huge hole underground. Smoke emanating from the Paramount was so dense that when the first units arrived at the scene, they could get no sense of what they faced. The dimensions of the disaster quickly became clear, however, and the fire went to five alarms in just seven minutes. Among the first to arrive was Rescue 1, and one of the men now assigned to the Rescue was Sonny's friend from Bowdoin Square, Bill Shea, now back on the job. Bill had won reassignment from Ladder 24 to the Rescue—and he cherished it.

When Bill and the other rescue men arrived, there was a man standing in the entranceway to the hotel. At his back, within the hotel, were flames. In front of him where the sidewalk and street had been, there was a vast hole. Bill and the others threw a ladder onto the ground and created a makeshift bridge across the hole, using sheet metal signs from nearby as a walkway along the ladder. They rushed to the man and led him to safety.

After that, Bill went through the smoke and dust into the hotel lobby and saw a spectacle of destruction. There were dead bodies that seemed to have been slung around. A young sailor lay draped over a railing, dead. And then Bill Shea saw a woman. She was moving; she was alive. In a huge, jagged hole about eight or so feet deep, the woman was amid mounds of debris and flames. The fire was all around her and it seemed to Bill that she was seconds away from being consumed.

Bill did what he felt he had to do: He jumped into the air and landed in the pit a couple of feet from the desperate woman. With debris and flames all around him, he struggled to take hold of the women and lift her into the air. Other firefighters squatted at the edge of the pit as Bill lifted the woman, who weighed in excess of two hundred pounds, and hoisted her up to the other rescuers.

In all, eleven people were killed in the explosion and fire, and fifty-seven people were injured. The *Boston Globe* characterized it as "Boston's most frightful disaster since the Cocoanut Grove fire killed 492 persons 23 years ago." The *Record American* reported praise of Bill by Lieutenant Paul Doherty, who said Bill "actually leaped into the flames, picked a woman up over his head and handed her to a man above. It seemed to me humanly impossible."

Deputy Fire Chief John J. O'Mara was a stickler about awards. O'Mara was such a stickler, in fact, that he had never before proposed that a firefighter receive an award for heroic action. Bill Shea was the first.

In spite of such remarkable events, as the 1960s progressed there was mounting animosity toward the fire department in the city's black neighborhoods. With the growth of the Civil Rights and Black Power movements came mounting hostility and violence against firefighters, particularly after the death of Martin Luther King Jr. Throughout the summer of 1968, firefighters responding to alarms in Roxbury and North Dorchester were sometimes greeted with showers of rocks, bottles, and bags of garbage raining down from nearby rooftops. Sometimes old refrigerators were pushed off the roof in an effort to crush a firefighter, and there were occasional Molotov cocktails. Some fire companies returning from alarms found their firehouse looted. There were drivers of trucks, as well as tillermen, who were struck in the face by flying objects.

In the fall of 1968, more than 800 Boston firefighters jammed into City Hall for a hearing on the violence problem—seeking, as the *Record American* put it, "protection against hoodlum attacks." The outcry by the members of the department got results: The city ordered police escorts for fire companies responding to calls in particularly violent areas, especially certain public housing projects. The city also constructed protective shielding around the tillermen on ladder trucks, and firehouses were protected while companies were out on runs.

But the violence generated another by-product as well—anger and resentment among white firefighters toward black neighborhoods. "We're risking our lives to help people and they're trying to hurt us or kill us," firefighters said. It was a growing racial divide that, in the years ahead, would only deepen.

———

In the first grade at St. Theresa's, my youngest brother, Tim, was a small child, wiry and energetic. It was clear from the start that the 50 to 1 student–teacher ratio did not work for him. During his first-grade year, he sometimes seemed a bit lost, yet he would go off to school quite cheerfully nonetheless, for Tim was a happy boy who took joy in being around his family and friends. He liked to talk and laugh, and around the house he was always upbeat and fun.

Tim's teacher was Sister Maureen, a member of the order of Sisters of St. Joseph, like Sister Cornelius had been. On this particular day, during a spelling lesson, Tim was chosen by Sister Maureen to go up to the blackboard in front of the class and spell a word. Standing in front of the class, knowing that he would almost certainly be unable to perform whatever task Sister Maureen would ask of him, made Tim very nervous. He was frightened and embarrassed even before he had been asked a single question.

The word assigned was "cabin." Tim went to the board and made several attempts. Sister Maureen urged Tim to sound out the word and he tried to, but this phonetic approach still did not work. Tim was not able to conjure up the correct spelling of the word "cabin." Sister Maureen, standing at the front of the room holding a long wooden pointer in her hand, found this unacceptable. She became angry, which caused Tim to become even more nervous. He wanted only to be able to go back to his seat, to shrink down in it and hide his embarrassment and fear.

Sister Maureen, however, did not send Tim back to his chair, not yet. She evidently viewed this as some sort of affront, some terrible transgression—that Timothy Kenney, age six, was unable to correctly spell "cabin." It was not that he had not tried. He had gone to the board, tried to sound it out and spell it, scratching crooked letters on the blackboard.

Sister Maureen was not about to sit idly by while Timothy Kenney failed in his spelling. She moved quickly, without Tim noticing it, positioning herself beside and behind where he stood. She took the pointer and whipped it in a hard, rapid forward motion, slashing Tim across the lower back, once, twice, three times, and again. The pain was terrible, the humiliation worse.

When Tim got home that afternoon, he said nothing to our mother, but Anne knew something was wrong. She asked him what the matter was and he said nothing. She reached for him tenderly and touched him on the lower back as he started upstairs to change out of his school clothes, and even though her touch was gentle, he cried out.

Anne was alarmed.

"What happened?" she asked.

"Sister hit me," Tim admitted.

"She *hit* you?"

Anne yanked his shirt out of his pants, pulled the shirt up and lowered his pants in the back several inches. She saw four thick, cherry-red welts across his lower back and buttocks. She gasped and led Tim up to his room and held him, comforting him, telling him everything would be all right and that he was a good boy. She left him there and ran downstairs, calling Sonny at work. She explained in a rush what had happened, and he left the shop immediately. It was unheard of for Sonny to come home during the middle of the workday, but he sped home and looked at the wounds for himself. He was sickened by it. But he was also enraged.

"What are we going to do?" Anne asked.

"Going to the school," Sonny said. He took Tim by the hand, and they rushed outside and drove down to the school. Sonny went into the principal's office and explained what had happened. The principal was hesitant, skeptical. Sonny went out of the office and brought Tim in. Sonny lifted Tim's shirt and nudged his pants down and showed the nun the welts. She was shocked.

While Tim waited outside the office, Sonny and the principal talked about a course of action. The nun said she would come to the house to apologize to Anne and comfort her, and to assure her nothing like this would ever happen again. Soon thereafter, the nun showed up at Wedgemere Road one day during school and spoke privately with Anne. But her apology was half-hearted, and our mother was disappointed in her attitude.

Sonny and Anne did all they could to comfort Tim and assure him he was safe at school. It was springtime, with not much left of the school year, and Tim finished out the first grade. In the late summer when teaching assignments were announced, it became known that Tim was again assigned to Sister Maureen's classroom. This was intolerable for Sonny and Anne.

Anne drove to the rectory and asked to meet with the bishop. No, she did not have an appointment. It was an important private matter. She had to see the bishop—no one else. After a few minutes, after hushed conversations within the rectory, Anne was given an audience with Bishop Minihan, the pastor. She explained the background of the case to the bishop and asked that Tim not have to be in Sister Maureen's class. The bishop seemed somewhat skeptical of the events as described by Anne. It was clear that he knew nothing of the case, which was incredible in and of itself. The bishop said he would think it over and in the meantime would contact the former principal, who had moved to another school. Bishop Minihan said he would consult with the former principal and get back to Anne. Soon thereafter, Bishop Minihan called one night and said he was sorry, but there wasn't much he could do. Bishop Minihan said he had checked in with the former principal and based his decision on her analysis of events. The bishop had therefore decided to send Tim back into a classroom with a nun who had beaten him.

Anne found it too much to believe. She was angry with the former principal. What could she have possibly said to the bishop that would result in Tim's remaining in Sister Maureen's class?

Anne wasn't going to let this go. She tracked down the former principal and asked her what she had said to Bishop Minihan. And then came perhaps the greatest shock of all: The nun said that the bishop had never called her about the matter, that she had never spoken to the bishop about Tim.

A bishop of the Catholic Church had told them a bald-faced lie, had looked at Anne and knowingly lied. She was heartbroken. A bishop within their church had cared so little for the welfare of a child that he had done *nothing* to check out the story.

The next day, Sonny and Anne made their decision. They removed John and Tim from Saint Theresa's and sent them to the local public school. Sonny had been born and raised a Catholic. He had once considered joining the priesthood. He had believed in the church, been comforted and guided by the church his entire life. And now this.

9

The Red Book

The Vendome Hotel, located at the broad corner of Commonwealth Avenue and Dartmouth Street, had long been one of Boston's iconic buildings. Constructed in the 1870s, the Vendome looked as though it had been uprooted from a Parisian neighborhood and transported whole to Boston. The building was constructed of white marble, with ornate carvings over huge windows. It was five stories tall, though it included one section of steeply rising dormers that rose an additional two stories. On a pleasant Saturday afternoon, June 17, 1972, fire broke out at the Vendome. The hotel sat a block from Newbury Street, the city's most fashionable shopping district, and a large crowd gathered to watch a dozen engine and ladder companies converge. By the time the first responding companies arrived, it was clear that the fire was out of control, and it took four alarms to summon enough men and equipment—sixteen engines, five ladder trucks, two aerial towers, and the Rescue—to contain and control the fire in an area where buildings were so close together that the blaze could easily have spread to nearby townhouses. Although the Vendome was a building with historic and architectural significance in Boston, it held a more personal importance to Sonny. On Sonny and Anne's first date, after the BC-Villanova football game, they had gone to the Vendome for cocktails.

It so happened that at that time of the fire, I had an internship working at a consulting firm on Boylston Street, a few blocks away. From the windows of the company offices, I could see the rear of the Vendome. As soon as the fire broke out, I called Sonny, who was at home on Wedgemere Road listening to events unfold on the BFD scanner.

"I'm going to go over and take a look," I said.

"Keep me posted," he said.

I walked over and saw engine companies parked at what appeared to be crazy angles along Commonwealth Avenue and Dartmouth Street. There were pumpers hooked up to several hydrants, with what seemed miles of hose snaked across the pavement. Though it appeared to be pure chaos, I knew there was a clear plan of attack. I knew that the engine companies had all dropped their lines in precisely the correct places and had hooked their pumpers up and sent a massive water supply through. I could see that the engine companies had made sure to get as close to the structure as possible, while still leaving prime positioning for the ladder companies. All four ladder companies had thrown their sticks to the roof, and the two tower companies—the trucks with huge aerial ladders with hoses like water cannons—were positioned at angles allowing them to cover different parts of the building. It was beautifully orchestrated, and I watched for a couple of hours as the crews brought the fire under control and, ultimately, put it out altogether. There were hundreds of spectators, awed by the flames and smoke and attack of the fire companies. People craned their necks, gazing up at the aerial towers firing continuous streams of water onto the building. When the fire was out, the crowd drifted away and I headed back to the office.

I was back in the office about 4:30 PM and I called Sonny and filled him in on what I had seen. He was pleased. An hour later, though, he called and said he heard a district chief ask that the department chaplain be brought around to the right side of the building.

"Can you see it from where you are?"

I went to the window, but all I could see was a cloud of dust and smoke, thick and billowing upward.

"I don't understand," I started to say.

"It must have collapsed," he said tersely.

"I'll head over now," I said, "and let you know."

I jogged down Boylston to Dartmouth and over two blocks to the Vendome. There were sirens wailing throughout the city. Four or five ambulances raced past me, while other fire trucks, speeding through the streets, trailed the ambulances.

When I arrived at the scene I couldn't believe what I was seeing: A huge part of the building that I had seen on fire just an hour or so earlier was gone. There was a massive pile of rubble, and dozens of firemen were frantically digging, some with tools, others with their hands. There were dozens of them, firefighters in black coats and black helmets hunched over the rubble, digging.

A crowd gathered again, but this time rather than a sense of awe, there was a sense of foreboding. A large number of policemen arrived and moved the crowd back half a block farther away from the site. It was difficult to see now because there were ambulances and fire trucks blocking the view, but I stayed and saw the faces of anguished fire-fighters as they arrived to pitch in with the digging.

As soon as he heard about the collapse from Sonny, my brother Patrick left Wedgemere Road and took the subway into the city. He reached the police line at Newbury and Dartmouth Streets and watched firemen digging in the rubble. At the time of the fire, my brother Tom was working as a volunteer for the Boston Ambulance Squad. Late Saturday afternoon, Tom was dispatched to the site of the Vendome, ready to help rescue any survivors. Though Pat and Tom and I were all there at the same time, none of us knew it then. Patrick told us later that he had overheard firefighters saying they thought several men were under there—but that others were unaccounted for. Tom would later assist in carrying a dead firefighter from the rubble.

In all, nine firefighters were dead, eight injured. Some of the dead were lieutenants: Thomas James Carroll of Engine 32, and John Edward

Hanbury from Ladder 13. Others were firefighters: Richard B. Magee of Engine 33; Joseph F. Boucher and John Edward Jameson of Engine 22; Charles Everett Dolan and Joseph Peter Saniuk of Ladder 13; Paul J. Murphy and Thomas W. Beckwith of Engine 32. Collectively, they were fathers to twenty-five children.

Sonny and Tommy Carroll had trained together at Egleston Square. Sonny had gotten to know Charlie Dolan at Bowdoin Square. John Jameson had been a friend of Sonny's for many years. When Sonny brought us boys into the firehouse when we were little, John Jameson would happily pick us up and toss us into the air. When Sonny got hurt, John Jameson frequently visited him in the hospital. Sonny had a picture at home of John holding one of the boys when they were very young. For years Sonny had known and worked with these men, eaten meals with them in the firehouse, maintained equipment with them during downtimes, fought fires alongside them. Had he still been on the job, Sonny might have been in there with them.

Just as the Cocoanut Grove fire had not deterred Sonny from joining the department, the Vendome did not deter Tom or Pat from their pursuit of a job on the BFD. Quite the contrary. The aftermath of the Vendome brought firefighters—active and retired, along with their family members—together in an outpouring of support for the families who had lost a husband, father, or son. Never before in my lifetime had the fraternity of firefighters come together so completely. Funerals for the men were massive affairs, with thousands of uniformed firefighters from all over the country coming to Boston to pay their respects. If anything, for Tom and Pat, it reinforced their intense desire to be part of the fraternity, to be among those men in their blue uniforms.

By the time of the Vendome, Tom had discovered what he called "a legitimate way of sparking." The Boston Ambulance Squad was a private, all-volunteer agency that operated an ambulance that sought to support the fire department. At the time, the City of Boston rescue operations were performed largely by the fire department itself. There were few ambulances—and those few were manned by people with minimal training—run by the city out of Boston City Hospital.

The Boston Ambulance Squad was composed of volunteers aspiring to one day join the fire department. Tom was assigned to an ambulance in Dorchester, and his team responded to any fire in that neighborhood. He remembered:

If there was smoke showing we'd go and we'd also go to any working fire in the entire city. At the time, the city was running an ambulance service, but it was nowhere near the magnitude that it is today or even a few years later. The city didn't have the resources to send an ambulance to let it sit and watch the fire. The majority of the stuff we did was first aid, but there were also cases where we had a burn victim or someone suffering from smoke inhalation or an automobile accident—a pretty wide array of calls. We were closely aligned with the fire department and had fire department radios in the ambulances so they could call us directly, and they knew that they could count on us to be there if there was a fire.

Working on the ambulance squad one evening, Tom responded to an alarm off Blue Hill Avenue. When Tom pulled in, there was heavy smoke showing and fire raging from the second floor of a wood-frame residence. Two of the men from Rescue 2, Ronnie Keating and Jay Donahue, rushed headlong into the burning building. Tom watched anxiously, waiting for Ronnie and Jay to reappear. The smoke grew thicker, the flames more intense. And then he saw them, emerging from the acrid smoke billowing out the front door. First came Ronnie, his coat open, without an air pack, charging forward. And then Tom saw the children—little kids around two or three years old. Ronnie was running, clutching a child under each arm, followed by Jay, who was also carrying a small child. Tom turned and sprinted to the ambulance as Ronnie and Jay jumped in with the kids. They sped through the city streets, headed for Boston City Hospital—Ronnie and Jay administering mouth-to-mouth in a desperate effort to save the lives of the children. When it was over and the children had been stabilized, Tom thought about what he had seen. He could see it in his mind's eye, and he watched it over and over again. He watched Ronnie and Jay emerging from the smoke and fire with the children, watched them run to the ambulance, watched them holding the children. And Tom knew without any doubt that this is what he wanted to do.

There were many young men like Tom who joined the ambulance squad, seeing it as good preparation for life on the fire department. The squad attracted devoted sparks, many of them from families with rich legacies on the job. Paul Carey was a young man who shared Tom's passion for rescue work on the ambulance, as well as his dream of becoming a Boston firefighter. Paul's father, uncles, and older brother were on the job, and eventually, Paul, along with his cousins and his son, would make it as well.

Tom and Paul spent countless hours working on the ambulance squad together, and much of that time was focused on talking about the fire department—about particular fires or rescues, about people they knew on the job, and about how their turn would soon come. There was a simple, pure passion for the department and the work, for its people and culture. They had been given a great gift, in a way; they had found something in life that they loved with a rare purity and passion.

Tom had obtained his standard first aid card from the American Red Cross, as well as a CPR accreditation in order to work on the ambulance squad, but he found that more and more of the volunteers were seeking emergency medical technician credentials as well. Tom enrolled in an EMT training program at Carney Hospital in Dorchester when he was nineteen. He knew that few firefighters had achieved EMT certification and thought it would be a great help on the job—and perhaps hasten his appointment to the Rescue.

Even as he volunteered on the ambulance squad, worked at Firecontrol, and studied for his EMT credential, Tom still could not resist the draw of going into the firehouse as a spark. Nelson invited Tom to ride the Rescue, and though Tom had sparked at various locations, this was unlike anything he had ever experienced. He said:

It was a different breed of guys and I was a little bit older and it had been [Sonny's] company. I could pretty much go in any time Nelson was working and ride. I just kept my mouth shut and stayed low. They knew I had an interest in it and those guys were interested in showing somebody who had an interest. So I'd go in the firehouse and Nelson might say, "Hey, we're going to check this piece of equipment. Do you want to know about that?" "Yes, I'd love to." So if they thought you were interested they'd go out of their way to take care of you.

In November 1973, Tom turned twenty. He had but one more year to wait before taking the Civil Service examination for the fire department. In the meantime, he heard about openings on the ambulance at Boston City Hospital. It would be work quite similar to what he was doing as a volunteer at Boston Ambulance Squad, yet it would be a paid position. The job required minimal training—nothing more than an advanced First Aid credential. With his EMT credential, Tom was highly qualified.

There was a posting in City Hospital that had said they had fourteen openings. I go to Personnel and I get the paperwork; and the lady gives me the paperwork and I fill it out. She says, "Okay, now you have to go across the street and see this guy who runs the ambulance." So I go over to him. He shuffles through all the paper. "No," he says, "we're not hiring right now." I say, "Okay." So I get up and I leave.

Tom thought this was odd—the posting at City Hospital said there were fourteen openings. It didn't feel right to Tom.

I had recently worked for the reelection campaign of Mayor Kevin H. White, and during the course of the campaign, I had come to know a number of city officials in a variety of departments. Minutes after being told there were no openings, Tom called me from a pay phone at City Hospital and explained what had happened. "Fourteen openings but we're not hiring" seemed odd to me, as well. I called a person within the White administration, explained what had happened, and listed Tom's qualifications for the job. By the time Tom reached home—it took him about twenty-five minutes—the Personnel Office from City Hospital had already called. His physical was scheduled for that same afternoon. He was hired the next day. Sometimes Boston can be a political city.

It was a clear autumn Saturday, a day when Pops, Sonny, and Patrick worked at Firecontrol from early morning until just after lunch. At the time, Pops was seventy-two years old, Sonny forty-seven, and Patrick seventeen. With work done, the three of them piled into Sonny's rickety Jeep and began the drive home, but they had traveled barely a quarter mile in the town of Dedham, near the Boston border, when they smelled smoke. A half mile down the main street, an old paper mill was on fire. Sonny guided the Jeep to the side of the road and the three of them studied the situation. The mill was an old structure built of red brick and wood—enough wooden beams and supports so that flames were roaring from the windows. There were a few fire engines from the Town of Dedham, but it was immediately clear to Pops, Sonny, and Pat that this would wind up being a multiple-alarm fire. They saw firefighters rushing to connect hoses to hydrants and pumpers, other firefighters working to advance hose lines as close to the fire as possible. They saw a loading dock at the end of a driveway where the fire was particularly intense. Someone had stretched a two-and-one-half-inch hose—known as a "big line"—partway down the driveway, but it was clear that there were not enough firefighters to man the line. The big line had already been connected to the pumper and was ready for action. Sonny knew several of the firefighters on the scene, and he knew they would welcome help until reinforcements arrived.

"Let's go," Pops said, and the three of them moved quickly down the driveway. Patrick seized the pipe (the nozzle of the hose), while Pops fell into position ten or so feet behind him and Sonny worked the hose line from farther back. The job was to advance the line as close to the fire as possible. Pops and Sonny had both worked to advance hose lines into buildings thousands of times, of course, and Patrick had done so numerous times as well, working as a spark. As they worked their way along the driveway, Patrick opened up the line and a powerful stream of water—enough to knock a man off his feet—surged through the line. Patrick trained it on the loading dock, thirty or so feet away, sending an intense stream of water into the flame. As he slowly moved forward behind the stream of water, Patrick could feel the intensity of the heat. An overhanging roof extended out over the loading dock to protect trucks from the elements, and Patrick moved forward and took a position under the overhang, at the entrance to the loading dock. Smoke billowed out the loading dock doors toward Patrick as Pops urged him forward with the line.

"It's getting smoky," Pat observed, coughing.

Pops kind of laughed. "This is nothing," he said, nudging Pat forward.

What was in Pops's mind at the moment? Did he think of other fires where he'd advanced a line into a smoky building? Is it possible he thought about the Grove, about the doorway on Shawmut Street? It had been thirty long years since Pops had last fought a fire—thirty years since he was in that Cocoanut Grove doorway on Shawmut Street. Was it possible for Pops to see a fire, to fight a fire, and not allow that image to creep back into his mind? Now, three decades later, he was a civilian clad in work pants and a plaid shirt, seventy-two years old and advancing a line with his son and grandson—three generations joined together doing what they loved most.

Every time he hit a solid wall or beam with the stream of water from the big line, it splashed back onto Patrick. The smoke billowed around him, penetrating his eyes, nose, and mouth. Even as it did, he heard Pops behind him urging him on: "Let's go, let's move," Pops said. Patrick laughed. They made some headway calming the fire on the dock, and Patrick adjusted the nozzle so that rather than sending a steady, gunlike stream of water, he sprayed the fire with a finer, foglike mist. The fog pattern drew cooler air in from outside and Patrick could feel it mitigating the heat.

After twenty minutes or so, Patrick, Pops, and Sonny had advanced the line to the dock and had knocked down much of the fire in that concentrated area. By this time, a number of other companies had responded, and there were enough firefighters to man all the lines. The three Kenneys turned their line over to Dedham firefighters and walked back along the driveway to watch for a while from the street.

As the three watched the firefighters battle the blaze, Patrick could not help but glance over at Pops and Sonny. They were watching with fascination—these two men who had seen everything there was to see in firefighting—yet they were still captivated by it, still drawn to it. Patrick loved the feeling, the connection to his father and grandfather. Pat knew of fathers and sons who had worked together on the Boston Fire Department, but he could not imagine that three generations of the same family fighting a fire was very common.

After a while, they hopped back into the Jeep and headed home. Each man knew at that moment that he would remember this for the rest of his life. There was something precious about that moment in time, something that linked the three generations as nothing else could.

It was called the Red Book, though its actual title was *Fire Manual for the Instruction of Applicants for Entrance or Promotional Examinations in the Fire Service in Cities and Towns of the Commonwealth of Massachusetts.* In the introduction to a particular edition, W. Henry Finnegan, the director of Civil Service wrote:

> Because of the importance and the hazardous nature of this work, the fire fighter engaged in it must . . . possess certain specific knowledge concerning the work if he is to perform his duties efficiently and with a minimum amount of risk to himself and to his fellow fire fighters. He should have a detailed knowledge of the dangers arising from heat, smoke, explosions, etc., caused by fire, of the haz-

ards presented by new industries, processes and materials developed by science, of the construction of buildings and the hazards involved in the materials used or stored in them, and of the dangers inherent in the use of water at high pressures.

This manual is . . . intended to provide those who are seeking careers in the fire service with a first course in the fundamentals of the work of fire fighting, and to provide a solid foundation of study for further specialization by those seeking promotion within the fire service.

Materials within the Red Book were drawn from a variety of sources, including the National Fire Protection Association, the American Insurance Association, the International Association of Fire Chiefs, and the American Red Cross. The Red Book was a paperback, crisp and clean when new, but inevitably, as an applicant carried it around, studying it when the chance arose, it grew soiled and dogeared. The Red Book contained detailed information about a broad array of firefighting equipment, including hoses, ladders, fire extinguishers, forcible entry equipment, first aid equipment, lights. It instructed on approaches to fighting fires in various sized buildings, the hazards of chemicals, precautions to be taken while fighting fire on a roof, the principles of ventilation, the dangers of back drafts and mushrooming, and gas masks. There were sections such as "Why Cellar Fires Are Hard to Fight" and "Factors Which May Indicate or Influence the Possibility of Partial or Total Collapse of a Building," and advice on breaching brick walls, artificial respiration, along with a glossary of structural and fire terms. In all, the Red Book was packed with 313 pages of practical information.

Tom would be eligible to take the fire department test after turning twenty-one in November 1974. Applicants for the BFD were chosen based on a Civil Service exam grade, combined with experience applicable to the job. Tom had built a superb résumé, so good that it was difficult to imagine any applicant scoring higher on the experience scale than Tom. And so he prepared for the exam by studying the

Red Book, the same book that Sonny had studied nearly thirty years earlier.

Tom got together with some of his pals, many also sons of firefighters, to work jointly to prepare for the exam. Red Harrison, a district chief in Boston, volunteered his time to teach a class on the Red Book to anyone who wanted to attend. Word spread from fathers on the job to their sons and sons' friends, and a few dozen young men showed up for Red's classes, held twice weekly, at a school in the Fields Corner section of Dorchester.

Tom recalled:

He would go through the Red Book and he'd pick one particular thing—explain five different ladders, for example; explain each one and how it differed from the others and what it was used for. He was a very good teacher and it was a really useful class. So things were looking good. I was in school studying the classes. I knew if I passed the exam, I'd get on the list; I'd have to do the strength test and then I'd be in. And word was they would be hiring fifty next year, or 150 or whatever. So things were looking good. Now a million guys want the job, but you know, we figured if I put the effort into it I'd have a good chance.

And then, on the night of March 8, 1974, Tom drove over to Fields Corner to attend Chief Harrison's class. Tom was well prepared as usual. He and the other young men settled into the seats, and the chief entered the room. He didn't seem himself. He was normally cheerful and full of energy, but tonight he seemed downcast.

"I have some bad news," he said. "I won't be able to do these classes anymore. They're not going to use the Red Book anymore." The chief explained that there had been a ruling from a federal court that day, and the ruling banned using the Red Book as a basis for the test. The chief packed up his things and left.

While Tom and Pat had been studying the Red Book, lawyers for the U.S. Justice Department and the NAACP were preparing lawsuits designed to change the firefighter selection process in Massachusetts. The cases were joined and argued before the courts in the summer and fall of 1973. Fundamentally, the case charged the City of Boston and other municipalities with discrimination against minorities in "qualification requirements and overall hiring policies for the position of firefighter." The case was brought by the U.S. Justice Department to enforce the Civil Rights Act of 1964 and the Equal Employment Opportunity Act of 1972. The presiding judge in the case, Frank Freedman, noted that the NAACP case was brought as a class action, "alleging discrimination in defendants' policies of recruiting."

An important issue during trial testimony had been whether the City of Boston and the Civil Service Commission, which administered the test, had made any efforts to go out and affirmatively recruit minority members. The judge found that the department had in fact made such an effort. Though it had been minimal in the late 1960s, the effort to spread the word within minority areas about careers in the fire department was stepped up. Part of the court transcript highlights the recruiting procedures:

Two black firefighters testified that for a period of weeks they talked to organizations, at high schools and to people on the street trying to promote interest among blacks in the fire department. Each of them had also at different times been sent out of state, at the department's expense, to conferences of black firefighters where recruitment efforts and techniques were apparently discussed. A Spanish-surnamed firefighter testified that he spent approximately two weeks in 1972 doing full-time recruitment work in the predominantly Spanish-speaking neighborhood of Boston. He passed out leaflets and arranged for announcements to be made over a Spanish radio program. About 100 people indicated an interest but he recalls only approximately 30 showed up for the first training class and that number rapidly dwindled.

All witnesses who were asked agreed that the greatest source of new applicants for the fire department is word of mouth and encouragement from friends and relatives already on the force . . . If indeed, for so many years those positions have been filled as the result of white firemen encouraging white friends and relatives to join the force, it is no little wonder that blacks and Spanish-surnamed persons represent such an insignificant percentage of the force. It is of course most understandable how this has happened and *the Court wishes to make it clear that it is not suggesting such an exclusionary policy has been followed intentionally or by design.* (Emphasis added)

A central question in the case was whether the test based upon the Red Book was relevant to performance of the job of firefighter. The judge wrote that

for a test to be . . . content valid, the aptitudes and skills required for successful examination performance must be those aptitudes and skills required for successful job performance. It is essential that the examination test these attributes both in proportion to their relative importance on the job and at the level of difficulty demanded by the job.

During the course of the trial, both sides had brought in experts to address this issue of whether knowledge of the material within the Red Book related to performance on the job. To the defendant (the City of Boston), it seemed self-evident. The Red Book was *all* about the tools, implements, and techniques used to fight fires. It was material that every firefighter needed to know. The plaintiffs, however, argued that there was little correlation between knowledge of the Red Book and an ability to perform as a firefighter. Both sides presented arguments on this question—with expert testimony from professionals in the field of testing. After sifting through the testimony, the judge said he was persuaded that the Red Book exam was not job related; he ruled that it did not correlate to an ability to perform well as a firefighter.

The most powerful evidence introduced at the trial involved statistics cited by the judge, who found a "comparison of population and employment statistics" to be "telling. Boston has a black population of approximately 16%. The combined minority population may exceed 23%. The city has a fire force of approximately 1,983 men. Of that total there are 16 blacks and 2 Spanish-surnamed persons who represent approximately 0.9% of the total force. . . ."

Whether discrimination against minorities was intentional or not (and Judge Freedman ruled that it was not), and whether recruitment had been robust or not—the judge could not get past the simple fact that although minorities composed nearly one-fourth of the city's population, they constituted just under 1 percent of the fire department. And so in perhaps the most significant court finding in the history of the Boston Fire Department, the federal court ruled that because department "policy has in effect resulted in the exclusion of . . . minorities from the fire department, the policy must be changed and present effects of past discrimination must be remedied."

Judge Freedman wrote that "plaintiffs will suffer irreparable harm in the nature of a lack of equal opportunity to compete for jobs on the Boston Fire Department, that the granting of preliminary relief will not cause irreparable harm to the defendants." The judge ordered a halt to hiring firefighters based on the most recent Red Book test and further ordered that future tests should be "demonstrably job-related."

The ruling, if upheld on appeal, would mean that the only white applicants with any real chance of getting on the job for some years to come would be two groups already given preferential treatment: veterans and children of firefighters who had been killed in the line of duty. An applicant who fell into neither category would have to achieve a perfect score to have even a prayer of making it on the department, and even that was no guarantee.

The City of Boston appealed the findings, seeking to have the judge's decision overturned by the United States Court of Appeals. Tom, Pat, Sonny, and Pops—along with our entire family and thousands of other families like ours in Boston—waited nervously.

10
Shattered Dream

Anne was not herself. She had been upset by the court ruling, of course, but there was something else troubling her. Throughout the spring and into the summer of 1974 she was anxious and irritable, and seemed distracted. The changes were subtle and most people didn't notice, but it was clear to me that there was something wrong. One night in late summer, while she and I were talking on the phone, she suddenly started crying for no apparent reason. I tried to probe, but she said she was just tired and feeling emotional. Her twenty-fifth wedding anniversary was approaching, and my brothers and I had planned a surprise anniversary party in September. In addition, Sonny and Anne had booked an anniversary trip to Bermuda for mid-September.

At the end of August, Anne went to the doctor and said she had discovered a lump in her breast. The doctor examined her and referred her to an oncologist, who diagnosed breast cancer. He said he wanted to get her into the hospital for treatment as soon as possible. "Take the Bermuda trip," he said, "but then into the hospital."

She was admitted to University Hospital in Boston the third week in September. She looked great and said she felt fine. She sat on the bed when she arrived at the hospital and smiled sheepishly, feeling as though she did not belong there. She looked and felt perfectly healthy. But she was not.

The same week, on September 18, 1974, the United States Court of Appeals issued its ruling in the case. It was the worst possible news: The court upheld Judge Freedman's ruling to kill the Red Book and order minority preference in hiring. The appeals court then pointedly stated: "What in our view conclusively tips the scale in plaintiffs' favor is the uncontroverted testimony, from experts called by both sides, that black and Spanish surnamed candidates typically perform more poorly on paper-and-pencil tests of this type."

The appeals court noted:

Other evidence at trial supported the view that the test bore more heavily on minorities. For example, the court found that Boston fire fighters were often recruited by relatives and friends. Minority applicants, lacking access to such sources of aid and advice, might find it harder to absorb the technical subject matter covered in the test. They could try to memorize the "Red Book," but such information is doubtless more easily absorbed by those exposed to fire fighters and firehouse routines. Such considerations do not, of course, invalidate the test; they are merely additional reasons for inquiring into its utility as a bona fide predictor of job performance.

Judge Freedman had ruled that there was no intentional discrimination by the Civil Service or the City of Boston. The appeals court characterized that as "immaterial," and wrote: "The result, not the specific intent, is what matters."

On the critical question of whether the Red Book exam was job related, the appeals court agreed with Judge Freedman that it was not. The appeals court decision stated that

a test fashioned from materials pertaining to the job . . . superficially may seem job-related. But what is at issue is whether it demonstrably selects people who will perform better the required . . . on-the-job behaviors after they have been hired and trained.

The crucial fit is not between test and job lexicon, but between the test and job performance.

... There is a difference between ... memorizing (or absorbing through past experience) fire fighting terminology and being a good fire fighter ... The test does not examine traits seemingly more relevant to a fire fighter's performance such as agility, stamina, quick thinking under pressure, poise, mechanical aptitude and the ability to work with others. Experts for both sides agreed that verbal memory is not a very important attribute for the job. And unlike the motor vehicle rules covered in a driver's test, it seems unessential whether the candidate absorbs the tested vocabulary before or after acceptance. Nomenclature and similar matters can be mastered during training and on the job. Testing them before acceptance puts a premium on ability to memorize terms that, at the time, contain only abstract meaning.

The appeals court ruling stated that selecting firefighters on the basis of the Red Book test would be akin to the Red Sox selecting players based on knowledge of baseball history.

The court later changed the passing grade on the test for minority applicants. For white applicants, the passing grade would remain at 70 percent. For minority applicants, however, the passing grade was lowered to 35 percent. New minority recruits would later be bitterly referred to as "thirty-five percenters."

This was a nightmare for the Kenney family. The opportunity to serve on the Boston Fire Department had always been there in the family, going all the way back to the 1930s. The prospect of a job as a firefighter was part of the family; the opportunity—the possibility—was like a living, breathing entity. And now that member of the family had died. And as is the case with the death of a family member, we reacted with a series of emotions: First shock and disbelief, then anger.

Looking back over thirty years of history, Tom said:

I know it probably wasn't fair every single time the way hiring was done. But I didn't institute that. And so now when it's my turn, for me to suddenly be saddled with the fact that somebody else made mistakes and I can't get the job that I want, I don't think that was fair either. And a lot of firefighters didn't think it was fair—and a lot of kids didn't think it was fair. A lot of guys took it personally because their kids had been studying and had been in the same position I was. And so, now, here's an opportunity for them to get the job. But because they weren't of color or they weren't a disabled veteran, their chances of getting on were pretty slim.

I was a white non-veteran. So of all the lists established, even if I got a hundred, they would have to execute all the other lists before they ever touched me . . . They changed the rules midstream. It was always if you wanted to be a firefighter, here's the Red Book. This is what you study. That was always the way it worked.

Tom and Pat had played by the rules, but now the rules had changed. The Red Book to which they had devoted thousands of hours of intensive study was gone, as worthless as last week's newspapers.

It was as though the federal court was singling them out. Tom and Pat were guilty of growing up in a family with a firefighting tradition—that was true. It was also true that they had learned about firefighting and the Red Book from people on the job. It was true, as the court put it, that Pat and Tom were "exposed to firehouses and firehouse routines." Certainly it was not the intent of the court to harm Tom and Pat, to deprive them of their dreams. But as the court itself had noted, intent is "immaterial . . . The result, not the specific intent, is what matters." Judge Freedman had written that the remedy he proposed "will not cause irreparable harm." Unfortunately, he was wrong.

―――――

We were raised in a segregated city. Growing up, we rarely encountered black people. Riding the elevated train downtown as kids, we saw black faces in the tenements twenty or so feet from the tracks. And though we sometimes saw black people downtown, we almost never saw a black face in our neighborhood, and we certainly never had any interaction with blacks. The reality was that Boston was a segregated city and had been for some time.

During the 1930s and 1940s, when Sonny was growing up, there was a small black population confined to an area within the South End and lower Roxbury. In *The Hub: Boston Past and Present*, historian Thomas H. O'Connor characterizes the city's black population as "isolated and generally unnoticed." Yet even in isolation, O'Connor wrote, there was vibrance to black life in the city, particularly around Massachusetts and Columbus Avenues in the South End, where black restaurants, bars, and nightclubs were clustered. Young Malcolm X was dazzled by life here, O'Connor wrote. The black population grew rapidly in the 1940s and 1950s, as blacks from the South migrated to northern urban areas. Soon, O'Connor wrote, black sections in the South End and lower Roxbury were badly overcrowded, and in the 1960s, blacks "were starting to move beyond the confines of their traditional, Roxbury boundaries, settling along the fringes of such formerly all-white neighborhoods as Dorchester, Mattapan, Jamaica Plain, Roslindale and Hyde Park." O'Connor continued:

> It was not long before the growing spread of the black population ran into a mounting wall of white resistance. Intensely proud of the distinctively ethnic characteristics that had distinguished their particular neighborhoods for more than half a century, and brought up with the strict admonition to "stay with your own kind," the Irish in South Boston and Charlestown, the Italians in East Boston and the North End, and the Jews of Mattapan, along with other residents of traditionally white areas, reacted in panic and alarm at the idea that African Americans were moving into their neighborhoods—their "turf." Racial tensions quickly mounted as whites raised fears of blacks taking their jobs, lowering the standards of all-white schools, bringing down property values, and adding to the danger of crime in the streets. . . .

The population shift in Boston's large Jewish neighborhood was perhaps most dramatic. According to O'Connor, in the mid-1950s, there were approximately 50,000 Jewish residents of Mattapan. Blacks began moving into the area, and "by 1972 the number of Jewish residents in the area had dropped to fewer than twenty-five hundred, and the subsequent flare ups of racial fears, panic selling, and blockbusting accelerated the exodus of Jewish families to the point where a once predominantly Jewish community was transformed into an almost all-black neighborhood."

Coincident with court rulings on the fire department had come a federal court ruling ordering the desegregation of the city's public schools. The NAACP filed suit, charging discrimination against black children in the school system. The matter was assigned to U.S. District Court Judge W. Arthur Garrity in 1972. More than two years later—on June 21, 1974, barely ninety days after the ruling in the fire department case—Judge Garrity ruled that the Boston School Committee had "knowingly carried out a systematic program of segregation." "The entire school system of Boston is unconstitutionally segregated," Garrity wrote. He ordered that the schools be desegregated by busing white children to black schools and black children to white schools. Beginning in September 1974, 18,000 children were bused to achieve racial balance in the schools. Black children boarded buses in their neighborhoods and rode to schools in white neighborhoods. White children boarded buses in their neighborhoods and rode to schools in black neighborhoods. Sometimes the buses passed one another on the street.

In Boston, it came to be known as "forced busing," and it was met with fierce—and sometimes violent—resistance in some white neighborhoods, particularly South Boston and Charlestown, where both Sonny and Anne lived as children. These were both gritty, blue-collar neighborhoods with narrow streets lined with cramped housing. The people of these neighborhoods were particularly enraged by Garrity's ruling, for it struck hardest at their children, who would now be forced to ride a bus to an unfamiliar part of the city.

The implementation of Garrity's order in the fall of 1974 met with chaos in Boston. Some white families responded to busing by boycotting school, keeping their children home for months. Other parents took to the streets and demonstrated. Some tried to physically block buses carrying black children. Other parents threw stones at buses with black kids, shouting racial epithets at them. Throughout South Boston and Charlestown, there were hand-painted and spray-painted signs on buildings, fences, park benches, everywhere: "Resist!" "Never!" Hundreds of police lined the streets of South Boston to make way for buses carrying black children—buses that were led and flanked by motorcycle police.

At the time, the situation was often portrayed as a purely racist reaction by ignorant whites, and there is no doubt that for some who resisted—perhaps for many—it *was* overt racism. But for many other white families, it was more nuanced than that; and in the overheated atmosphere, nuance was the first casualty. The anger of many white families was not about racism but about powerlessness. Sonny hated the busing order not because he was racist—he certainly was not—but because it was a betrayal by the federal government he had gone to war to protect.

For many working people in the city's blue-collar neighborhoods, the busing order evoked memories of the ugly historical times when their ancestors were treated like immigrant riffraff. The busing order heightened a sense of pride and solidarity among many Irish and Italian Americans. Many older Irish folks could still recall job ads in the newspaper from the earlier part of the century that would bear the mark: "Irish Need Not Apply."

For these families—the ones who did not object purely on racial grounds—this was as much about class as anything else. Sonny observed bitterly that Senator Edward Kennedy supported the busing.

"Of course his kids all go to private schools—it doesn't affect his family at all," Sonny said. Sonny made similar observations about Mayor Kevin White, who lived on Beacon Hill in a bubble of privilege (though Sonny was not among those who bitterly called White "Mayor

Black" for his perceived favored treatment of black Bostonians). The *Boston Globe* was a passionate supporter of the busing order. The publishers and editors of the *Globe*—overwhelmingly—lived in affluent suburbs. "Of course they're for busing. It has no impact on their families at all," Sonny observed.

But it would very soon have an impact on the Kenney family, with John and Tim both in public schools in West Roxbury, having been withdrawn from St. Theresa's. The initial stages of busing focused largely on South Boston and Roxbury, but the desegregation plan spread throughout the city in the ensuing years. This plan was enforced by Judge Garrity, earning him the undying enmity of Sonny and others who felt a sense of betrayal from this Irish Catholic who had been nominated to the bench by Senator Kennedy. The judge was despised throughout the city's white working-class neighborhoods. Sonny and thousands of others considered him wholly insensitive to the white families he affected. Countless white residents of the city were enraged at this man who lived in the lily-white suburban town of Wellesley—a preserve of the wealthy—and thus had zero personal understanding of the impact busing had on families. None of Garrity's family, neighbors, or friends were impacted by it. Each night, while the city roiled in turmoil, the judge escaped to the tranquil streets of Wellesley, never having to face any of the consequences he imposed on the lives of Bostonians.

While 18,000 students were bused the first year of desegregation and 21,000 the second year, the youngest Kenney boys were forced to deal with the fallout from busing. John escaped the Boston public schools by winning a scholarship to a prestigious private school in West Roxbury, but Tim went on to English High School, which was overwhelmingly black.

The resentment grew more profound with each passing school day that fall of 1974 and pervaded white working-class Boston, including the fire department. The men of the department had played by a certain set of rules: Work hard on the job, save some money, and buy a single-family home with a yard in Hyde Park, Roslindale, Brighton, Dorchester, South Boston, or West Roxbury. And now the rules were abruptly changed—not just the rules for admittance to the fire department, but rules for where their kids would go to school.

Ultimately, busing in Boston was a colossal failure. Not only did it fail to achieve its intended result—racial balance—but it deeply divided the city for years. By 1980, just six years after busing had started, the census found that 80,000 people (nearly all white) had left the city since 1970. In this "white flight," one-third of the white families with children under eighteen left the city. Twenty years into busing, the share of Boston schoolchildren who were white had plummeted to just 19 percent.

It is ironic that a city with such a rich history in the abolitionist movement, with so many storied thinkers, writers, ministers, and philosophers, would become one of the most racially divided cities in America. The city that had provided a safe haven on the Underground Railroad had become a city of raw racial animosity.

Tom's hopes were raised after he scored well on the written exam and was subsequently called for the strength test. Historically, applicants called for a strength test were on the verge of being hired. Tom received written notification of the strength test three weeks in advance, bought a new pair of sneakers, and began running every day, working to improve his conditioning. By this point, he was six feet, three inches, about 170 pounds of solid muscle. He had enormously powerful hands and was so strong he could lift a refrigerator on his own.

On the day of the test, he drove out to the old Massachusetts Fire Academy in Stowe, a small town about an hour from Boston. He found a field office in a trailer and about forty or so guys waiting to be tested. Tom checked in and, like the other candidates, was given a light vest with a number on it. The test was composed of a series of stations, each one measuring some aspect of strength, speed, or agility.

Before the testing started, an administrator emerged from the trailer and beckoned the young men to gather round. He explained that each man would perform once at each station. He asked whether there were any questions. One young man raised his hand and asked how many people typically flunked the test. The administrator looked around, gazed out over the group of exclusively white faces, paused for a moment, then replied: "Today, none."

Jesus, Tom thought, *This guy is thinking, "Here's my way to fuck the system. I'll automatically pass all the white guys."*

A ripple of excitement spread through the crowd, with everyone eager to get the test over, knowing there would be a passing grade, knowing this would take them to the brink of the job they all so badly wanted. The men dispersed, dividing up into equal groups at the various stations. They had barely begun—in fact, Tom was still standing in line waiting to do the obstacle course, his first event—when the man reemerged from the trailer.

"That's it," he announced. "No further testing today."

And everyone was sent home.

The job candidates were all now a mixture of anger and bewilderment. Some of the men talked with the administrator, and word spread that there had been some eleventh-hour ruling—from Civil Service or a court or somewhere—invalidating this very strength test.

Tom stood there feeling numb. *Five minutes ago, I thought I had it made. And now nothing.*

One night, Patrick was in the kitchen of the firehouse in Grove Hall—Engine 24, Ladder 23. There were a few firefighters there as well as a number of younger guys who had hoped to get on to the department. The talk focused on the exam—just a few days away—that all of these young men would be taking in the hopes of getting on the job. There was intense anger about the court ruling and the guys were talking about whether there was any hope. On this particular night, a Boston police officer stopped by the firehouse for coffee. Pat listened as the cop explained that there was a way for all of them to get the job. He said that on the Civil Service exam there was a box to identify black applicants. He said he knew for a fact that no one at Civil Service actually followed up to check on who was black and who wasn't. The cop said all they had to do was check the box saying they were black and as long as the received a thirty five on the test they were home free.

The guys couldn't believe this. Surely someone would check.

"Of course you'd get caught," someone said.

"Nope," said the cop, shaking his head. "They don't check."

That night, some of the men vowed that they would do just what the cop was suggesting—they would claim on the Civil Service form that they were black.

Pat was amazed by the conversation. He couldn't believe that anyone would actually go to that extent, but even he considered it briefly. He knew, though, that he couldn't do it. He knew it would be dishonest. He knew it would be crazy—and it was just plain wrong. But there were others there that night who didn't think it was so crazy; who really were willing to do *anything* to become firefighters. Two of the men there that night were twin brothers—Philip and Paul Malone. They would claim to be black. And they would get away with it—for eleven years—before they were discovered and thrown off the force. (The Malones insisted to the state Civil Service commission that they had black ancestry but they could not prove it and the commission did not believe them.)

Sonny thought it was all sheer madness. He had trouble grasping the idea that his boys—who had worked so hard and long, who had devoted themselves to preparing for their calling—were prevented from joining the department because of the color of their skin. Sonny considered this a profound betrayal by his government. He had gone to war at eighteen, his friends had died in service to their country, and now the court system of that country—a court system supposedly devoted to justice—was shattering the dreams.

It was a fucking disgrace.

Sonny called his old friend Leo Stapleton, with whom he had worked as a young firefighter. Leo was now Chief of Department, soon to be commissioner. Sonny asked Leo if he could help the boys, do anything for them. Leo was sorry, truly sorry. He could not.

Sonny was disconsolate. It was too unfair, too cruel. It hurt too much.

It was heartbreaking for Pops and Sonny to watch Pat and Tom keep trying, over and over again. Between the two of them, Tom and Pat took the test ten times—four times for Tom, six for Pat—before they gave up on their dream.

11
Tom Saves a Life

Sonny sits in the wood-framed, vinyl-covered hospital room chair. His hair is somewhat unkempt. He wears green work pants and shirt, having come directly from Firecontrol. He sits in the chair, not staring, exactly, but eyes wide, jaw set, lips pursed. His hands grip the chair, and I see that his knuckles are white. My brother Michael is here and has been here for some time. He was the only one with our mother when she died. I come over to Sonny and look at him.

"Dad . . . ," I say.

He blinks, his eyes wide. He is stunned, disbelieving. I want to take him in my arms, my father, and hold him and feel his warmth and convey to him that we will hang in there together and carry on, and yet this is not done in the Kenney family. Sonny does not move to touch or embrace me or Michael, though he will later hug the younger boys. I reach down and touch my father's hair but then pull my hand away.

Hospital personnel recede, allowing us to be with her for some final moments before her body is removed. On the seventh day of November 1974, our mother—Sonny's wife of twenty-five years—has lost a brief and terrible battle with cancer. She never reached her fifty-second birthday. She lies in a hospital bed, milky white. We stand around and nothing is said. A nurse will later tell us that on her final day, semiconscious, she said, "I cannot leave my family."

Sonny knew little of how the house operated. Anne had done everything at home—all the cleaning, laundry, grocery shopping, and cooking. She did whatever clothes shopping was necessary, and all the Christmas shopping. She was in charge of the schedules for the boys, and she drove them or walked them where they needed to go, getting them there on time and ready for whatever it was they were doing.

Sonny tried. He worked up a shopping list and from it derived a meal plan for the week ahead. He was partial to chicken with mushroom soup, which he let simmer in a Crock-Pot throughout the day, to be ready for 5:30 PM supper. Friends and neighbors dropped by with precooked meals, but that receded after a few weeks. He cooked blade steak (as she had), made grilled cheese sandwiches, and heated various canned vegetables from Jolly Green Giant. He invariably referred to the "fresh, whole kernel corn" from a can.

He took John and Tim out to Old Sturbridge Village, a re-creation of an early New England colonial village. They stayed in the hotel there, ate dinner in the restaurant, and toured the farm and the various old-world village shops. The boys loved it. Sonny took them to the Sheraton Wayfarer Hotel, a weekend special, in Bedford, New Hampshire. John and Tim both had the prime rib; then John had seconds, another massive cut of beef. Sonny loved that.

He was trying, but he felt disoriented. This was not his life, not the life he had built for himself, not the "ideal life."

It was around Thanksgiving when the glass appeared on the kitchen counter—an odd size, slightly larger than a juice glass, quite a bit smaller than a water glass. Sonny would later refer to it as a "pony glass." He kept it to the left of the sink, tucked over by the wall next to the sugar and flour canisters. The first time I saw him use it, he reached into the cabinet above the counter and produced a fifth of

Chivas Regal. Sonny had always enjoyed scotch whiskey, and there was always a fresh bottle around Christmastime. After the wake and funeral, a number of friends had come by with bottles of Chivas in ornate silver gift boxes. The bottle, rounded and squat, carried a certain appeal with its rich amber color. The label was distinctive, silver with a red background—Blended Scotch Whiskey 1801. There were two or three bottles in gift boxes tucked into the cabinet above the sink.

I first saw Sonny with the glass on Thanksgiving weekend. It was midafternoon on Saturday or Sunday, and I happened into the kitchen. He was standing at the sink with the pony glass half filled. He stood straight, the glass in his right hand, his left hand on his hip. He raised the glass to his lips, then threw his head back and consumed it all at once. He stood for a moment letting it settle. He rinsed the glass, filled it with water, and drank that. Then he set the glass back down on the counter.

I was surprised because I had never seen him do that before, but it certainly was not as though he was drunk. I did not speak, and neither did he. And I really did not think much of it. The guy had lost his wife three weeks earlier. I figured he was entitled to deal with it in whatever way worked for him.

Christmastime had always been the highlight of our year. Anne had always decorated the house with festive wreaths, ribbons, and candles. This year, the other boys and I did the decorating she had always done, though it somehow did not look the same. We thought it important to stick to the routine, and the routine meant family and friends joining us on Christmas Eve for food and drink. People streamed through, cramming the small kitchen and living room, sitting on the stairs. There was a lot of drinking. One of our neighbors crashed face-first onto the floor. He was helped home by some friends. I noticed during the course of the evening that Sonny was never far from the Chivas Regal. What was remarkable, I noticed, was his ability to handle it. Any normal person drinking what he was consuming would be dead drunk. I was not alarmed by it because I assumed that after Christmas, the Chivas along with the pony glass would be returned to storage. I assumed we would do whatever we needed to do to get back to reality.

Sonny got through the Christmas holidays and the winter months reasonably well, but then, come spring, he seemed to sag under then weight of it all. And it was not just the death of his wife. It was the collective weight, borne over the years, that seemed to slow him, confuse him, set him off his game. Anne's death, along with the federal court ruling—at virtually the same time—proved crushing. And these had come on top of other losses Sonny had suffered in his life, losses which he had absorbed but which now, fused together, combined to create a new, much weightier burden than he had ever had to bear. He had watched his father lose the job he loved back so many years ago. Sonny had returned from the war to learn that he had lost his friend Swede Wilson. He had been blessed with an appointment to the Boston Fire Department, but a venal captain had deprived him of a chance to continue at Boston College and so he had lost a crucial opportunity to establish the foundation for perhaps greater things in life. He had lost the job he had loved so dearly, the job that had defined him in so many ways. In losing that job, he had lost the partnership with Nelson Pittman, his closest friend since Swede. And he had also lost the unwavering confidence he had once had in the Catholic Church. He remained a man of faith, yet the incidents involving the accusation of my cheating and, more important, the beating of Tim and subsequent dishonesty of the bishop, had shaken the foundation of Sonny's belief in the Church and its leaders.

And so it seemed, half a year or so after Anne died, that Sonny had begun to lose his way.

It was a family function of some kind, a party for a cousin or aunt or uncle twenty minutes' drive from Wedgemere Road. It was a long social affair, and later that night Sonny was driving his mother home, with Tim riding in the backseat. As they rode along, the car was weaving, Sonny's hand unsteady, his vision uncertain. The car lurched up onto the median strip and Molly, by then also called "Nana," began to scream and shout at Sonny. He was drunk, he was going to get them all killed. He steadied his hand somehow, but then, again he swerved and the car bumped up onto the median, again and again. Nana kept yelling at him. Soon enough, he was able to guide the car to her apartment building, dropping her off. He then drove home, managing to reach Wedgemere Road safely.

We were out to dinner one night, with a few of my friends, Sonny began to slur his words. I was surprised in part because I had not noticed how much he was drinking. It was so pronounced that after a while it was hard to focus on anything else. He was clearly unaware of it and continued telling stories and drinking. He had told a story about the war years midway through the evening, and now he was sipping scotch after dinner and repeating the identical story—this time with a thick tongue and slurred words. Soon enough, we left, and I dropped him off.

I arrived at Wedgemere the following morning with coffee and doughnuts. Sonny had just returned from mass at St. Theresa's with John and Tim. Sonny and I settled in the living room. It had now been just about six months since Anne's death. In the interim, Sonny had turned fifty-one.

"I want to tell you that I was concerned last night about the drinking," I said. I spoke in a soft voice, in part because I did not want to be overheard by the boys, but also not to sound accusatory or harsh. Sonny sipped his coffee as though unsure what exactly I was talking about. Then I could see he realized I was talking about him, about *his* drinking.

"I wasn't aware . . . ," he started, then stopped.

"It was pretty obvious," I said.

"Obvious?" he said, a bit surprised.

"Yeah."

"How so?"

"You didn't sound quite right."

He sat contemplating this, then gave a brief sigh. "There's a lot going on," he said.

"I know that," I said. "Look, I know. I don't mean to get on you but I think you should be careful."

I didn't mention it but the first thing I had checked upon arriving at the house was whether the pony glass was there on the counter—and it was. It stood in exactly the same place, just to the left of the sink, over by the wall and against the canisters.

"No, I've got chicken in the Crock-Pot for tonight," he said. "The boys love that. Whole kernel corn and French fries."

He had been doing this for a while—reciting the menu for various meals. Whenever I called during the week, he would rattle off the menu: franks and beans, sausages and mashed potatoes, meat loaf, Crock-Pot chicken, whole kernel corn. Putting a hot meal on the table at suppertime became the benchmark for Sonny; it became the essential responsibility that measured his performance as a single parent. With food on the table all was well.

I guess he had heard what I had said, but it was certainly not an easy thing to do. Now it was done, and I thought everything would be fine. Six months since his wife died; six months since his world had been turned upside down, shaken, and dropped on its head. He was working his way through it. He was a smart man. He'd been through an awful lot in his life and he would get through this. That he needed a crutch to help him through—was that such a bad thing?

Patrick had gotten a job like Tom's, working the Boston City Hospital ambulance. Pat was eighteen at the time, a graduate of Catholic Memorial High School. In addition to working as an EMT, Patrick continued part-time at Firecontrol, where he noticed a disturbing trend. Sometimes he went out on calls and found that the client had been promised service months earlier. Some clients were angry and even verbally abusive about Sonny. Some said they had called him repeatedly without having received a return call. Some had paid for services in advance. A few had already gone out and found another company to do the work.

Patrick noticed there were more and more nights when Sonny stayed out late. Pat came home from work one day at 5:00 PM, and Sonny was sound asleep on the living room sofa. At Firecontrol, Pat saw that increasingly Sonny would go out for lunch and sometimes not return for hours, invariably smelling of alcohol. It was a far cry from the fifteen-minute lunch Pops had mandated years earlier.

Patrick's anger and discouragement built over time, until one day he came home to Wedgemere Road from working on the ambulance and walked into the house to find Nana cleaning and redecorating. Patrick was alarmed. The place smelled different from the way it had always smelled. There was something—some polish or something that gave the house a very different smell. Patrick was upset. He didn't want anything to be different from the way it had been when Anne was alive. And then Patrick noticed that the colonial-themed curtains, the ones Anne had loved, were gone, replaced by something else, some flowery thing.

"What are you doing?" Patrick asked. "Why are you *changing* things?"

There was an edge to his voice, an intensity that struck Nana. She responded in kind with a sharp comment about how she was not appreciated.

But all Patrick could think about was how hard Anne had worked to get the house right; to suffuse it with the colonial theme she loved. Finally, Patrick noticed that some things had been rearranged, things of Anne's replaced by knickknacks from Nana's apartment, set up on the dining room table. Patrick went into the kitchen, picked up the phone, and called a taxi. He went back into the dining room and said to her: "A cab is coming. You should get in it and go home."

"I know when I'm not appreciated," she said, gathering her things together and taking the taxi home.

There was a rawness to this time, a time when nerves were badly frayed, when life had been altered in such a wrenching fashion for all of us that we were disoriented to one extent or another. An air of unease settled over the house on Wedgemere Road. Within six or so months of her death, Tom, now twenty-one years old, moved in with a group of friends in an old house in Dedham. Mike and I had long since moved out, which left Sonny with Patrick and the two younger boys.

As the months passed, Pat found more and more Firecontrol customers angry that Sonny had not delivered as promised, had not even returned their many phone calls. Pops, too, could see that things were slipping at Firecontrol. Pops felt some of the servicemen were taking advantage of Sonny's growing disengagement. He saw servicemen returning to Firecontrol at the end of the day and transferring bags of groceries from the Firecontrol truck into their cars. He would see guys come back who had gone out with a shaggy mane in the morning, their hair freshly trimmed in the afternoon. Pops told Patrick he thought the men should get haircuts and do grocery shopping on their own time. The slow decline of the business grieved Pops, who had always believed, and still did, that there was enormous potential for growth, if only others in the family—particularly Pat and Tom—would join in the business and give it their full attention, really work it hard. Now, not only was that not happening, but Sonny was clearly letting the place slip.

Patrick felt he had to say something to Sonny, but it would be hard. He was eighteen years old, and who was he to tell his fifty-one-year-old father about responsibility? After all Sonny had been through? But Patrick was determined that things—at home and at Firecontrol—would slip no further. He spoke to Sonny one evening in the kitchen, just the two of them.

"You know, Dad, things aren't going so well around here," he said. "With you drinking and out all the time. Things around here aren't getting done. And at work these guys are really pissed off when I go out there and you haven't delivered on your promises and you haven't even called back, and more and more of them have taken their business to somebody else. And you have a responsibility here and at Firecontrol."

Sonny didn't like it.

"That's my business," Sonny said. "I'll take care of the shop. And I'll take care of the house. What I do in the evening is my business, not yours."

It degenerated quickly from there, and soon enough Patrick rented a room in Brighton and moved out of Wedgemere Road, never to return.

For myself, I wanted to spend time with Sonny—I wanted to show him how much I cared about him and how much I understood him. I did not want him to feel as though his sons disapproved of everything he did, to feel a chill coming from us. He was changing, coping, adapting to a new life and I wanted to be part of that life.

"How about if I join you for a drink this weekend," I proposed—at The Hollow, his favorite haunt. After work, he usually cleaned up, put on a decent shirt and pair of pants, and drove down to The Hollow, where he had become friendly with a group of middle-aged and older people who preferred to while away the hours drinking. Over time, it became clear that Sonny would rather be at The Hollow than any-where else.

And so on a Saturday evening, around nine or so, I drive down with a friend to Quincy, a blue-collar city just south of Boston. The Hollow is a modest-sized restaurant on the main street, surrounded by a spacious parking lot. When my friend and I arrive, we head around to the side and enter the lounge. It is crowded with men and women in their for-ties and fifties, for the most part. It is warm, faces are flushed, a bluish cloud of cigarette smoke hanging in the air. There is the sound of clink-ing glasses, of many voices, much laughter. The men and women stand in clusters, some at a few small tables, others lined along the bar. The men tend to the heavy side, fleshy faces and necks. Their hair is neatly trimmed, turning gray. The women are well coiffed, many with a frosted look. They wear dresses, nearly all of them, not skirts or pants. The men wear pressed slacks, a few have ties and jackets, and a number sport turtleneck sweaters or shirts. I notice a few flashy watches, several pinky rings on men. The impression is of people having a fine time, loose, enjoying one another. Every right hand, it seems, holds a glass, and if not a glass, then a cigarette. Ashtrays are everywhere—along the bar, atop tables, on a few laps.

We go to the bar and have not yet spotted Sonny. My friend orders wine, and I realize hers is the only wineglass I see—the glasses people hold are small tumblers with dark brown or clear liquids—either that or highball glasses.

Sonny appears and we chat. He introduces us to several of his friends. At the time, I was a reporter at the *Boston Globe*. One of the first people to whom Sonny introduces me is a middle-aged woman who smiles, shakes my hand, and tells me she considers the *Globe* too liberal.

"I never read it," she says, still smiling. *Ah,* I think, *never read it but it's too liberal.* Of course! This is the millionth time someone has told me they consider the *Globe* too liberal—and sometimes it is too liberal—but usually people wait until we're a few minutes into conversation before the anti-*Globe* comments start up.

Sonny is by my side, a wry, satisfied smile on his face. He seems comfortable here, and over time it becomes clear he knows everyone. People come by, and he introduces them with a quip, often an inside joke of some kind. Each time, he introduces the woman with me as my "lady friend." There is an old-fashioned air about the place, I realize, and perhaps that is, in part, what makes Sonny so comfortable. Highballs, cigarettes, Joey Bishop–Dean Martin-type quips. It suits him. When Sonny's glass is empty, I notice that he merely nods to the bartender and, within seconds, a fresh scotch is in his hands. As the evening wears on, we have a second, then a third round. Sonny insists. Sonny's friends insist. *How long had they been here before we arrived?* I wonder. I'm on my third round—what about Sonny? The cloud of smoke thickens, clinging to my clothes. Sonny breaks out a fresh pack of Lucky Strikes. The air is thick with smoke, and the temperature has risen. I stand off to the side, away from the crowd, talking quietly with my friend. I watch Sonny engage with his friends, his dark wavy hair in place, his manner easy and fluid. I'm feeling the liquor after three drinks, but there is no indication that Sonny is feeling his after—what? Three? Four? More?

"How often does he come here?" my friend asks.

Oh, I think, and then I realize I am embarrassed to tell her the truth. "Couple times a week," I lie. It's got to be four or five, actually.

The bartender comes by with another round—bought by a friend of Sonny's, so I cannot say no. The man who bought us the round comes over with the woman who thinks the *Globe* is too liberal. Sonny joins in as well.

"I read the *Herald*," the woman blurts, still smiling, referring to the *Globe*'s main competitor.

"Me, too," I say.

"I read it because it's accurate."

"I like the sports," I say.

"The *Globe* has good sports," says the man who bought us the round. He is thick waisted, with oversized rims on his eyeglasses, reminding me of the schlock comedian Charles Nelson Reilly.

"Really good," I say. "Good writers."

"I don't read newspapers," the man says. "I like Channel 7."

It's late, and I tell Sonny we have to head out.

"I'm glad you came," he says. I thank him, and as we are saying our good-byes to the woman who hates the *Globe* and the man who bought us the round and doesn't read newspapers, another fellow I have not met suddenly steps into our circle, arches his eyebrows, and says: "Did ya hear the one about the Polish ballerina? She did a split—" And at this point, the woman who hates the *Globe* pipes up—"and she got stuck to the floor!" They all burst out laughing.

My friend drives. During the ride home I feel agitated. I am hot, sweaty, smoky, a bit drunk, and angry. Sonny will stay there and get drunker and then sometime during the night or early morning, he will get behind a wheel and drive home, and then he will get up and repeat the process tomorrow and the day after and the day after. *What is going on here?* I wonder. *What is happening?*

While Sonny was losing his way, Tom was finding his. Tom was absorbing the blows of Anne's death and the court ruling, and he was carving out a life for himself. He had moved out of Wedgemere Road to a house only a mile away, but it might as well have been the other side of the earth. Tom was working as an EMT, devoting himself with a passionate intensity to the job, and he wasn't around the old house much anymore. If there was a family event, a holiday, something like that, he would come around; otherwise, he stayed away. He needed to get on with his life, and he was doing so, looking forward, not back.

This was a time of opportunity for Tom. Historically, Boston City Hospital ambulances were stationed at the hospital itself and responded to calls—no matter where they were in the city—from that central location. That strategy had clearly become outdated. There were countless ambulance calls in high-crime areas of the city, particularly Dorchester and Roxbury, and sending an ambulance from the BCH wasted valuable minutes. Thus, the hospital administration decided to experiment with dispersing ambulances to a couple of key locations, in East Boston and Roxbury, and Tom was fortunate to get the Roxbury assignment. Roxbury was an inner-city neighborhood, overwhelmingly black, an area with the highest rate of violent crime in Boston. Tom's shift was 4:00 PM to midnight, which would prove to be the busiest ambulance in the city—just how Tom wanted it:

> I learned very quickly how violent the city could be, because I don't think I was there but a few days and saw my first murder, then my second murder, and after a couple of weeks I'd had six murder cases. I think in 1974 in the city there was something like 135 murders, mostly shootings and stabbings, and I was at about 70 percent of those.

On his first day on the job in Roxbury, Tom responded to a call where he found a man had been bludgeoned to death with a hammer. A few days later, he responded to a call for a stabbing on Dudley Street:

> There had been a fight, and when we pulled in there was a crowd and a guy on the ground about thirty years old clutching his chest and sweating profusely. He had lost an awful lot of blood but he was still conscious and talking, and we took a look at him and the guy that was with me on the ambulance was older and more experienced, and he said, "Kid, this one we got to go quick." And we're putting a dressing on him and the guy's telling me, "I'm gonna die,

I'm gonna die." And I said, "No, no, you're going to be fine, you're going to be fine. We're going to rush you to City Hospital. They'll take care of you. They do this all the time." We threw dressing on his chest, threw him on the stretcher. We didn't have sheets on the stretchers when I first started. Into the truck, no straps, nothing, and then flew to City Hospital, and by the time we got there he was dead. I was surprised—wide awake one minute and dead the next. Over the years, obviously, I've learned that happens in an instant. It happens all the time. But the first time you see it, it's like, "I didn't know that was going to happen." But it happened very fast. I found that to be a common factor in a lot of cases. People knew.

Heroin was very popular at the time in the city, and we'd get heroin overdoses on a routine basis and they would come in clusters. We could always tell when there was a bad batch of heroin in town or an unusually pure and powerful batch because we'd get a rash of overdoses in the same area literally within hours of each other. And you've got to get there fast, because one of the problems with a heroin OD is that it slows down the respiratory rate and they stop breathing. If you catch them early enough, you can revive them. We'd find them overdosed in every imaginable place—the bathroom in a bar, the front seat of a car, the hallway of the projects—everywhere. A lot of times we'd show up and the guy would have ice packed down his pants around his groin. I don't know why, but addicts thought ice on the groin was kind of a home remedy for heroin overdose. I think they felt like the cold would revive the person. So we'd show up and the guy's pants would be soaked or he'd have all this ice packed in there. It was useful because when we'd show up, seeing the ice packed in there we'd know right away it was a heroin overdose.

———

In the summer of 1975, a fire broke out in an apartment building at 129 Marlborough Street in the Back Bay. Television stations and newspaper photographers responded to the scene and captured dramatic pictures of a woman named Diana Bryant and her goddaughter, a two-year-old child named Tiara Jones, trapped on the third-floor balcony as the fire raged in the floors beneath them. A radio-station helicopter pilot flew over, saw the scene, and set his chopper down on the roof of the building in an effort to rescue them, but he could not reach them from the roof and fire officials ordered him to take off.

The fire department was maneuvering a ladder company into place and was seconds away from sending the stick up to the balcony and rescuing the woman and the girl. Stanley Forman, a photographer from the *Boston Herald*, was on the scene photographing the god-mother clinging to the child on the balcony, when suddenly, without warning, the balcony gave way and the woman and little girl tumbled through the air three stories down. Stanley followed them all the way down, his camera firing away as they fell, capturing their flailing arms, twisted bodies, the expressions of horror on their faces—photographs so dramatic they later won the Pulitzer Prize. As they fell, the god-mother was slightly below the child and the godmother hit the ground first and was killed, yet the child landed atop her, the blow cushioned somewhat.

Tom remembered:

I was working with Jimmy O'Neil in Ambulance 10. We were the Roxbury truck assigned to the Dudley area, but we had just come to work so we were still at City Hospital on Mass Ave. when they gave out a reported building fire at 129 Marlborough Street. And they said they had people injured. That's all we know as we throw the siren and lights on and head over there, and as we're moving comes an update that there's more than one person hurt and now they're going to multiple alarms and calling for more ambulances.

So we were the first ambulance in, Jimmy O'Neil and myself and when we got there, we pulled up and everybody is pointing down the side street. As soon as we got out of the truck, I grabbed my bag and they're all yelling down the side street to an alley behind the building. I start running down there and as I come around the cor-ner, there's a guy on the ground and he's got a little kid in front of him. This guy picked up the two-year-old kid and handed her to me and the kid smelled like smoke—and I wasn't sure she had a pulse, but she definitely wasn't breathing. So I immediately started to do mouth-to-mouth resuscitation and I'm running with her as I'm doing this back up into Marlborough Street, and we get in back of the ambulance and go like hell for New England Medical Center.

Tom worked on her in the ambulance as they raced to the hospital, about six or seven minutes away. By the time they pulled into the medical center ER, Tom had gotten her breathing again and the child was gasping for air and he could detect a strong pulse.

Tom Kenney had saved her life, and the drama of the event captivated the imagination of the city.

The Stanley Forman photographs were plastered across page one of the *Boston Herald* and were shown on television news programs over and over again, and Tom became an instant hero for saving the life of the child. Coming as it did nine months after the federal appeals court ruling and eight months after Anne's death, Tom's life-saving rescue lifted the entire Kenney family. Pops and Sonny were deeply proud of Tom.

It seemed, though, that there was always a counterpoint to glittering moments like these. Tragedy and triumph did not come in equal measure, but sometimes it seemed that way.

That fall, on October 23, 1976, Tom responded in the ambulance to a fire in an old mattress factory in Roxbury, an abandoned six-story brick warehouse that had been the site of previous fires. The firefighters knew the building from previous alarms, knew that it had been weakened and they would not be permitted inside to fight the fire. Tom and the other members of his ambulance crew watched as fire companies worked the exterior of the building, knocking down the flames. One of the firefighters on duty that night was Richard Sheridan of Ladder 16. That night, however, Aerial Tower 2 was short a man and Richie Sheridan, age twenty-nine, was dispatched to fill in with the tower vehicle. At the time, Richie was divorced, living with his widowed mother in Hyde Park.

It was a warm fall night, and the city seemed particularly quiet. It was shortly after 2 AM, not long after Tom had responded to the scene, when he heard a terrible sound—a crack, then a deep rumble. And then, for just a moment, it seemed that the scene froze before Tom's eyes: There was the building on fire, and there were the firefighters, and there was the dark sky and the eight or ten fire trucks, and there was this terrible sound. And in his mind Tom knew what was happening, knew in the instant before it happened what was to come. It was just then that a massive brick wall crumbled, cascading down upon firefighter Richard Sheridan. Then all hell broke loose. All three dozen or so men at the scene—firefighters and members of the ambulance crew—rushed to the pile of rubble and began digging. Tom and most of the others dug with their hands, pulling away chunks of brick and cement. Other men near Richie had been struck by falling debris as well, and had been injured, but Sheridan had borne the brunt of it.

Quickly, Tom and his crew found Richie and cleared the bricks from his head and chest. Tom and the other men began administering CPR while the firefighters cleared the rubble away from the rest of his body. Richie was transported to Peter Bent Brigham Hospital, where he was pronounced dead.

To me at the time, there was something particularly disturbing about Richard Sheridan's death. It was shocking to me that a twenty-nine-year-old could die like that. I was disturbed by the unpredictability of it, by the reminder that any fire at all—even one where the men were ordered not to enter the building—could prove fatal. Richie Sheridan had been a meter reader for Boston Gas Company before becoming a firefighter. Had he stuck with that job, he might well have lived until age eighty. But he had become a firefighter in Boston, and he had not lived to thirty.

As Tom settled into his role as a skilled EMT, things seemed to deteriorate elsewhere. Pops's lungs—never quite right after the Cocoanut Grove—began giving him even more trouble. He was coughing more often and more violently than in the past. Since Pops had long carried an aversion to any sort of medical treatment—all you could get going to the doctor was bad news, he would say—he avoided getting a checkup for years. But soon his condition was such that he had little choice. He was suffering, laboring for breath sometimes. More ominously, there was pain in his chest that steadily grew over a period of months and reached the point where it doubled him over at times.

Sonny drove Pops over to the VA hospital in West Roxbury, where Pops was examined and subjected to a series of tests. The news was not good: Pops had lung cancer, and it was in a fairly advanced state. The doctors said it was terminal.

Pops continued to work at Firecontrol for some time after the diagnosis. Work had sustained him throughout his life. He had started out working as a boy because he had to provide for his family. He had worked most of his life to place bread on the table but also because he loved work; he loved to be active, to produce, to contribute. And so Sonny would pick him up at his apartment in the morning, and some days would go better than others. Some days the pain was so great it forced Pops to sit down, alone in the back of the shop, and fight for air. Pops always won those battles because he would look about him and see fire extinguishers that needed recharging, extinguishers that should be out at some restaurant or school or factory or hospital protecting people. Pops could see that Sonny was going through a dark time and knew that Sonny needed him. Pops was there for Sonny, taking care of business at the shop, even when Sonny did not. Pops knew about the long lunches Sonny was taking. He could see Sonny's condition some days, and then he knew he would leave early and go home to crash on the sofa.

As a teenager, Pops had been a ferocious opponent in the ring—relentless, determined, crouched behind raised fists, fists that flashed out and hammered an opponent into submission. Pops had been a champion and he wore the gold ring to prove it. He had been a fighter—and now he fought with all his might. And day after day, he would get up in the morning and fight his way to work and fight his way through the day, and remain standing at the end of the day—each one a triumph of his iron will.

12

"It's Not As Bad As You Think"

A crowd gathered in the street when the old woman shuffled along the ledge three stories up, her back to the wall as she moved carefully sideways and came to a stop on the narrow ledge well away from the nearest window. In Boston and any other city, for that matter, there are rescues and then there are rescues. There were countless situations where Boston firefighters guided confused or elderly people from smoky apartments or nursing homes, countless instances of firefighters herding a family together and leading them to safety. Dramatic life-or-death rescues, however, were rare.

Bob Mackey was a firefighter on Rescue 1, and on the job, he was all business. A quiet, reserved man, his standards were lofty and he was unflinching in making sure he and those around him measured up. This did not always endear him to other firefighters, some of whom were a bit more relaxed in their approach. Though often gruff and direct—and sometimes blunt and critical of other firefighters—Mackey was so intense and competent that he was widely considered to be one of the most professional firefighters in the department.

Tom's friend Paul Carey, now a captain, worked with Mackey on Rescue 1, and remembered:

Bob was not a very large man, physically, but he was a *giant* on Rescue 1 when I went there as a new guy. I already had 4 years on the job, but Bob wouldn't even acknowledge me, treating me like a Probie [a new firefighter on probation] because now I was on the Rescue. He waited to see how you did, kept an eye on you, giving little tidbits of advice, and reserved any judgment until he saw how you performed at a fire. He had no patience or tolerance for incompetence and expected guys to *do their job*, and he paid attention to detail at everything he ever did. He was very "squared away," and a creature of habit. He did the same thing every day, rode the bus into work, and walked a good distance—in fact, he walked everywhere. He had his gear in the same exact spot in the back of the rescue . . . He was old fashioned, but extremely smart, and well read on a variety of subjects. He was a navy vet of World War II, and I believe his ship was sunk and he spent some time in the water awaiting rescue.

An alarm sounded for Chauncy Street in downtown Boston, just a block or two from the central retail district. When Rescue 1 arrived, the men found a crowd gathered in the street and an elderly woman standing on a ledge of the old building—threatening to jump.

Stanley Forman, the Pulitzer Prize–winning photographer from the *Boston Herald* who had photographed the falling child whom Tom had saved, arrived at the scene and began shooting pictures. One of his photographs, which appeared in the newspaper the following morning, showed a frail, elderly Chinese woman, back against the stone building, standing on a narrow ledge. She appears in the photograph to be at least three and perhaps four stories up. The woman stood about thirty feet or so from the corner of the building, and when Stanley Forman looked up he saw a Boston firefighter come around the corner, slowly, carefully, walking along the ledge. Stanley had photographed thousands of fires and rescues, and he knew at once it was Bob Mackey from the rescue company. Stanley watched, shooting pictures, as Bob Mackey—entirely untethered—made his way along the ledge. The woman did not see him, for he came from around the corner and her attention was on the street below. Perhaps, with age, her eyesight had weakened as well. It seemed as though Mackey was counting on this—counting on the woman not seeing, hearing, or even sensing him. His plan was to sneak up on her, get hold of her, and bring her back inside through a window about fifteen feet away.

Of course, anyone watching this scene—and hundreds of people in the street were doing that—could see that what Mackey was doing was utter madness. He was moving steadily along a ledge no more than a few inches wide. Should his balance shift *even slightly,* he would fall to his death. And what if he reached the woman? What could he possibly do with her? What if she pushed him or pulled him, or did anything that might cause his weight to shift? There was nothing on the building to hold on to.

In spite of the obvious danger, Forman could see that Mackey moved along, without hesitation, carefully, not recklessly—but by no means timidly. And why was he doing this? Why was he risking his own life—in one of the most dangerous rescues anyone on the Boston Fire Department could ever remember—to save the life of a woman who might be eighty years old? A woman who was so distraught she wished to end her life?

And the answer, of course, was simple. Bob Mackey was doing this because it was his job. He arrived with the Rescue and after the crew sized up the situation, there seemed no alternative but for someone to go out and try to bring her back inside. And Mackey was ready to do it—not because he had a death wish or sought the glory—but because it was his job. And there he was, through the lens of Stanley Forman's camera, moving ever closer. Still the old lady did not realize he was there until, finally, he reached out and took hold of her. And she looked at him, surprised, then surrendered and allowed him to walk her back along the ledge to the window, where he placed her safely inside.

The photographs went out on the news wires worldwide, and Mackey was awarded a medal for his work, which he added to the collection of medals he kept at home, never wearing them on his uniform in public as other firefighters did. And he did not discuss the rescue because he was only doing his job and he wanted no attention.

Sometimes very late at night, when John and Tim were thirteen and eleven, one of them would awaken and look outside and see that the car was still not in the driveway. It would be a school night, 1:00 or 2:00 AM, sometimes later. And they would be concerned and then afraid. What was happening? Where was Sonny? What was he doing? Why wasn't he here, asleep in his room, like other parents were? Why did he leave them alone in the house?

There came a time when John was truly afraid. He went through a period of being petrified that when Sonny was away, someone would come into the house and kill him. He often asked Sonny in the early evening whether he planned to go out that night, and Sonny would say no. Then John would feel a sense of relief and try to relax. And sometimes Sonny really would stay home. But often enough, around 9:30 or 10:00 PM, he would put on his coat and say he was going out for a bit to have one drink. John knew what that meant: He would be wide awake, waiting in fear, until Sonny returned. John used to wait until Sonny drove home down Wedgemere Road—it could be 11:00 PM or 3:00 AM, it made no difference—and he would run to bed and pretend to be asleep.

One morning John got up for school and went outside. Something was not quite right, but the absurdity of it did not strike him immediately. He stopped and looked, and then it registered: The car, a navy blue Pontiac, was parked not in the driveway or on the street in front of the house, but in the front yard.

Sonny drank throughout the afternoon, making no effort to hide it from John, age fourteen. At suppertime, Sonny somehow managed to cook fish sticks and macaroni and cheese. At the table were Sonny, John, and Tim, and John could not help but watch his father eat. Sonny's hand shook. He moved very slowly, deliberately, trying to focus on edging the fork through a fish stick. He cut off a piece, then attempted to balance it on his fork and lift it—*very* slowly—to his mouth. But halfway there, the food fell off his fork, landing on the plate. He closed his eyes to steady himself, then tried again, but he was unable to do it, unable to get the food from the plate to his mouth.

With increasing frequency, Sonny stationed himself at the sink, reached for the pony glass, poured a liberal amount of scotch into the glass, brought it to his lips, tilted his head back, and drank it all down. He would do this throughout the day. At bedtime, he might have two. After drinking the scotch, he would stand at the kitchen, run the cold-water tap for a moment, fill the glass, then drink the water.

One night when Sonny had gone out, John seized the glass, dropped it into a brown paper bag, and took it outside. He twisted the top of the bag and smashed the glass against the pavement again and again. He brought the bag back inside and placed it exactly where Sonny always kept the glass. John was fearful and angry. He could not stand what his father was doing. I reassured John that this was a phase that would end soon. I told him I would talk with Sonny.

There is an invisible line in time that when crossed, reverses the roles of parents and children. A parent is the authority figure, strong and sometimes distant but unquestionably in charge. Until, that is, it gets turned upside down. A parent's classic role is to prevent a child from actions that are self-destructive. There is authority and weight in a parental voice when warning a child about the dangers of, for example, drugs or alcohol.

So I try to fulfill my promise to John. The time has come that at age twenty-five, it is my job to warn my father that he is on a path of self-destruction, it is initially jarring. But Sonny's drinking has gotten so bad that he expects this, expects me to speak with him in this way.

"It has to stop," I say in a firm voice, as he and I sit in his living room, both smoking in the late afternoon. John and Tim are out, and we have the house to ourselves. I have made two mugs of tea, Sonny's strong on sugar, and we sit talking. When I had spoken with him before about this, he had seemed surprised that it was obvious he had had too much to drink. Now, there is no sense of surprise at all.

"I know it's hard," I say. "We all miss her but we have to move on. Let's worry about the kids now," I say, referring to Tim and John. "They're at a vulnerable age. They really need you. They need you to be there for them and to be clear-headed." He nods, knowingly. He understands. He is quiet, and there is a kind of dignity in the silence, a feeling that this man of pride is quietly taking stock, silently reconciling what it is he must do. I sit there fighting an urge to lecture him. I feel superior to him in some ways now, and I hate that I feel that way. But it seems clear to me that I have a clearer understanding of the nature of responsibility at the moment than he does.

"It's not as bad as you think," he tells me. "Maybe you're exaggerating it a little bit, making more out of it than really exists. You're not around during the week when things go smoothly. Food on the table, the boys on time for school, homework."

He pauses. "Maybe there's some exaggerating. I've had some bad nights, it's true, but Jesus, Mary, and Joseph. . . ." And here, he looks away and frowns. What he has been through; how he has been forced to adapt.

"It's a lot, I know, Dad," I say softly.

My father is a smart man. He knows how to talk. He knows what to say. He assures me that things are under control. He assures me that his devotion is to the boys. He looks me in the eye and says: "I'm doing the best that I can. It's not perfect, but I think things are okay." He stabs a cigarette out in an ashtray with one of the Bruins stenciled on it and tells me that he has chicken in the Crock-Pot with cream of mushroom soup. "The boys love that," he adds.

———

Sonny drove Pops into the VA for checkups and tests, and the doctors confirmed that the cancer had advanced. One day, when Pops had completed the testing, the doctor suggested that Pops "get his affairs in order." He smiled and said to the doctor: "I've been married for fifty years and never had an affair in my life."

But his sense of humor could not hide the pain. The doctor prescribed Brumpton solution, a powerful mix of morphine and heroin intended to ease acute pain in terminal patients. Pops was supposed to take it every three hours, but an hour or so after each dose he pleaded for more. It was horrible for Sonny, watching his father suffer like this. The disease robbed Pops of his perpetual smile—that warm, welcoming smile. It robbed him of his sunny nature. It was horrible to see what the end of life could be, shocking in its way and very different from the way Anne had gone. Sonny didn't know which was worse. He only knew he hated seeing his father suffer.

Why was this happening? Sonny wondered. *Why did they all have to die? Why did he have to lose the people closest to him, one after another, through the years?* Swede had been only twenty years old, his whole life in front of him. Anne's death had left a massive hole in Sonny's life, had knocked him off balance, confused him, sent him spinning off his well-ordered path. And now this: The closest person to him throughout the course of his life: the man who had raised him with love and kindness in a home where his mother had often been cold and severe, the man who had set an example for him, whose footsteps he had followed—into the navy, onto the Boston Fire Department. The man with whom he had worked each and every day, father and son side by side now for fifteen-plus years. He was dying, lying there on the bed, skin and bones, wracked by an agonizing pain. Sonny could not bear it.

Out of the blue one day near the end, Pops asked Sonny about the Cocoanut Grove. He asked whether Sonny thought they would ever figure it out—solve the mystery of how it had actually started and why it had raced with such ungodly speed. Sonny said he didn't think so. Pops shook his head. "What a shame," he said.

Pops died on a crisp November day in 1979. He was seventy-nine years old.

13
Thanksgiving

Bobby Greene was a legendary firefighter at Engine 24 and Ladder 23 in the Grove Hall section of Roxbury, one of the most dangerous neighborhoods in the city. Like most firefighters, Bobby Greene was a modest man. He was also short and muscular, invariably chomping on a cigar. His desire for action had led him to serve in the U.S. Navy during World War II and in the Marine Corps during Korea. Bobby Greene was blessed with remarkable skill as a ladderman, a catlike ability to move with speed and certainty up over a ladder. Paul Christian, the commissioner of the Boston Fire Department, is careful with words of praise for anyone, yet he characterized Bobby Greene as "the number one ladderman in Boston." For years, co-workers marveled at his ability to accelerate up a ground or aerial ladder, nimbly ascending to a window or rooftop. He seemed to descend with ease and a sure-footedness that was a gift. He was also a skilled tillerman on Ladder 23.

On November 25, 1978, Bobby Greene sat in the kitchen of the Grove Hall firehouse sipping tea when an alarm sounded. The box was for a small, single-alarm fire on Alpha Road in Dorchester, not all that far from the Dorchester neighborhood where Bobby lived. When the companies pulled into Alpha Road, they saw a modest amount of smoke and fire coming from a two-and-a-half story wood-frame house. It was a nothing fire, the type of fire these men had quickly extinguished literally hundreds, perhaps thousands of times.

Bobby Greene, age fifty, ascended the stick and set to work clearing a window in the attic. And then it happened—a shout that someone has fallen. And there on the ground lay Bobby Greene, bleeding badly, immobile. He was rushed to Carney Hospital nearby, where his condition was listed as grave.

No one knows what happened, just that he fell about thirty feet from atop the ladder. No one knows what happened because no one saw it happen. The fire department estimated damage to the structure at about $2,000.

Two days later, Bobby Greene was dead, and men throughout the department were stunned. Bobby was the last person anyone ever thought would get killed on the job. It was shocking news on a job where it was difficult to shock anyone. Everyone had the same reaction: "If it can happen to Bobby Greene, it can happen to anyone."

———

Tom grew increasingly expert at his work. And he was always working to better himself, to become smarter, more competent, and more knowledgeable.

In the late 1970s, a young physician named Len Jacobs took over Emergency Services at Boston City Hospital and instituted a program to train paramedics. The training for paramedics was deeper and broader than that for EMT certification, and Jacobs wanted ambulances out in the city manned by personnel with the most advanced possible training. The theory was that a paramedic would possess enough additional knowledge and skill to know how to keep people alive longer than an EMT—long enough to be transported to the hospital for emergency treatment.

An examination was given, open to any current BCH employee with EMT training. Those passing the written test were given an oral interview. In all, sixteen young men and women were selected for the rigorous paramedic program, including Tom. The new group started classes in June 1978, which coincided with Tom's wedding, requiring him to postpone his honeymoon. Tom and the others were taken out of uniform and instructed to wear a shirt and tie to classes, which were held at Boston City Hospital. The program was full time, five days a week, 8 AM to 5 PM, and the homework was considerable. The course was a sophisticated effort to provide Tom and the others with a strong clinical sense so that they would be able to discern quickly just how sick a patient really was and what treatment was most appropriate. For the first two months, the program was exclusively classroom work. After that, in addition to classroom sessions, the group began a series of clinical rotations. In all, Tom went through seven or eight rotations, learning to draw blood and use syringes, to insert intravenous solutions, to place a tube down the trachea enabling a patient to breathe (a mistake in this procedure could be fatal). He learned to read and interpret electrocardiograms and to administer drugs used to treat abnormalities of the heart.

During training one day, Tom was out on a call for a man who had been stabbed. The program protocols were strict. Students out on a call were supervised by a medical proctor, in this case a registered nurse. Even with her present, there was a strict prohibition against treating patients without radio communication with an ER physician.

It was about 9:00 PM on a cool fall night when Tom and two other students in the paramedic program—Richie Serino and Nick O'Neill—pulled into the scene of a stabbing on New Heath Street in Roxbury. There was a taxi by the curb, its doors open, police officers standing nearby. A large crowd of bystanders had gathered, pressing in for a glimpse of the cabdriver. A couple of Boston cops moved the crowd back as Tom, Richie, and Nick moved quickly from the ambulance to the cab. The crowd was mumbling and complaining, hurling taunts that had become routine during Tom's time on the job: "If he was white, you would have got here sooner," someone said. Tom and the others ignored it and focused on the work.

The cabdriver, a man named Thomas Kosonen, had been stabbed with an ice pick. Tom, Richie, and Nick examined him and found that the ice pick had been plunged directly into his heart. Mr. Kosonen was unconscious and unresponsive but alive, his pulse faint though detectable. Among them, Tom, Richie, and Nick had about fifteen years experience as EMTs on the streets of Boston. They had seen everything and they knew that unless they acted very fast, Mr. Kosonen would die; and they suspected that even if they moved very fast, he would likely die anyway. They also knew that this was *precisely* the type of situation where paramedic training could make a life-or-death difference. They swiftly got Mr. Kosonen onto a stretcher and into the ambulance and began racing toward BCH.

Thomas Kosonen urgently needed two things: First, he needed help breathing, which would require an endotracheal intubation. Second, he needed fluid to ward off shock. The problem was that EMTs were not trained or permitted to intubate a patient or to insert IVs. Paramedics, however, are trained in both of those procedures and Tom, Richie, and Nick had been given this training—but not the official certification required to actually perform such procedures in the field. An ER physician was normally available to them by radio, but Richie was getting no response. Tom looked at Nick and Richie—said nothing—and knew what they had to do. While Nick ran an IV line into Mr. Kosonen, Tom slid a tube down his throat to intubate him. This was a tense moment, for it was a tricky procedure. If the tube went down the wrong way, Mr. Kosonen could die. Still no luck raising the doctor.

Even as they neared the hospital, they had not reached a doctor, and they were nervous. They had obviously violated a critical rule, and as they were about to pull into the hospital there was a moment of hesitation. What if they had done something wrong and Mr. Kosonen died? Should they stop? Should they undo what they had done? He was probably going to die any minute anyway. But they knew they could not undo what might be his only chance, so they decided to take whatever heat came.

They rushed him into surgery, and as it turned out, Tom, Nick, and Richie had done precisely what they were supposed to do—and they had done it perfectly. They had performed so well that Mr. Kosonen reached the hospital in a stabilized condition, enough so that surgeons were able to repair the damage to his heart muscle.

Two weeks later, Thomas Kosonen walked out of City Hospital.

Soon thereafter—nearly a year after starting the program—Tom, Richie, Nick, and the others graduated as certified paramedics, adding a significant new dimension to Boston Emergency Medical Services.

Perhaps the most disturbing aspect of Tom's time as a paramedic in Boston was the animosity directed at him and his colleagues by people of color.

The everyday reality being played out on the street meant an often harsh reception for Tom and his colleagues in many black sections of town. Tom and the other paramedics were certainly welcomed into many black homes by families who deeply appreciated their professionalism. But routinely, they were greeted with resentment, the basic theme being that they would have gotten to a white address faster. The fact that the ambulance was stationed in the heart of the black community, positioned specifically to respond to black neighborhoods, was either unknown by many black Bostonians or ignored as inconvenient to their bias against the ambulance squads.

Tom has somber memories of those days. He told a series of stories from those difficult times, beginning with one about responding to a report of a man hit by a car and suffering cardiac arrest outside Edward Everett Square in Dorchester:

We step on it and as we pull up, two of our guys from another ambulance are being pounded by six guys. We go in to support our own people, and we end up in fistfights with half a dozen guys.

Another night we get a call for an emotional disturbance and we respond with two cops. And we're up on the third floor talking to the guy in the kitchen trying to calm him down. All of a sudden he's out on the porch trying to go over the railing, and we restrain him and end up in a fight with him.

Another night we get a call to an apartment on Mass Ave. between Shawmut and Tremont, up on the third floor. We found out later the guy had a massive dose of PCP, and as soon as we walk through the door the guy grabs [Tom's partner] John McLaughlin and slams him into a window. We try to get the guy off, but he's got this incredible strength and so he's got John and we're beating him with a flashlight and we mace him, and after a while we finally get him down on the floor.

There were a lot of summer nights—especially weekends—when we'd get a call to go into one of the projects, and it would be just me and another white guy, and everybody in the project was black and you just prayed that you didn't get stabbed or shot. Any of these assaults or stabbings could turn into more violence in the blink of an eye.

We'd call the police if we were in trouble, of course, and they knew when we called there was a problem. They were extraordinarily helpful. But those were tough minutes waiting for the cops. There'd be a stream of anti-white racial slurs and you'd have your tail between your legs waiting for help and then when help arrived you'd have the biggest mouth in the crowd.

One night in 1979, we got a call for a child hit by a car in Grove Hall, one of the most dangerous parts of Roxbury at the time. It's a warm Friday night around 8:30 and when we pull in, there is already a police presence and there's a huge crowd gathered around. Fortunately, the kid turned out to be okay, but when we pull in and get out of the truck, there's this one lady, a black lady, she had to weigh 350 pounds. Her ankles were as big as my head. And she looks at us and says, "Well, look who's here. The last one to come is the ambulance. Well, take your time it's just another colored child dying in the street." And she looks at me and says, "And the last one here is the slim-whitey-looking-motherfucker." And my partner Nick O'Neill hears this and he bursts out laughing and he says, "Oh, lady, you're right. He is a slim-whitey-looking-motherfucker." And she starts laughing and it immediately turns the tide, so that now instead of a racial incident, it's "make way for the doctor, the child will be all right." She tells everyone to get out of the way and let us through. And, as I say, fortunately the kid was okay.

There was animosity not only in the street but within firehouses, as well. In the years following the federal court ruling, racial tension and conflict mounted dramatically as black firefighters began to enter the companies. There were instances of white firefighters cooking meals and refusing to eat with blacks. There were racial epithets. Anecdotes about black firefighters' incompetence or lack of courage or laziness were passed around. Some of the stories were true, some exaggerated, and some fabricated. Morale throughout the department was abysmal. A disproportionate share of minority firefighters washed out of the job after only a few months. A few years after the federal court decision, estimates were that as many as half of all new minority firefighters quit or were fired.

And then things got worse.

Massachusetts and Boston faced a fiscal crisis in 1981 so serious that layoffs of thousands of public employees were required. Layoffs on the fire department, though quite rare, had always been done according to seniority—last hired, first fired. But the federal court stepped in and ordered that even with layoffs, the percentage of minority firefighters on the department had to be maintained. This meant nearly all the firefighters laid off were white, and many were senior to blacks and Hispanics who kept their jobs. For white firefighters, this was a disaster—one that engendered as much or perhaps even more bitterness than the original federal court ruling in 1974. It took half a dozen long years for those laid off to get rehired, but the resentment lingered much longer.

It was a balmy Friday night in May 1981, and Tom was working the 4:00 PM to midnight shift on the Paramedic 2 wagon covering the southwestern part of the city. Fortuitously, Paramedic 2 was on Hyde Park Avenue in Hyde Park when a call came for a motor vehicle accident near Cleary Square. There was nothing unusual about the call—it was like a dozen others every day. On the wagon this night were Tom and Steve O'Rourke, a man some years older than Tom with extensive experience. Also riding with them was a registered nurse from BCH Emergency Services. They pulled up to the scene at the intersection of Hyde Park Avenue and West Street, a blue-collar neighborhood of three-deckers across the street from a doughnut shop.

Tom recalled:

We pull up to the accident and get out of the truck and there's a police sergeant, an old-timer, and he said, "You're not going to believe what has happened here." And O'Rourke says, "We'll believe anything," because between the two of us we'd seen everything. Or we *thought* we had.

And so now we go around in front of the ambulance and we see the car, a Ford Country Squire station wagon smashed into this huge tree. The car has hit the tree dead center, and the front end of the car has wrapped itself around the tree with the headlights practically touching each other. It looks as though the guy went from fifty miles an hour to a dead stop in the blink of an eye.

There's the smell of gasoline in the air and steam billowing up from under the hood. And as we approach the car, we can see a steel bar absolutely right through this guy's head. It came from the back and it entered his left rear side of his head and came through his left forehead and continued on another couple of feet through the windshield. So the bar is sticking through the windshield, sticking through his head, and sticking into the back section of the station wagon. Obviously what happened was that this huge bar—seven feet long and an inch in diameter—was in the back of the station wagon and this guy smashes into the tree and the impact is such that the bar rockets forward and pierces his head.

The cop had already called the fire department, but Tom told him to call them back and make sure they sent the Rescue. Within a couple of minutes, several fire trucks arrived along with a district fire chief and Rescue 2. With the smell of gasoline and the possibility that the car could ignite at any moment, the engine company stretched out a hand line at the ready.

The man in the wreck was John Thompson, thirty-nine years old. He was wearing work clothes, and there was alcohol on his breath and a few beer cans in the car. And Tom and Steve O'Rourke had thought they had seen everything and, in a way, they had—heart attacks, gunshots, knife wounds, severed limbs, virtually every conceivable type of trauma. But *nothing* like this.

It was really very rare to see something new, but this was beyond new—this was beyond comprehension. If someone had said "Okay, so you arrive at the scene of a car accident and there's a guy in a station wagon with a seven-foot-long steel bar through his head, three feet sticking out the back, three feet sticking out the front"—if you asked a thousand EMTs and paramedics and doctors, every one of them would say, of course, the guy's dead. Not a prayer. Not a chance. Forget it!

I'm leaning over the wreck and looking at this guy—and of course he must be dead because how could anyone ever survive such trauma. He is covered in blood and I'm looking at this scene and I cannot believe what I am seeing because all of a sudden the guy's hand came up and he's trying to grab hold of the bar.

Miraculously, John Thompson was alive. The urgent question was how to get him out of the wreck and somehow keep him alive during transport to the hospital.

It's pretty clear we cannot transport the guy with the bar in his head—he wouldn't fit into our truck. So we're going to have to cut the bar behind and in front of his head. But as we were talking this through with the firefighters, the guys from the Rescue, someone said, "We've go to be careful not to burn the inside of the guy's head" with heat generated by the power saw. We didn't have enough room to work inside the wreck so the Rescue 2 guys cut back the car's roof to give us some space. We worked to immobilize him, because now he was getting kind of aggressive reaching up for the bar, and if he were to get a hold of it and start pulling on it, that could easily kill him. We're in the wreck treating him and I'm holding his hands down while the firefighters start cutting the bar about a foot behind his head. Each cut took about a minute. We made the inside one first—the cut behind his head. Then they went around and stood on the hood and cut the bar outside the windshield. While this is happening, I'm next to the guy on the seat holding the bar in place and holding him. He's moaning and groaning. He was kind of combative. So I'm trying to restrain him and keep the bar from moving around and doing any more damage.

While they were making the first cut in the bar, the sparks actually set a fire inside the car, and because the line was right there, all they had to do was open the line and immediately knock down the fire. Then they ran water over everything that had been covered with gas.

As they're cutting, we're pouring water over the bar to keep the temperature down so it doesn't heat his brain. After the firefighters cut the bar at both ends, it was sticking out about a foot in front of his head and a foot behind, which allowed us to move him and lay him gently on a stretcher on the street next to the car. Normally the stretcher locks into the side of the truck, but the bar stuck out on each side—thick solid steel—so you couldn't lock the stretcher in. So we put him in the middle of the truck and we go like hell to the hospital.

Now we have to transport him and one of the things we do in trauma cases is communicate ahead to the ER so that the doctors there know what's coming and can be prepared. And one of the things prized in paramedic training is an ability to communicate clearly and effectively so there is no doubt what the situation is when you arrive at the ER with the patient. Steve O'Rourke, a well-educated and eloquent man, gets on the radio and explains to them that we have a bar, but at City Hospital they have no idea how big it was. They were kind of thinking it was maybe the size of a tire iron. They couldn't imagine it.

When we pull in, Dr. Len Jacobs is there, the head of Emergency Services and with him is Dr. Joseph Ordia, a neurosurgeon, and other doctors and nurses. And when we opened the doors and pulled out the stretcher, all of them were just like, "You've got to be shitting; this guy is still *alive*?"

When journalists around the city heard about the incident, they were in disbelief. The *Globe* ran a front-page story on the following Sunday morning, headlined "A Prayer Card in His Pocket" by Loretta McLaughlin, a veteran *Globe* writer:

The prayer card was in his shirt pocket as he sat trapped in the demolished station wagon, his head impaled on a crowbar. John Thompson always carried the card with him. It commemorated his mother's death: Theresa Thompson 1979.

The prayer beseeches St. Jude, patron saint of the hopeless, "when help is almost despaired of . . . come to my assistance. I am so helpless and alone."

Late last Friday night, Thompson, 39, of Hyde Park suffered massive head injuries when the seven-foot bar, used to move large granite blocks, flew through his head when his vehicle slammed into a tree alongside Hyde Park Avenue.

Yesterday, less than four days later, he could see. He could hear. And he understands everything that is said to him.

Thompson was sitting up in a chair beside his bed yesterday afternoon, his head propped on a pillow, when the two men who rescued him came to visit him in the intensive care unit at Boston City Hospital.

When Thompson's wife, Madeline, saw the paramedics, she reached up and kissed each one. "I'm so thankful for what you did for Jack," she said over and over.

They had met the night of the accident outside the neurosurgery operating room, but she had been preoccupied then.

Boston Department of Health and Hospitals paramedic Thomas Kenney, who directed Thompson's rescue Friday night, immediately spotted the prayer card.

"Oh, I'm glad you got it back," Kenney said. He'd found the card in Thompson's pocket.

It's pinned now to Thompson's hospital johnny.

Kenney and his partner, paramedic Stephen O'Rourke, had reached Thompson's side within one minute of the police call reporting the car crash.

"We just happened to be nearby," Kenney shrugged.

Thompson's progress amazes them, as much as it does the team of BCH specialists looking after him.

Yesterday, the tube that had been inserted in his throat to keep the airways open was removed.

The respirator that had been used to assist his breathing was also dispensed with.

As he sat in the chair—and except for his head which is swathed in bandages and protected by a heavy white knit cap—Thompson was the picture of strength—a big shouldered, broad-chested, burly man.

His face was still somewhat swollen, but his eyes were wide open. He could just about manage a flickering smile.

He shifted himself in the chair from time to time to adjust to a more comfortable position.

Kenney asked him if he remembered putting the crowbar in the back of the car.

Thompson nodded, made an acquiescing sound—his speech is still impaired—and rolled his eyes up, ruefully.

At this point BCH specialists are cautiously optimistic about the extent of Thompson's eventual recovery. He's done remarkably well so far, they said.

Kenney and O'Rourke had brought the crowbar with them to show Thompson's wife how the accident happened.

They demonstrated how it went through the left side of his head, the front end protruding out three feet through his forehead and the other end, three feet behind his head.

Still speckled with blood when they examined it, the chisel end of the bar is six to eight inches in length and more than two inches wide.

Paramedics Kenney and O'Rourke explained that the chisel end went through O'Rourke's head with the blade vertical, like a spearhead standing on its side.

Had the blade been horizontal, they said, the blow unquestionably would have been fatal, driving through the center of his brain.

Kenney told her how they had immobilized Thompson's neck in a brace and sandbagged it while Boston firefighter Steve Cloonan had cut the ends off the bar.

It was so long that one end rested on the windshield frame and the other on the top of the front seat. Thompson's head was frozen in position halfway along the shaft of the bar.

They told her of their anxiety as a fire broke out in the back seat when gasoline was ignited by a spark from the saw.

Kenney showed her how he held on to the bar with one gloved hand nearest the saw and a bare hand next to it.

"The friction from the saw was heating up the bar. We kept hosing water over it to cool it down and I kept feeling it to make sure it wasn't getting too hot up near his head."

Again and again Mrs. Thompson's eyes widened in incredulity.

She, in turn, told them how she and her mother, Mrs. Eileen Loughman, were at home Friday night when the accident occurred. The Thompson house is on Edson Street, less than a mile from the point on Hyde Park Avenue where the station wagon Thompson was driving slammed into a tree.

"We heard the sirens from the police cars, fire engines and the ambulances," she said.

"And we said, 'Oh God, help the kids.'" You know we just assumed it was kids in a car crash. It never entered our minds that it was Jack.

"The whole thing is just a miracle," she said.

"Jack's mother must have been looking out for him that night."

It was not often that the *Boston Globe* editorial page would weigh in on a car accident, but the John Thompson story was so huge that an editorial ran on the following Monday morning, May 7, 1981, under the headline "Trauma and Triumph":

The more details one learns about the rescue of John Thompson, the Dorchester man whose skull was impaled by a crowbar in an automobile accident last week, the more incredible it seems—and the more pride Boston can take in the four Boston firefighters and the five members of a City Hospital emergency medical team who performed the rescue.

Imagine the scene: a man, trapped in the front seat of a demolished station wagon, encased by twisted metal, anchored in place by a seven-foot crowbar which the impact of the crash had hurled through his skull with the force of a missile.

Senior Paramedic Thomas Kenney and his team—Paramedic Stephen O'Rourke, emergency medical technicians Carlos Grau and Gary Winitzer, and nurse Rose Lorencen who was on her first night with the team—were at the accident scene on Hyde Park Avenue within a minute. Fire Lt. Stephen McLaughlin and firefighters John Nemes, Stephen Cloonan and Joseph Hughes of Rescue 2 arrived just minutes later. None of them, nor perhaps anyone else, has ever been confronted by such a challenge.

For 34 minutes the two crews worked to keep Thompson alive, and to free him from the wreckage. During part of the time, the rear seat of Thompson's station wagon was aflame as sparks from the cutting saws ignited the gasoline in the ruptured fuel tank. "It was pretty hairy for a while," is all Kenney will say.

When he was finally free, the two teams inched him onto a stretcher and into an ambulance. Eleven minutes later, Thompson was at Boston City Hospital. Often seen as a poor cousin to the city's world-renowned hospitals, BCH is a nationally-rated full trauma center, capable of handling any disaster, any emergency. In the entire annals of emergency medicine, however, there is no record of a situation similar to that which then confronted Dr. I. Joseph Ordia, the Nigerian-born neurosurgeon who was waiting for Thompson at the emergency room door, and the trauma team headed by Haitian-born Dr. Lenworth Jacobs. Six days later, Thompson remains in critical condition, but is alert and responding well. "It is all quite remarkable," says Dr. Ordia.

It is remarkable, and incredible; most of all, however, it is a testament to the skill of Boston's medics and firefighters whose accomplishments last Friday night out on Hyde Park Avenue deserve the community's warmest gratitude and respect.

Tom received a commendation from the Department of Health and Hospitals. In addition, Governor Edward J. King invited Tom to his office for a ceremony in which the governor presented Tom with a citation and posed with him for a picture.

As great as things were going for Tom in Boston, the truth was that he had always wanted to be a firefighter, and it was now clear—seven years after the original court ruling—that his chances were essentially nil. He repeatedly took the Boston Fire Department test whenever it was given and would await the results, but with no real expectation that his name would climb high enough on the list to be appointed. He was scoring high nineties in the test, but it mattered not; he was neither a veteran nor a minority. As he put it, "A list was usually good for three years so I'd take it and three years later, take another and I got on the tail end of one but I wasn't appointed and then I'd take another one. But I never gave up the idea completely. I was just kind of still waiting for the opportunity."

Then one day Tom was at Ambulance Supply and met a member of the fire department for the Town of Sandwich on Cape Cod. For a second job, this man worked for a company delivering medical supplies. Tom said, "So we're talking as we load the ambulance at the start of our shift and he hears that I had spent quite a bit of time as a spark in Boston, and he said the Hyannis Fire Department was looking to hire people but you had to be a paramedic. I said, 'Well, I am a paramedic.' He said if I was interested I should check it out. The idea of possibly being able to become a firefighter and also use my paramedic training, that definitely appealed to me."

Tom went down to Hyannis and drove around for hours, looking, getting the feel of the place. It certainly wasn't Boston. But he also talked with people on the department, and found out that with its location at the center of the cape, it was one of the busiest rescue operations around. After a few months, Tom took the Hyannis exam and passed it. He was subsequently offered a position as a firefighter-paramedic on the Hyannis Fire Department. His whole life had been in Boston—he didn't know any other place, really. He had been born and raised in the city and loved it in so many ways. His family and friends were there, but the reality was that he could not see it working out for him on the fire department. "I just didn't think the opportunity was ever gonna be there," he said.

Meanwhile, Tom thought Hyannis seemed nice. He thought he and his wife could raise a family there. And that was that. Tom left Boston to accept a position as a Hyannis firefighter.

My brother Mike and I talked about the drinking and what to do about it. We agreed that we had to talk with Sonny again. We sat down with him one night, just Mike, Sonny, and I, and we spoke in supportive, warm tones to him about how much he meant to us and the other boys and how important it was to get this thing under control. Sonny listened and nodded his agreement. He appreciated our concern. He agreed with us. And he would change course—he would get it under control. More than that, he had recognized the problem and already had it under control, he assured us.

On a day when we were all supposed to get together to move my grandmother Nana from one apartment to another, Sonny was supposed to meet us with her keys. He didn't show up. We called and called but there was no answer. Later in the afternoon, I drove to Wedgemere and confronted him in the kitchen. My anger had built up over time. He had placated us, parrying each and every attempt we had made to help nudge him toward sobriety, but the situation had deteriorated.

"You fucked the whole thing up," I said. "We were all there—everyone arranged their schedule around this. Tom drove up from the Cape. Where were you?"

"Watch your mouth," he said.

"You were shit-faced," I said.

"Watch what you say."

"Really? Watch my mouth? Watch what I say? How about this—You're a fucking drunk. You're a fucking bum. How about that?"

His face grew dark. This was unknown territory—*unheard of* territory.

"Get out of my house," he ordered.

I had actually believed him earlier when he had told me—and told me and Mike together—that he would get it under control, that he had it under control. And now I felt like a complete fool. Of course I should have known he was lying. I hated what he was doing to himself.

For some reason I thought back to a night in the late 1960s. It was summer, a warm evening, and he and my mother had gone out to somebody's house in the neighborhood for a party. Before they had gone out, my mother had told me my hair was too long (about a half inch over the tops of my ears) and that I had to get a haircut. I was a typical teenager and asserted my independence. "I don't want to get it cut," I said. "I want to grow it." She had not liked that but had not pressed the issue.

Late that night I was asleep in the bottom bunk bed in the room I shared with my brother Michael. At the time, I was probably seventeen and Mike sixteen. It was late when our parents came home, after midnight, and my mother came into our room to check on us and say good night. Sonny was standing behind her in the hallway a couple of feet away from where he used to sit telling us Smokey and Joe stories. After she said good night, he said something about me getting a haircut. He said it in a kind of nasty way. I said, sorry, but I wasn't going to get a haircut.

"You Goddamn well will do what you're told," he said, coming into the room. I could smell the alcohol from several feet away.

I sprang out of bed.

"No," I said. "No, I won't."

And then it happened: He charged forward, brushing past my mother, hunched over, head forward.

"You fucking . . . "—and began punching me in a series of rapid-fire motions, punches all aimed at the body, at my stomach and chest and rib cage. I stood straight and did not respond, for I could not strike my father. I was stronger than he was, I knew, and I certainly could have defended myself, but I chose not to. I suppose I was in a kind of shock, because I could not believe this was happening. Mike jumped down from the top bunk and, with my mother, restrained him. They moved him away from me as he flailed a few more times, and I stood there trying to absorb the reality of what had just occurred.

How could he kick me out of this house—my home. The very idea that he would try and throw me out of this home so enraged me . . .

"I ought to fucking . . . " I said, making a fist with my right hand.

"Get out!" he ordered, pointing to the door.

I just shook my head.

He grabbed the phone and called the police. "Yes, my son is threatening me and refusing to leave my house. Right. Twenty-seven Wedgemere Road in West Roxbury. Thank you."

When the cops came, I left.

———

On a crisp Thanksgiving Day, the year Tom has decided to make the move to Hyannis, Sonny is at home preparing Thanksgiving dinner for four. There is John, then in college, and Tim, still in high school, and one of Tim's friends. Tim and his friend went off somewhere briefly, so John and Sonny are alone in the house. John, in the living room, hears a loud thud from the kitchen, just a few feet away. He goes in to investigate and sees the door to the oven open, the tray holding the nicely browned turkey halfway out. There are oven mittens. There is the table with platters for serving turkey, a container and ladle for gravy, serving dishes for carrots and corn from a can. Atop the stove there are pots and pans, and there is steam in the room, a moist holiday warmth. And there on the counter, over in the corner, tucked away a bit, is a bottle of Chivas Regal—a bottle, if John is not mistaken, that was quite full not all that long ago. And now John sees that there is mostly daylight between the bottle top and the level of brown whiskey.

And here is John, who loves these holidays, taking in the entire scene.

Sonny is passed out cold on the floor.

My brother John stands quite still and looks down at his father, whose thin, somewhat elongated face is flat against the speckled linoleum, whose mouth is open, whose breathing is steady. In any other house there might be the thought of heart attack, but here, with Sonny, John knows what has happened. And the beauty of John is that he gazes down at his father, and he feels swelling in his breast that is not anger or resentment or disgust, but sadness. Sadness not for himself—for he knows that he and Tim and Tim's friend will make the best of the day—but sadness for Sonny.

John is six feet, one inch, broad shouldered and powerful. He squats down and reaches under Sonny's arms, lifts his upper body, then slides his other arm under Sonny's legs, hoists him up as though cradling a child, and carries his father upstairs and places him gently in his bed, where Sonny spends the remainder of the Thanksgiving holiday.

14

27 Wedgemere Road

Shortly after eight o'clock on the morning of February 5, 1987, fire broke out in an apartment of a multiple-family wood-frame residence on East Third Street in South Boston. In the apartment were Paula Walsh, her ten-month-old infant, and her two young children, ages three and four. Paula and a friend were able to get the children out of the apartment and into the hallway where she thought the kids would be safe. As the fire progressed and smoke thickened, Paula managed to get the four-year-old and the ten-month-old out of the house.

But in the rush and confusion, three-year-old Mark was lost.

It was a cold morning, a dusting of snow on the ground, when Ladder 19 responded. Jimmy Hardy of Ladder 19, a fifteen-year veteran of the Boston Fire Department, arrived to discover a familiar location: He had once lived in the house that was now on fire. When Hardy stepped off Ladder 19 to survey the situation, he saw thick smoke billowing from the building and heard a "really crazed" woman screaming, *"My son's in there!"*

"Where?" Hardy shouted.

"I don't know . . . I can't find him!" she replied.

Hardy charged in through the front door, intending to head up the stairs, but dense smoke and searing heat drove him back outside. He knew there was a window on the third floor, and he also knew the aerial ladder would be raised to the roof adjacent to that window. He ran back outside, climbed onto the ladder truck platform and moved quickly up over the stick to the third floor, entering the building through the window.

Inside, Jimmy Hardy and another firefighter, Jimmy Prokop, also of Ladder 19, encountered heavy smoke and almost no visibility. They crawled through the rooms, searching everywhere—under beds, in closets, along walls. The two firefighters split up and searched the entire apartment with no luck. They got to a window where the smoke had cleared somewhat, but Prokop had run out of air for his mask and was forced to head back outside.

"Go on down—I'll check one more thing," Hardy said to him. "I'll be right there."

The alarm indicating he was nearly out of air sounded on Jimmy Hardy's mask. It was time to go—time to get back outside so he could breathe—so there would not be a double tragedy, a dead firefighter along with a dead child. But Jimmy Hardy had a clear thought in his mind: *If there's a kid in here, I'm going to find him.*

It occurred to Jimmy that the boy might have tried to get to the stairway to make his escape. He had to check the stairway.

Jimmy Hardy made his way across the apartment and opened the door onto the hallway where the smoke seemed impenetrable. It was pitch black. He could see nothing. He went four or five steps and recalled that the stairway went left at that point. He moved another four or five steps and was feeling his way along, using his hands to pat the stairway, touching everything along the way, hoping to stumble on the child.

He felt some clothes in the stairs along the wall and near the clothes he felt what he thought might be a head, but he was not sure—he thought perhaps it was a doll. It felt lifeless. He picked it up, felt that it was very light, and carried it to the window, where he could see it was the boy, but Mark looked as though he was gone, as though it was too late.

Jimmy Hardy carried Mark out through the window, tossed aside his mask and helmet, and began administering mouth-to-mouth resuscitation as he descended the aerial ladder. He then laid Mark down in the street, where Mark's mother, along with neighbors, was screaming frantically.

Mark was unconscious as Jimmy set the boy down on his back in the street. People were wailing that he was gone.

As he knelt next to Mark, Jimmy Hardy shouted: *"Are there other children in there?"*

Assured that all the children were out, Jimmy turned back to Mark and thought he saw Mark's eyes move.

"Breathe—breathe hard!" Jimmy encouraged Mark. Jimmy was practically shouting, his voice urgent.

"Breathe hard!" he repeated, the words coming with his thick Boston accent.

"Breathe haahhd!"

In a photograph taken by Boston Fire Department photographer William Noonan, Jimmy Hardy is kneeling on the ground, his fire coat disheveled, his wavy hair mussed, his eyes searching, pleading.

The EMTs whisked Mark away to the hospital and then to the Shriners' Burns Institute at Massachusetts General Hospital. The initial days were rough and it appeared that Mark would not make it, but then came a turn for the better and he survived. Jimmy was elated at the news and visited Mark, bringing gifts and getting to know the boy and his mother. Jimmy knew Mark's dad had fallen on some tough times and was not able to visit his family, so Jimmy helped fill in a bit.

Over time, Mark received skin grafts to treat burns on his neck, face, fingers, and back. As the years passed, Jimmy always made a point of buying Mark gifts for Christmas and for his birthday, and he took him to Christmas parties.

Jimmy Hardy received the John E. Fitzgerald Medal, the highest award from the Boston Fire Department. The photograph of Jimmy hunched over Mark found its way into newspapers around the world. During his career, Jimmy Hardy also saved a woman from jumping off the Mystic River Bridge in Boston. He saved a drowning woman in Fort Lauderdale, Florida, while he was on vacation.

But it was the rescue of Mark Walsh that stood out in a particular way. Jimmy Hardy is long retired now, but as he looks back upon his years as a rescue man, he thinks perhaps it was a path he was meant to take.

"Maybe I was supposed to do that," he says of his rescue of Mark. "Maybe that's why I got on the fire department."

Sonny had nurtured Firecontrol from its infancy. He had begun it in the most modest of circumstances—in that tiny vacant room behind Reid Brothers Laundry just off Washington Street, around the corner from Forest Hills station where the elevated tracks start their downtown run. That had been two decades earlier, back when Sonny had sat alone in that room at a solitary desk, filling out cards, copying the names of companies from the Yellow Pages.

But now he wanted out. Sonny didn't want to run the company anymore. He had no interest in managing it, dealing with irate customers, or returning their phone calls. He didn't want to be tied down in an office each day. He was also concerned about legal liability. In a recent court case, the owner of a company similar to Firecontrol had lost everything when a fire in a restaurant had done extensive damage. As the sole parent of two young boys, Sonny felt he couldn't risk that sort of legal exposure.

Sonny was proud of having won some of the best accounts in New England. Nonetheless, the accountant said the business had always been marginal. And Sonny was glad to be moving on.

With the sale of Firecontrol, most of the certainties in Sonny's life were now gone—his wife, his father, the BFD, and now the place he had gone to work each morning for twenty years, the company he had created and nurtured for so long. There had been enormous sweat equity in this company where Pops and Tom and Pat had all worked, the company that had yielded an award for Sonny—that shiny brass extinguisher full of 500 weighty silver dollars. And now Sonny was getting rid of it as though it was a burden. The fact that selling Firecontrol was an act of liberation for Sonny made it all the sadder to see. He sold it to a firefighter who worked for him—and Sonny walked out the door.

I went to see Sonny about a week after our confrontation over his drinking when he had called the police. "I'm sorry," I told him, as I walked through the side door of Wedgemere Road. "I went too far. I was pretty upset and angry and I'm really worried about your drinking, but I said things I should not have said. And I'm sorry."

Sonny looked hard at me and nodded his head slightly.

"I'm satisfied," he said. "I'll accept that."

At this point, I was working out of town, traveling to various cities. From hotel rooms in New York and Washington, Atlanta and Montgomery, I kept tabs on Sonny at home, usually calling in the evening, after a day's work.

This time, when I ask how things are going, he recites, "We had meat loaf with whole kernel corn and French fries," his voice thick. French fries comes out as "Frrennch friesssh." He struggles to enunciate the word. Then he repeats the same sentence, verbatim.

I sit up on the tidy hotel bed, my legs extended, tie loosened, shirt collar open, and I look around the institutional walls of the Holiday Inn or Ramada or Hilton as though I am going to find some sort of answer or explanation.

It is the same, night after night. Some nights I do not call, though I never forget about it. I always remember. Every night, without fail, there is the impulse to call, to connect with the people at 27 Wedgemere Road. Even in my mid- and late twenties, it remains the center of my universe. Some nights I sit, hand on the phone, and make a decision not to call because I do not want to hear him slur his words. I fail to call, generally, on a night following one when he has repeated some filthy joke he picked up at The Hollow or referred to one of his friends at The Hollow one too many times.

"You know so-and-so, used to be married to a mobster, that guy, wasshisname, the hit man? She's a lovely girl."

Oh, I'm certain she is, Dad.

"My friend from the Hollow told me the one—have you heard the one—" and here he laughs for a moment, playing the punch line of the joke over in his head—"Have you heard the one about the Polish ballerina. She does a split and . . . ?"

And I hold the phone away, at arm's length, and I think for a moment, *If I hang up will he notice? Will it matter? Can this really be happening?*

"Jeez, Dad, I'm supposed to meet someone downstairs for dinner five minutes ago. Gotta run. Bye."

I jump up from the bed and walk briskly out of the hotel room, wait impatiently for the elevators, stride through the lobby and out into the street. I walk quickly up the block, moving so fast I soon work up a sweat in the humid night air. It's just as he always told me in baseball: "Don't think—react." And so I am not thinking, I am reacting, and my reaction is to get out of the hotel and away from that phone as fast as I can. I am breathing heavily and wondering why it is I am here; wherever "here" is this week. Why am I here when I should be at 27 Wedgemere helping out? And even as I resolve to go back there—to go home, even though I do not technically live there anymore—I wonder about Sonny.

Why is he doing this?

What has happened to him? I try to understand. Maybe he has played by the rules for so long he is fed up. Half the society in the 1970s seems to be in rebellion of some sort and maybe this is Sonny's rebellion. Maybe he has played by the rules for so many years—for his whole life—that he has just had it. Or maybe it is the cumulative weight of the losses. I worry that Sonny's sense of history eludes him. His grandfather suffered from a serious alcohol problem—so serious he was unable to care for all of his children after his wife had died. How is Sonny different? Isn't he following in his grandfather's footsteps? Sonny has heard the stories of Pops's upbringing—how he was all but on his own by age fourteen—but has he taken that to heart? What has he learned from it?

As time passes, Sonny becomes increasingly red-faced. His appearance grows more weathered. The Chivas is replaced by cheaper brands, some I don't even recognize. After a while, nips appear—many small bottles of amber liquid. Nips, I think, have only one purpose—to be concealed. They can be secreted away almost anywhere and everywhere. From Chivas to cheap brands to nips seems to me an ugly downward spiral. I am struck by the coarseness of his language during these evening phone calls. Under the influence of alcohol, Sonny is unguarded. I have never before in my life heard him utter the word "asshole," but now I do. So and so is an asshole. The term "bitch" is used—"She's a long-legged bitch." These words, which are merely part of the din of the world most days, take on a piercing quality when uttered by my father. I cringe; I feel a physical reaction.

One night in Boston I drop by the house, and one of his friends from The Hollow is there. Sonny has clearly been drinking—his eyes are bloodshot and unfocused and he is slurring his words. I am uneasy and make an excuse to leave just as Sonny's friend, between sips of his drink, says: "Hear the one about the Polish ballerina?"

For a year or so, Sonny worked freelance, conducting inspections for companies writing fire insurance. He inspected residential properties, noted their general condition, remarked on any fire hazards, and took a Polaroid snapshot. He was paid a fee for each inspection. After that, he found a job as a door-to-door salesman for the American Legal Association, a small regional competitor to the American Automobile Association. Sonny sold memberships for car owners seeking insurance against a dead battery or flat tire. It was difficult work walking all day, knocking on doors of people who did not wish to be bothered.

Few memberships were sold on Sonny's route. Both of these were jobs with no set schedule and no boss breathing down his neck, affording Sonny wide latitude. Stay out half the night and sleep half the day? This he could get away with. Show up in the morning with a thundering hangover? Who would know?

After a while, the new owner of Firecontrol called Sonny and said he was having trouble running the business. He asked whether Sonny would be willing to come back for a few months and help him through the transition. Sonny agreed to return on a temporary basis, and he did, straightening out some problems.

He was only back at Firecontrol for a matter of six months or so when he heard about a position at the U.S. Army Material and Mechanic Testing Laboratory at the Watertown Arsenal in Watertown, Massachusetts, about a twenty-minute drive from Wedgemere Road. There was an opening for a chief fire safety officer. Sonny applied and got the job. The position suited him. It was full time, though not particularly demanding.

My brother Michael called Sonny one afternoon and said he was coming by to say hello. Fine, said Sonny. Mike pulled into Wedgemere and was driving down the narrow lane to our house when he saw Sonny's car coming toward him, headed out of the dead-end street. They had to come to a near stop to pass by each another, but Mike watched Sonny slowly drive right past him. Sonny did not look in Mike's direction, nor did he turn his head or wave or acknowledge Mike in any way. A dark-haired woman was sitting in the passenger seat of Sonny's car. Mike continued on down to the house and went inside to wait. But Sonny was gone.

My brothers and I got on with our lives. Some of us talked with him regularly, others, well, not so much. Sometimes it was too much—too painful and infuriating to talk with him when he was drunk. So for some of the boys, weeks and then months passed between conversations. By the early 1980s, my brothers and I were doing our best to make our way in the world. My youngest brother, Tim, worked as an apprentice for two plasterers and lived in an in-law apartment in my house in West Roxbury, about half a mile from Wedgemere Road. It was not long before Tim learned the business well and struck out on his own. John worked at a variety of jobs but was about to land at a job at an advertising agency, where his writing career began. Patrick shifted gears from firefighting and became a police officer in a beautiful suburban town just west of Boston. It was not firefighting, but over time he came to enjoy the work and, as it happened, he was extremely talented in law enforcement. Tom was, well, Tom. Mike went to work for the city's leading advertising agency, and I was working at the *Boston Globe*, assigned to the State House bureau.

"It's been hard, I know, but this drinking. . . ." I could not finish the sentence. Sonny and I were sitting across the kitchen table from one another, and he nodded in agreement and frowned. He reached over and tapped a cigarette out of an open pack of Luckies. He snapped open his silver lighter—the one with the submarine vets' logo on it—and lit up. He drew the tobacco deeply into his lungs and slowly exhaled, the smoke drifting out the kitchen screen. It was a warm summer evening, and so it occurred to me that this was exactly where Sonny was sitting that night so long ago when he brought home the polished brass fire extinguisher and the 500 silver dollars. On that night my mother sat where I was sitting—I could see her smile, her pride in him and what he had achieved.

"What are you gonna do?" I asked.

Sonny considered this for a moment as he reached up and removed a piece of tobacco from the tip of his tongue.

"Get it under control," he said.

He looked at me and sighed. This promise has been made before.

"How?" My question sounded more pointed than I intended and he regarded me closely, surprised by the sharpness of it. The word hung in the air—part challenge, part accusation.

"I'm going to work on it," he said, not looking at me, stubbing the Lucky out in the Bruins ashtray.

"Work on it?" I replied, making no attempt to conceal my skepticism. "What does that mean?"

Now I was a bit red-faced myself, clearly angry and impatient with him. He looked at me and was taken aback, but he seemed uncertain how to react. Should he challenge me in return? Tell me to watch myself? Should he express sorrow? There was a prolonged silence.

"You need help," I said. "I think you should go down and spend some time with Father Tom." Father Tom Barry, a former Franciscan missionary and my mother's younger brother, was a parish priest in Miami. He was a beloved, iconic figure within our extended family. Sonny looked at me, surprised, but seemingly intrigued, as well.

"I spoke to him last night," I continued. "I told him exactly what's going on. He's very sympathetic. He has great respect for you—you know that. I said I thought it might help if you went down and spent some time with him, talked some things through. He would love it if you did."

So it was arranged that Sonny would fly to Miami and spend a week with Father Tom. He stayed with Father Tom at his apartment, and they dined at various restaurants—some owned by Father Tom's friends, where everything was on the house. The Cuban émigrés loved their parish priest. Sonny and Tom took walks and sat around and talked quietly. Father Tom was a practical man, a man of wisdom. They prayed.

Sonny started dating a woman he had known growing up. Theresa McCauley was from South Boston originally and had married a Boston firefighter. In fact, Joe McCauley had been on the Rescue with Sonny. It was Joe McCauley who had once said that Patrick was "a natural born firefighter." Theresa had been a widow for several years when she and Sonny got reacquainted through mutual friends and began a courtship. The only obstacle was that she lived on Cape Cod, about eighty or so miles away. Sonny used to drive down and they would have dinner on weekends. As the relationship developed, Sonny wanted to be closer to her. In 1986, he found a position at the

Otis Air Force Base on Cape Cod as a fire captain for the base, a job comparable to the one he had at Watertown. Sonny thus went from firefighter to Firecontrol to fire safety officer to fire chief—over the course of nearly forty years.

I sensed it coming. I sensed that he would eventually move down to the Cape to be with Theresa. But, still, it was jarring when he announced he was going to sell our house at 27 Wedgemere Road. This was where our lives together had unfolded over thirty years.

My brothers and I went through the place, gathering up our possessions, sorting through old pictures and sports equipment. Everyone took what was theirs, and suddenly the place that had been our base— the place where we had come together as a family—was gone. I walked through the house in those final days and paused in each room, remembering. Here was the exact spot in the upstairs hallway where Sonny sat in the darkness telling us stories—mesmerizing tales of Smokey and Joe, the heroic firefighters. Here was the place where the plaster had been repaired—obvious by its rough surface—where I had punched a hole in the wall in anger when Sonny said I could not borrow the car to go to a school dance. Here was where Tom used to lock the bathroom door in winter and, as a teenager, lean out the back window, smoking. Here was where Patrick fell off the cellar stairs and landed on his head. Here was where Mike and Tom and I used to wrestle on the carpet in the living room, inches from the fireplace brick. Here was the mantle above the fireplace where, during a living-room hockey game, one of my mother's prized Hummels was knocked off its perch and shattered. And there—still sitting there so many years later—was the replacement that Michael and I had paid for ourselves, had walked all the way up to the House of Leslie to purchase. I stood staring at the Hummel—"the original Hummel figure"—a child sitting on a fence with a bumblebee nearby.

I had grown up in this house; it had all happened here, everything that was important, everything that was precious to me in my life. And now we were leaving it, and things would never be the same. We had all scattered and now had no common plot of earth to call our own.

15

"One of the Happiest Moments
I Ever Experienced on a Rescue"

S onny married Theresa, moved to the Cape Cod, and a few months later, at age
sixty-three, he decided to retire. He was sick of working, had been
working virtually his entire life and wanted to be done with it. He had
few financial responsibilities. All of us boys were now adults out on
our own. He had tucked away the proceeds from the sale of the house,
and he received monthly checks from Social Security and the Boston
Fire Department, along with a small one from the federal government
for having worked at Watertown and Otis. Sonny was not one of those
retirees itching to pack a bag and see the world. Quite the contrary. He
had never had much of an inclination to travel, and after he remar-
ried, it soon became clear that he and his new wife preferred to remain at home in Harwich, a quaint little town on Nantucket Sound.

The question was, what would he do with all that time? And the answer came on the first day of his retirement. He put it this way:

If I were in the house all day with Theresa—with anyone, with the
Virgin Mary—I would be a basket case within a matter of months. I

had to have something to do and I felt an inclination to the Grove. There had been only two published books about it, and they didn't tell me all that much as a firefighter. And my father having been there and knowing some of the firefighters there from my boyhood—it was just a very natural thing for me.

He started off by rereading Paul Benzaquin's book and by reading a newer book—similar to Benzaquin's, called *The Cocoanut Grove*, by Edward Keyes. Upon completing the two, Sonny decided his book would come at it from the point of view of a firefighter.

There was something startling about this because Sonny had never written anything in his life, never mind a book. He had never before expressed any real interest in writing, yet this was what he said he would do with his retirement years. And he pretended with nonchalance, all the while, that he had simply happened upon this idea.

His explanation for delving into the Grove—"I didn't have a boat"— was meant to suggest that this was a casual endeavor, one that Sonny chose because, well, you just couldn't sit on the porch and stare into space all day. But beneath that casual air was a deeper truth—Sonny wanted to tackle the Cocoanut Grove because it was the ultimate issue for a firefighter, for the son of a firefighter who had been there, and who, on top of it all, had been injured there. It was the worst of all tragedies in Boston fire history, never, God willing, to be repeated. He would be taking on an event that had been relegated to the dusty archives, an event that remained—forty-six years after the fact—a mystery of sorts. How had it started? How had it raced with such demonic speed, consuming all in its path? He was taking on the event that had defined his father's life and that would, though Sonny didn't know it yet, come to redefine his.

Sonny wanted to start by talking with eyewitnesses who could help put him inside the club that night. He wanted to hear firsthand what it was like. He mentioned the idea to Theresa, who just so happened to have recently spoken to a friend who knew a Cocoanut Grove survivor. Sonny tracked down Henry Gaw in Clinton, Massachusetts, about fifty miles west of Boston, and set out early one morning for the three-hour drive to Clinton. He was excited at the prospect of looking into the eyes and hearing the words of someone who had been there that night. Sonny realized that the vast majority of people who had been there were dead. Nearly 500 had died as a result of the fire, of course, but hundreds of others had died of natural causes during the intervening forty-six years. Sonny knew that the youngest among those at the Grove that night were already quite elderly. He wondered how many Grove survivors were still alive. It could be dozens or it could be only a handful. Thus, he drove to Clinton with a sense that this was something special.

Henry Gaw was a short, stocky man living alone in a pleasant house in a blue-collar neighborhood. He appeared fit, with trimmed gray hair and a genial manner. He was surprised anyone wanted to discuss the fire after all these years, but he was more than willing to help Sonny if he could. He and Sonny sat at the kitchen table having coffee as they went back through time. Henry Gaw's memory was remarkable concerning the details surrounding the Grove disaster. Sonny would come to find, in fact, that everyone he encountered who had been involved in any way with the fire that night had the event indelibly imprinted within their memory. For many people, it was as though there was a sort of video reel of the night's events that they could call to mind and replay with perfect clarity.

In the more than two hours of conversation, Henry created an invaluable picture of the scene. During high school, Henry had worked at a movie theater, and every evening before the pictures were shown, the theater manager had insisted that Henry check to make sure the emergency exits were in working order. Henry used this experience, along with quick responses, to save himself and his wife from dying in the fire. After their conversation, Sonny thanked Henry warmly, feeling as he left that something important had happened: Henry Gaw had brought him inside the Cocoanut Grove. In the days after meeting with Henry, Sonny sat down at his Selectric on the Cape and wrote a section about Henry for his book:

It sometimes seems that spontaneous happenings, as opposed to those well-planned in advance, result in the most memorable and enjoyable of times; and this was exactly what was happening to the three close married couples from the tiny Massachusetts town of Clinton. The six, Bob and Eleanor Coleman, Joe and Catherine Salmon, and Henry and Loretta Gaw, during their weekly get-together decided they would like to attend the upcoming football game in Boston featuring their favorite College of the Holy Cross versus the favored and formidable Jesuit rival Boston College. The improbable chance of obtaining tickets to the "sold out" event was, by chance, overcome with a quick telephone call to a close friend and prominent Holy Cross alumnus. With tickets in hand, weekend reservations were confirmed at Boston's stately Copley Plaza Hotel. Dinner reservations for Saturday evening at the renowned Latin Quarter nightclub were placed and the group anticipated an exciting, fun filled weekend!

On the bleak rainy Saturday the shocking result of the final score of the heralded football game between the two bitter rivals brought nothing but joy and exultation to the Clinton six, since their under-dog favorites had drubbed the highly acclaimed Boston College Eagles by 55 to 12 . . . Happily leaving the stadium the little group dispelled the chill and dampness of the rainy afternoon with a few celebratory cocktails while looking forward to an evening of pleasant dining and entertainment at the plush Latin Quarter.

On arrival at the nightclub their expectations were dashed when they were informed by the Maitre D that there had been a mistake made in communications, their reservation could not be honored and they could not be accommodated at the already jam-packed club.

Disappointed but undaunted, the little group wandered through the theatre district seeking admission to a half dozen clubs and restaurants but, with growing concern, they were turned away from each one because on this Saturday night it seemed as if everyone was out celebrating. As they were leaving the filled to capacity Mayfair Club on Broadway, they saw, across the street, the glowing neon sign of the Cocoanut Grove nightclub. It was now well after 9:00 PM and their immediate concern was for a hot and satisfying dinner before returning to their hotel.

Entering the ornate Foyer through the Piedmont Street revolving door main entrance the three couples approached the tuxedoed headwaiter who stated, "we are very crowded," but after Bob Coleman quickly pressed a sizeable tip into the man's hand, they were informed that there would be but a five minute wait for their table. And in a very short time they were ushered to a table located on the ultra-chic "Terrace," usually the province of the wealthy and famous.

After ordering a round of drinks they were able to enjoy an unobstructed view of the entire Dining Room, Caricature Bar and the stage upon which the second floor show was about to be presented. In response to a request for dinner menus, they were informed by their waiter that there was virtually no food remaining for dinner since the crowd in attendance was twice what would normally be there, but, he said, he could try to provide something in the way of sandwiches. The famished six quickly placed their orders and settled back to what promised to be a top-notch floor show, a fitting climax to a memorable day.

Within a very few moments, Henry, while sipping his drink and listening to the animated conversation, became aware of a crowd "shuffling around" near the Lobby area. Facing in the direction of the main entrance and having a clear view he saw "a trickle of flame over the Lobby area." He said quietly to his tablemates, "There's a fire over there, probably a small one, but I don't think this is a good place to be." In the very next instant flames flashed across the entire ceiling of the Dining Room. "It just went WHOOSH, right across, all flames," Henry recalled. Reaching across the table Henry grabbed Loretta and, pulling her to her feet, said in a voice tinged with anxiety, "Hold onto me, put your arms around my waist." Pulling the terrified girl with him Henry jumped down the few Terrace steps to the main floor level and looked briefly in the direction of the Foyer

where he saw "a mass of people clawing and pushing each other."
Clutching Loretta tightly he turned away from the direction of
the milling mob and started toward the rear of the now-flaming
nightclub.

A cloying, blinding, impenetrable pall of smoke dropped instantly from above and sounds of panic erupted from all directions.
Choking and blinded, Henry doggedly moved toward the rear of
the Dining Room, attempting to hold his breath while clinging
tightly to his terrified wife. Somewhere in the rear of the building
Henry knew there had to be an exit—he knew that from his high
school days as an after-school usher at the tiny neighborhood theatre in Clinton where the Manager (a call-fireman) had repeatedly
insisted on daily inspection of the function and access of exit doors.

Now burning fragments of the fabric ceiling were raining down
upon the screaming crowd. Loretta, with her head tucked tightly
against Henry's shoulder, was actually biting him in an attempt to
gain a breath of air. Crashing blindly against over-turned tables and
chairs, bumping into panicked people seeking safety and sensing the
skin on his hands and face burning . . . he staggered on until . . . he
saw, through a wall opening, light from outside the building. He was
close to the Shawmut Street exit door! Out of the darkness the strong
hands of a Boston firefighter propelled him through the open doorway into the street and the cold, clean air of the November night.
Henry sprawled, face-down, in the street with his badly burned
hands splitting open with agonizing pain. But he had been separated
from his beloved Loretta and, turning back into the inferno, he
rushed through the open exit door only to be confronted by a firefighter who softly said, "You're going the wrong way, buddy," and
Henry was once again thrown into the winter cold of Shawmut
Street. Now, with his torn hands bleeding, as he raised himself to
rush headlong into the Cocoanut Grove to reach Loretta, there appeared in the blackened doorway . . . the diminutive burned, but still
alive Loretta.

Hours later the firefighters would remove the four charred bodies of the Colemans and the Salmons.

Sonny sat back in his study at home after typing out his report from the interview. It was incredible how it had happened: A group of close friends on an impulse to have a fun weekend and four of the six were killed. In that instant when he had looked to the front and seen smoke and a panicked crowd jamming the revolving doors, Henry had known that there would be another exit. He knew it! And when the crowd surged one way, he and Loretta went the other.

Sonny felt a sort of reverence for Henry and what he had been through. He felt as though there was something almost sacred about the experience. Sonny felt his connection to the Grove had grown stronger. It was a powerful connection because of Pops, of course, but now Sonny had spent time with a man who had actually been inside the club that night nearly a half century earlier. He had sat with Henry and seen the pain in his eyes as he described the scene; as he talked about the loss of his four friends. He had sat with a man who had shared what were surely among the most intimate and painful memories of a lifetime. And Henry had been entirely open and trusting and Sonny was honored to have received that trust.

He was thrilled to have met Henry; to have recorded his story, and the truth was that Sonny was pleased with his writing for he felt it captured the experience Henry had described to him. He could not help but conjure in his mind an image of Henry and Loretta fighting their way toward the exit and finally making it to the Shawmut Street door where they escaped. In Sonny's image, there was Pops—for that was precisely where he had been stationed pulling people out. And Sonny could not help but wonder whether it was Pops who had saved Henry and Loretta. He could never know for sure, but he also knew that for a critical part of the evening—most likely the part when Henry and Loretta made it out—there was only one firefighter at the Shawmut Street exit.

———

Every week, Sonny drove up from the Cape to attend to the needs of his mother. Nana was living in a one-bedroom apartment—a public housing project for the elderly—just off Cummins Highway in Hyde Park. Sonny would take her food shopping and on other errands, all the while listening to her complain: about her health, her sisters, her grandchildren who visited infrequently. After starting his Cocoanut Grove research, Sonny decided that on his trips to Boston to help his mother, he could also conduct some Cocoanut Grove research. He knew Joe O'Keefe, the Massachusetts Fire Marshal. Some years earlier, when Sonny had been at Firecontrol, Joe had asked Sonny to serve on an informal advisory committee to help develop state regulations for fire extinguishers. Sonny had offered his thoughts. Subsequently, regulations were drafted, hearings were held at the State House, and eventually, regulations were adopted.

In the spring of 1988, Sonny drove up from the Cape to visit the fire marshal at 1010 Commonwealth Avenue, the state fire and safety headquarters. He was greeted warmly by Joe O'Keefe and they sat talking of old times. Sonny explained that he was interested in researching the Cocoanut Grove fire and wanted to start with the official state records. Joe called in his assistant, who, as Sonny put it, had worked there "since Christ was a carpenter."

But she shook her head. "No, we don't have any records on the Cocoanut Grove."

"Nothing?"

"Nothing."

A couple of weeks later when Sonny was at Nana's apartment, he decided to get in touch with George Graney, an old friend of Pops's who had been at the Grove. When Sonny was finished shopping with Nana, he called George from her apartment. George said, "Well, I'm sitting here right now being interviewed by Casey Grant from National Fire Protection Association about the Grove and we were just talking about your father."

Jesus! Sonny thought. At the very moment he called, George was being interviewed by someone from the NFPA and they were talking—*at that moment*—about Pops. There was something happening here, something powerful, something larger than himself. Sonny felt in an odd way—and he had never felt this way before—as though he was somehow meant to do this work.

George invited Sonny to join in the conversation, and Sonny immediately drove over to George's house on Athens Street in South Boston. George, now in his eighties, had always been called Red, for the red hair he had had when younger. George introduced Sonny to Casey Grant, a handsome young man in his late twenties with a compact build and pleasant manner. Casey had earned a master's degree in fire protection engineering from Worcester Polytechnic Institute and was new to the NFPA. It so happened that he had been charged with the responsibility of putting together a report on the Cocoanut Grove fire for that year's annual meeting of the NFPA, and he had come to George seeking firsthand information.

It was fortuitous. Here was Sonny, barely having begun his work, sitting and talking with a firefighter who had been at the scene, a man who had not only worked alongside Pops but had been assigned to the same firehouse. And he was talking with a well-educated fire protection engineer whose focus at the moment was the Grove. Casey Grant was generous of spirit and encouraged Sonny in his work, and he said anytime Sonny wanted access to the NFPA library, with its vast amount of technical information about fires and firefighting, Casey would arrange it.

The three men, all with their varying interest and connections to the Grove, sat chatting about the fire for a while longer. Mostly, Casey listened as George and Sonny reminisced about various firefighters, virtually all now dead and gone.

A week or so later, Sonny took Casey up on his offer and visited the NFPA library. "It turned out one of the librarians was an off-duty Watertown firefighter," Sonny recalled. "I had access to records, reports, clippings. I read the original NFPA report on the fire by Bob Moulton."

Bob Moulton was something of a legend in firefighting and fire-prevention circles. Moulton served as the technical secretary of the NFPA and was thus the organization's lead expert on fires, from their origins to prevention. Throughout the worlds of firefighting, fire

prevention, and code enforcement, Bob Moulton was a towering figure, widely respected for his intellect, seriousness of purpose, and devotion to his work. The Moulton report had been published early in
1943, barely a month after the fire. The report was vintage Bob Moulton: serious, thorough, and precise. The report's twin imprimaturs—
Bob Moulton and the NFPA—gave it a gravitas few other individuals
or organizations could match.

The small staff at the NFPA library provided Sonny with comfortable, quiet accommodations in the library, where he was literally
the only visitor at the time. He was in no rush and intended to read
through slowly and carefully, seeking to absorb and understand everything Bob Moulton had written.

"In any disaster such as this," Moulton wrote,

> it is difficult to determine the exact circumstances of the fire and
> the sequence of events in the few moments in between the start of
> the fire and its fatal results. . . .
>
> No exact figures are available as to the number of people in the
> building, but it appears that the number was about 1,000 as compared
> to the reported official seating capacity of something over 600. . . .
>
> Fire started in the Melody Lounge, a basement cocktail lounge.
> Feeding on the highly combustible decorations, artificial cocoanut
> palms and cloth covered ceilings and walls, it spread with great ra-
> pidity . . . Some of the surviving witnesses said the first they knew
> of the fire was when a girl with blazing hair ran screaming across
> the room. Others first saw flames flashing through the air just below
> the ceiling. There was a mad rush for the exits . . . *So rapid was the
> travel of the fire and the noxious smoke and gases that many appar-
> ently collapsed at their tables without even making a move towards the
> exits.* (Emphasis added)

Jesus, thought Sonny. It was unimaginable to him—after all of his
experience as a firefighter—that a fire could move so quickly that
people would not at least have time to get up from their tables and

run. He could not fathom it, could not understand what sort of monster had been created here. Sonny continued reading:

> Much comment has been made in the newspapers over the reported confession of a 16-year-old bus boy that he struck a match for light while replacing a light bulb and that an imitation palm tree thus was ignited. *However, other testimony indicates that flames were also observed breaking out near the false walls of the lounge, and that the walls had been hot for some time prior to the fire.* Other testimony indicated that . . . defective wiring or some other cause of fire may have precipitated the disaster. Actually, however, the exact source of ignition was a factor of considerably less importance than was the inadequacy of exit facilities and the extensive use of combustible decorations. (Emphasis added)

Sonny paused. This was really interesting. He had never heard anything before about the possibility that flames broke out from the false wall of the lounge and that the wall had been hot for some time. Not only was it fascinating, but it suggested greater complexity to the cause then the conventional wisdom that it had been the busboy. Also, Sonny wasn't at all sure he agreed with Moulton's observation about the source of ignition. In fact, Sonny thought the source of ignition was critically important because it could conceivably have some bearing on the nature of the fire and its speed. Moulton recounted that bodies had been piled up behind the jammed revolving main entrance, that an exit door at the top of the Melody Lounge staircase had been concealed and locked shut, that perhaps 100 victims had been trapped in the Broadway Lounge behind a door that opened inward and had jammed shut under the crush of people trying to flee.

As he reviewed the NFPA report, Sonny marveled at the scale of the rescue operations: 500 American Red Cross workers mobilized in under half an hour; 150 Motor Corps ambulances converging on the scene; 500 nurses' aides assisting hospital personnel; 300 volunteer nurses; 400 officers and men from the First Naval District of the U.S.

Coast Guard. As Sonny read through Moulton's report, certain facts caused him to pause and reflect on the staggering scope of the tragedy. "The dead who were extracted from the fire," Moulton wrote,

> were placed in a garage across the street from the night club. Those who died en route or after arrival at hospitals were placed in hospital morgues to await collection and handling by the Emergency Mortuary Service. The Mortuary Service, by 1:30 AM, had over 400 bodies accounted for in the various morgues throughout the city. . . .
>
> Most of the victims died from burns and inhalation of smoke and flames. It is interesting to note the statement of Dr. William H. Watters, associate medical examiner for the Southern Suffolk District, who said that he remembered only one broken bone—a rib—in the hundreds of bodies he examined, indicating that people died too quickly to fight for their lives. . . .

In his report, Moulton explored a variety of possible theories to explain the fire. There had been the suggestion, for example, that so much alcohol was consumed in the confined club space that alcohol fumes triggered the start and spread of the blaze. But Moulton rejected this notion, saying that "it does not seem possible that there could have been sufficient alcohol vapor in the breath to have created a flammable mixture in the Melody Lounge. Evaporation from drinks on tables in sufficient quantity to furnish a flammable mixture is not theoretically possible unless the liquor is served straight and warm. . . ."

Moulton discussed and rejected theories that proxylin (cellulose nitrate), used to make leatherette banquettes, was the cause. Moulton said there were insufficient quantities of proxylin to cause the fire. Since the building had once been a warehouse that housed cellulose nitrate motion-picture film, some had theorized that "a quantity of scrap film may have remained in some concealed space . . . A few reels of motion picture film, wrapped in an ordinary paper parcel rather than in the standard metal container and placed against a hot steam pipe or some other source of heat, could have gradually decomposed with the evolution of flammable and toxic gases. This, however, does not seem particularly consistent with the first observation of the fire around the artificial palm tree. . . ."

Moulton discussed briefly and set aside theories pertaining to flame-proofing chemicals, insecticides, and gasoline vapors. And then there was the "refrigerant gas theory." Moulton rejected that as a possibility, writing that "none of the commonly used refrigerant gases is flammable so this would seem to rule out any refrigerant gas being in any way responsible for the initial flash." Moulton wrote that as had been the case in many other fatal fires, there had been panic at the Grove. "The prevention of fatalities due to panic . . . can only be accomplished by eliminating the conditions that are conducive to panic. . . ." He elaborated on this point:

> Experience shows that as long as people are moving freely toward an assured place of safety there is little danger of panic even though fire may be rather close behind them. This emphasizes strongly the importance of free and unobstructed exit with nothing to delay or block the flow of people. Doors must swing with, rather than against, the exit travel. There must be no reduction in exit width along the path of travel as, for example, by a narrow door forming a bottleneck at the foot of a flight of wide stairs. Exit details should be designed so as to minimize the danger of stumbling and falling, for when one person falls others are likely to pile up and the exit becomes blocked . . . Above all, the path of escape must be clearly marked so that there is no question from any point in the room as to the direction to go to reach an exit. . . .

Moulton was clear in his condemnation of the revolving main entrance door and of various locked emergency exits throughout the nightclub. He noted:

> The NFPA Building Exits Code prohibits revolving doors as exits in places of assembly, and furthermore requires that in other occupancies where revolving doors are used swinging doors must be immediately adjacent or within twenty feet. . . .

It should be obvious to anyone that all exit doors in a place of public assembly should be kept unlocked whenever the place is occupied. This is so elementary that no code or law should be needed, but experience all too often shows that this elementary factor of fire safety is disregarded. . . .

Sonny found himself shaken by Moulton's report. The level of negligence—particularly the locked exits—seemed almost incomprehensible. With so few changes, so many lives could have been spared. With Moulton's overview, Sonny wanted to dig deeper, particularly from the perspective of the fire department.

Sonny paid a visit to fire headquarters to see his old friend Leo Stapleton, who had become commissioner of the department. As a young man, Sonny had fought fires with Leo. Leo's father was one of the renowned firefighters in the city and had worked with Sonny's father-in-law.

Sonny and Leo chatted for a while, again, about old times, and Sonny explained the project he had embarked on. Leo said he could have access to any and all department records on the fire. They were kept upstairs, above the commissioner's office, and Leo had an assistant guide Sonny up there and open up the files.

The repository was a small dusty room with large boxes containing various files, along with several large albums, two by three feet, containing newspapers from the period. Aided by one of Leo's assistants, Sonny carried the material to a desk on the third floor of fire headquarters, where he sat comfortably going through the pages. He was very pleased with the response he had received from the commissioner and felt a sense of pride that here he was, back at headquarters, given a desk in a quiet area and full access to the files. He was part of the family and that was how he was being treated. And he was exhilarated undertaking this search for—what? For this bit of history, for nuggets, for his father's story—perhaps for the origin of the fire itself?

Sonny discovered the Form 5s from the night of the fire—official fire department records made out by every company that was on the scene. The Form 5s contained information about response times, listed the names of each firefighter responding, described what each company did upon arrival and throughout the events of that night. For Sonny, the Form 5s were gold. He read through them, fascinated by the details of each company's actions, delighted when he came across the form for the rescue company listing his father's name.

"I read through all the Form 5s and I realized that within eight minutes, twenty-five engine companies were working at the Cocoanut Grove," Sonny says. "The response system worked beautifully."

Sonny spent a good deal of time reading through the files and returned again for several weeks, until it occurred to him that he could get a lot more done if he copied the files and brought them home to the Cape. He carted the files over to Crown Copy Center in West Roxbury, which was owned by a friend. Sonny had the entire haul photocopied, then returned the originals to fire headquarters.

Back on the Cape, now surrounded by the treasure trove from the BFD, Sonny began to examine the commissioner's report on the three weeks of hearings held in the immediate wake of the fire, all twelve volumes containing testimony from about 100 witnesses. He read through the transcript of the hearings, and then reread it. The fire did not behave as an ordinary fire. Witness after witness spoke of the speed of the fire, yet no one offered convincing testimony to explain exactly how the fire had started or how it had gathered so much speed. Sonny jotted down some notes:

- source of ignition
- point of origin
- spread of fire

Sonny sat back thinking about the Grove. He remembered the area well from when he was fifteen years old. Back then, Sonny worked after school as an elevator operator in a small hotel that served the theatrical community on Warrenton Street, steps from the half dozen or so major Boston theaters. On breaks, Sonny would often eat at

Eddie's Lunch, at the intersection of Broadway and Shawmut, which later become the Broadway Lounge within the Grove.

Back at fire headquarters, Sonny obtained a printout of all the living firemen who would have been old enough to have been at the Grove. He then went through and eliminated all those designated as having been on active military duty, as well as the men belonging to engine or ladder companies that he knew did not respond to the fire. Sonny was struck by the number of firefighters, Cocoanut Grove veterans, who had died during the intervening years. After sifting through the various lists, Sonny had compiled names of a number of men who were alive and who had been at the fire.

Sonny wrote up a letter that asked firefighters who were at the Grove to write or call him and share their recollections. He sent a couple of dozen or so letters and quickly started receiving responses. One of the first came from Johnny Rose. Sonny was astonished by this because he knew Johnny well—had, in fact, worked with him at Bowdoin Square for ten years and had never known Johnny had been at the Grove. Johnny had never spoken of it. Sonny drove out to Dedham, just outside Boston, to visit with Johnny, who was then quite old and not in the best of health. Johnny Rose, like Henry Gaw, was surprised that anyone was interested in the Grove after so many years, but his memory of events of that night was sharp. He particularly recalled, he told Sonny, "the terrible screams" when he first pulled into the scene. Johnny Rose with Engine 22 had been at the car fire that Pops had been sent to near the Grove, and when Johnny arrived on the scene of the Grove, flames were spewing from the building. Johnny provided some new perspective:

> We knew there was a lot of fire in there, but of course, we had no idea how many people were involved. Shortly, there seemed to be a slackening off of the crowd's activity as the people inside were being overcome, burned and trampled. We were able to gain entry and started to take some people out of the doorway. We didn't get too far in because the door in the vestibule swung inward and was blocked by bodies of those who had fallen. . . .

It took us a good half hour, I would say, to get from the doorway across the lounge to the bar. There was still a lot of heat and smoke, and the bodies were piled and intertwined one on top of the other. And still there were people in there, at first hollering and screaming, moaning, and then there were no moans at all. When we reached the cocktail bar there was a tremendous pile of bodies, people who had fled through the corridor from the Caricature Bar and the main dining room, seeking safety from the flames. Unable to reach the Broadway door before the heat and smoke overcame them, they jammed up, milled around, and that was it. We just continued to remove body after body.

Soon thereafter, Sonny received a letter from a firefighter named John Crowley, who was long retired and living in Florida. Sonny could hardly believe it when he read that the night of the Grove was John Crowley's very first night as a Boston firefighter. Based on the letter, Sonny wrote the following for his book:

John Crowley was justifiably excited. This was his first night as a fire-fighter in the City of Boston. Standing beside the Patrol desk of Engine 9, in the East Boston section of the City, he was learning under the watchful eye of Bobby Quirk of Ladder 2 how to count the fire department tapper, answer the department phone and the many other requirements of properly attending to the duties of the "man on patrol." At 10:20 PM Box 1521 sounded on the tapper and was recorded in the house journal but, since the location of Box 1521 was on the other side of the city, no further action was required from the crew of Engine 9. Within minutes however the tapper chattered out a 3rd alarm and Quirk leapt to his feet saying, "What the hell is going on? They never skip an alarm." Within seconds Engine 9 hose wagon and pumper were out the door heading for the Sumner Tunnel that ran under Boston Harbor and was the sole connecting link between East Boston and the downtown area of the City. . . .

As they pulled in to the fire location and reported to the Deputy Chief they were directed to run and operate a hand-line to a door on Shawmut Street. As they hurriedly stretched the 2½ inch hose-line down the narrow street they passed people "who were dead or dazed and delirious on the streets and the sidewalk." Upon entering the building they "passed people piled shoulder high on each side of the doorway." When temporary lighting was restored the inside of the building was a gruesome sight. There were people dead at tables who had died without moving. At this time the fire had been virtually extinguished and Engine 9 crew was directed toward the Piedmont side of the Club to aid in body removal. "On the way out I seen so much money of all denominations on the floor, it hit me of how insignificant money was." While removing charred bodies to waiting taxis, trucks and ambulances he noted "two police cars with ladies pocketbooks completely filling the back seats." Shortly thereafter the crew was ordered up on to the "very badly burned stage and told to shovel up burned debris that could contain body parts. I prayed that this did not happen."

John Crowley had seen the worst possible horror—the worst fire in the city's history—on his very first shift as a Boston firefighter. He struggled with the question of whether he would continue on the job. "I had to battle with myself as to whether or not to stay on the job. I stayed—for thirty-one years."

Talking with men such as Johnny Rose, Henry Gaw, John Crowley, and others was enthralling to Sonny. He was thrilled by their vivid recollections, and he felt a surging sense of excitement that these men were within yards of where Pops had been that night.

Sonny initiated more and more phone conversations with me during this period, calls to bring me up to date, to tell me about someone he had interviewed or about some particular fact. To me and my brothers, this project seemed like a godsend, a cause, a passion—a *calling*, in a way. This drive and passion he felt was reminiscent of his commitment to the navy and the fire department.

It became clear over a period of months that this project was changing Sonny. He was sober more often than before—certainly not always, but more often and noticeably so. The research and gathering information on paper, but particularly the interviews, had energized him as nothing had in a very long time. The work changed him, giving him a focus. It connected him with his old world—the world he loved best—and with his father. He could sit around with men from BFD and talk about firefighting and the Grove, and his father's name inevitably came up. Some of them knew exactly what Pops had done at the Grove and the others, well, Sonny had the pleasure of filling them in. He had not displayed a passion for anything in so very long, and about this he was passionate. He loved doing it and cared about each and every man he spoke with; he treated every story with unending curiosity and reverence.

There were nights when he would call to talk about a particular aspect of his work, and it was clear he was stone sober. He excitedly filled me in on some new piece of information or new insight he had gained about the speed of the fire, for example. And he recounted his conversations with various people and told me about a document or record he had dug out of the files. It was thrilling to hear the excitement in his voice. And often on such nights, I later got a phone call from one of my brothers, recounting how Sonny had just called them, as well, to tell them precisely the same story he had told me. We did not know where this Cocoanut Grove thing was going, exactly, but one thing was for sure: It was the tonic he needed at the moment.

Tom was ambitious. He wanted to be the best firefighter he could possibly be, just as he wanted to be an outstanding paramedic. But he wanted more than that: He wanted to push himself and test his mettle. Whenever there was an opportunity to take advanced rescue courses, Tom signed up. The department would pay for the training, though Tom would have to do it on his own time. Nonetheless, he took advantage of every chance he got to take any type of rescue course.

In 1990, Tom saw an ad in a trade publication for a conference in Montgomery County, Maryland, sponsored by the Montgomery County Fire Department and the International Association of Fire

Chiefs. The conference, designed to teach rescue personnel techniques for saving lives in building collapses, drew experts from around the country, and Tom learned a tremendous amount in just a week's time. Near the end of the conference, federal officials began discussing an intriguing idea. Consideration was being given to forming regional teams in building collapse, and Tom was immediately drawn to the concept.

They told Tom, "Look, ultimately the government wants to have these teams all across the country, and if your state comes up with money, the federal government will match it up to $2 million."

One of the main advocates for the idea was an instructor at the program, a New York City fire captain named Ray Downey. Tom recounted how he first got involved in the effort:

> Ray was a captain on Rescue 2 in Brooklyn, and he and I got to talking and he asked about various guys I knew in Boston and it turned out we had a few friends in common. At the conference Ray was teaching concrete (breaching) and breaking. Over the course of the week we became friendly, had dinner and hung out.
>
> When I came back to Hyannis, I was pretty excited about the challenges of structural collapse. Though they occur infrequently in this country, a lot of the skills that I learned about lifting heavy objects and breaching and cutting things were applicable to everyday fire department stuff, either in accidents or forcing your way into a building during a fire. I was definitely also interested in this idea of putting together a Massachusetts team. The idea grew out of the Federal Emergency Management Agency (FEMA) and I made sure I kept current with what their plans were. But quite a bit of time passed and there was no movement.
>
> And then one day I get a phone call from Ray Downey and he says, "You'd better get the firemen together up there because I heard that Beverly, Massachusetts, Civil Defense is getting the team." So I said, "Well, who do I call?" He gave me a number and I found out this group up in Beverly was putting the team and holding a meeting the following week. So I drove up to Beverly [in summer 1992]

and they explained how they were forming this team which would be funded and managed by FEMA. They said there would be training once a month, but we would not be paid for training. We would be paid only when we were activated. I didn't mind that—I wanted the additional training—and the idea of being part of a select team responding to building collapses really appealed to me.

So we began training and after a while we learned that teams in other places were getting substantial sums from their state governments to match the federal money. It allowed them to significantly improve their equipment and their ability to do the job. The team in Virginia Beach was getting a million dollars and Ray's team in New York was getting a million and a half, but in Massachusetts we had received next to nothing and all of our equipment was surplus or used. And then came Oklahoma City and the federal building and pretty soon we had the funding we needed and we were ready.

Back in Hyannis, Tom also had ambitions to make lieutenant, a difficult achievement on any department but particularly so on a department the size of Hyannis, where openings are rare. Preparing for a test requires six to seven months of study for several hours a day. This was not something Tom had ever enjoyed, but he was willing to put the time in because he so very much wanted to be promoted. Tom's view was:

The thing is in the small departments, if you want the job, really, you've got to be number one. They can take any one of the top three. But historically they take number one. You've got to strive to say, "I'm not going to pass the lieutenant's exam, I've got to *top* the lieutenant's exam" in a small department.

The first lieutenant's exam I ever took I think I was like number three or number four and they made one guy. A couple of years later I took it a second time and I was number two. They made one guy. The third time I took it I was number three. One guy got made, then one guy quit and left for another department. When that happened I moved up to number one and I got made.

As Tom saw it, one of the most painful aspects of the job was seeing preventable tragedies that were far more common than they should be.

One night we responded to a fire on Bay Shore Road in Hyannis and there was heavy fire through the roof. It was an L-shaped house and we got a hand line on the building and I ran to the front to give horizontal ventilation. I went at the door leading to the living room and took out the windows, and when I did, I could see somebody lying on the floor face down, about ten to twelve feet inside.

The chief was pulling in, and I yelled to him that somebody was in there. I went in and started crawling, and I went over and I grabbed her but she was burned so bad her skin came off in my arms and on my gloves. The chief followed me in, and he and I sat her up and I picked her up, bear-hugged her, and ran backwards out the door. She was unconscious and unresponsive and she was rushed to the hospital.

When the fire was out I went inside and had a look around. It was pretty obvious what had happened. She had been sitting in the living room having a cigarette and somehow an ash had gotten into a stuffed chair. She didn't realize it at the time and she went to bed. As she was asleep the fire ignited in the chair and then spread across the living room. When she realized what was happening she opened her bedroom door into the hallway leading to the living room and there was heavy smoke. She started forward, probably heading for the front door, probably stumbled and fell, overcome by smoke, and that's where we found her.

But the tragedy was that instead of coming out of her bedroom and going toward the front door, all she had to do was go back inside her bedroom—remember we're on the ground floor here—open the window and step outside. But people almost always try to exit a building the way they came in. The other thing, and it's really sad, was she didn't have a smoke detector in the house. A $7 smoke detector could have prevented the whole thing. She was taken up to Mass General and a week and a half after the fire she died.

There were other types of moments, Tom said, when experience and the right equipment made all the difference.

One afternoon we got a mutual aid call for a car accident on Route 130 near the old Mashpee Town Hall and we responded in the heavy rescue. Evidently there had been a woman and her child in a Ford LTD driving towards Mashpee on Route 130. They were going to take a left by the old town hall and in front of her was a box truck, so her view of the road ahead was obscured. She should have waited for the box truck to clear, obviously, but she went ahead and turned into the oncoming lane and a cement truck—huge thing with no time to react—hit her broadside and drove her car off the road and into a gully. Then the cement truck came to rest on top of the passenger side of her car—which was where the woman's two-year-old daughter was sitting. And the child was not in a car seat. The mother was just running an errand, so she didn't bother to use the car seat. It was in the back seat and the child ended up getting thrown face forward onto the passenger side floor. And when the truck landed on top of the car, it completely crushed that whole side of the car.

The mother, who was fine physically, was screaming for the child when Mashpee got there, so they knew there was a kid in the car, but you really couldn't see her. They did some digging and all they could see was kind of like her diaper from the back. You couldn't see the head or the shoulders, the lower part of her legs. The Mashpee rescue squad was able to get the mother out but the child was underneath everything and they didn't have the equipment to get to her. We are fortunate to have the big rescue truck, fully equipped for heavy rescue. We used a Hurst system—a hydraulic tool known as the Jaws of Life, which has the power of seven tons of force.

We went over there and there were four or five of us on the truck that day—Dean Melanson, Danny Clough, Donnie Chase, and myself and it was a horrible wreck, the cement truck had just demolished the car—one of the most devastating entrapments I'd ever seen. I mean this kid was down in there under all kinds of twisted metal. It was a mess. The first thing we had to do is lift the cement truck high enough so that we could get under it, and we did that with a mechanical jack, which I had trained on down in Maryland. Then we placed air bags under the cement truck. Now, this truck weighed thirty tons. But the strongest of these air bags can lift seventy-four tons as much as one inch. We placed four bags in position and inflated them slowly, raising the cement truck enough so that we could place lumber underneath it, to level it, and allow us to try and get to the child. With the air bags, we were able to lift the truck nearly a foot, which enabled us to get the Hurst system underneath. The Hurst tool gave us some more room and we were able to get a power saw in there and cut off the car door.

Tom found that the experience of having trained down in Montgomery County, Maryland, prepared him exceptionally well for precisely this type of rescue operation.

Once we got the cement truck up, we had to cut away the whole dashboard to be able to get at the kid. And we finally got her out—I guess it took about two hours—and there was a helicopter waiting to fly her to the hospital. We put her in the ambulance and it was just about a mile to the field where the helicopter flew her to Boston, and the miracle was that she had a very small chest injury and fractured wrist. That was it. It was one of the happiest moments I ever experienced on a rescue.

16
Sonny the Author

Eddie Loder was a squat, powerful man with some of the characteristics of a bulldog. Lest there be doubt about Eddie's love for the job in general and Rescue 1 in particular, he proudly displayed a tattoo of a Rescue 1 bulldog on his upper arm. Eddie Loder was forty-one years old, and during his two decades on the job he had gained a reputation for fearlessness. Both Tom and Patrick considered Eddie one of the finest firefighters they had ever met—an opinion shared throughout the department.

On a balmy evening in late May 1990, Eddie Loder and his mates from Rescue 1 responded to an alarm at the Ritz Carlton Hotel at the corner of Arlington and Newbury Streets in Boston's Back Bay. The Ritz was the city's most enduring landmark of old-world Boston elegance, an attractive brick structure overlooking the lush public garden where the swanboats ferried passengers around the duck pond.

On this particular evening, however, there was a young woman in her twenties, who had just left a psychiatric hospital, seated on the ledge of her top-floor hotel room threatening to jump. Hundreds of spectators gathered below, and the event was carried on local television. A police unit had gone up to the woman's room and, from the entryway, had urged her to come inside, but she threatened to jump if they stepped closer.

After some time had passed, it became increasingly clear that the police officers were making no headway. Eddie Loder and the other firefighters were told that someone had spoken by phone with the woman's doctor, who was convinced she was deadly serious about jumping.

Eddie and the rest of the Rescue 1 crew—Paul Carey, Bobby Breen, Jimmy Hardy, and Lieutenant Jack Joyce—headed up to the roof, where they found a number of good anchor points to secure their ropes. The question arose as to who would strap on the harness and go over the ledge.

"I'll go," Eddie Loder said.

The plan was simple: The officers inside the room would distract her, and at that moment, Eddie would drop from the roof and push her back inside.

"I wasn't going to go down and sweet-talk her," Eddie said. "My game plan was to come right down off the roof and get her inside, whatever it would take."

Word came from police that she might have a razor. When Eddie heard that, he said, "I'm going to give her a kick. I'm not going to be nice about it. I'm going to have to do what I have to do."

There was a serious logistical challenge that wasn't presented by other rope rescues. Normally, firefighters using ropes rappelled down the side of a building or the inside of an elevator shaft, but if the rescue crew threw ropes over the side to rappel down, the woman would see them and possibly jump. Eddie would have to jump off the building, and get to the woman before she realized what was happening. So the crew tied Eddie to the end of a rope and guessed how far down the woman's window was—about eight feet from the roof. When Eddie was ready to go and the rescue crew on the roof waited for a signal from the officers in the woman's room, Mike Walsh from Ladder 17, who was on the roof, said to Eddie: "You sure you really want to do this?"

Eddie laughed. "Someone's got to do it."

"Don't you want me to go downstairs and get a bottle of the best booze they have in this hotel so we can have a couple drinks before you do this?"

There were half a dozen men on the roof holding the ropes tied to secure anchor points. Paul Carey had the job of holding onto Eddie, who was in position on the edge of the roof, sitting like a scuba diver with his back to the water, ready to fall in. The rescue crew on the roof was in radio contact with men outside the woman's room, waiting for a signal. Eddie could lean a bit and see over the edge of the roof; he could see the woman sitting there on the ledge. Paul Carey held onto Eddie awaiting the signal. Standby, they were told.

"Jeez, Eddie," Paul Carey joked a moment before releasing Eddie, "I hope we tied the knots right."

And then the signal came. Paul let go and Eddie Loder went over the side, into the dark night. And when he did, the city seemed covered in a massive flash of light, an explosion of light from powerful television klieg lights and the flashes of still photographers below.

As he fell, Eddie thought of the razor. "Is she going to jump out at me, lunge at me, is she going to reach for the rope?"

"When I went off the roof, you know sometime when you see something move at the side of your face; well, that's what happened. She'd seen me there. And she turned around and she let out a scream and as she let out a scream, my foot was across her chest. I mean I kicked her so hard she ended up halfway in the room. Of course they tackled her and wrestled with her and she did have a razor. They got that away from her."

While the team inside subdued the woman, Eddie swung at the end of the rope, extended several feet away from the window. He reminded himself not to look down as he waited for someone inside to reach out and pull him in through the window. Inside, the young woman looked up at Eddie Loder and swore at him.

Sonny was reaching out in all directions, responding to any leads that came his way. He would hear of a survivor from a friend of a friend or from a firefighter or from another survivor, and then he would try to track the person down, though his pace was unpredictable. There were days when following up on a lead was an urgent matter, when he felt the need to get an interview scheduled and completed right away. There were other times, though, when he would be drinking and would slip off track. Weeks would go by when he would do next to nothing, and then, suddenly, almost frenetically, he would reemerge, determined to plow ahead gathering material.

On April 29, 1991, Sonny tracked down his old friend Howie McLennan, a Boston jake living near Washington, D.C., who had gone on to become president of the International Association of Firefighters. Sonny called, and he and Howie reminisced for the better part of half an hour. That night, Sonny wrote to Howie:

> Howie—
> After talking with you I just sat out in the back yard with a cold beer and a flood of memories came back; of Lt. Red McNamara, John Hernan . . . And to walk into headquarters last week and shake hands with the new commissioner—Marty Pierce's kid . . . Where the Hell did all those years go??

Sonny asked Howie to "jot down whatever you remember" about the Grove "while you are lazing around in retirement." He concluded his note with "take good care of yourself."

Looking for survivors, Sonny pored over the list of people who had been injured at the Grove. He went through the list of people who had testified at the fire commissioner's hearings held in the wake of the fire. He dug into the tedious work of looking up phone numbers for people, hoping they still lived in the town where they had been five decades earlier. Sonny got lucky with Hewson Gray, who had testified before the commissioner's hearing and had been living in Waltham, a town just west of Boston. He still lived there.

Sonny visited Hewson Gray at his modest home. He was retired and a widower. He appeared to Sonny to be in his seventies, a man of medium height and build with a weathered face and wispy gray hair. He was quite surprised that anyone was interested in the Grove so many years later.

Hewson told Sonny that he and his wife, Hilda, along with three other couples, had reservations for a table across from the stage in the center of the room, but when the party arrived, they were told that no tables were available in that area. They were led to a table against the rear wall of the room—not perfect, but they would still be able to see the band and enjoy the show. After a round of cocktails, Hewson got up from the table and went to the men's room, which was all the way across the club, just inside the revolving door at the main entrance. Emerging from the bathroom, Hewson encountered a friend, and they stood in the foyer near the stairway to the Melody Lounge and the front door, chatting for a moment. Then Hewson walked back across the dining room to his table.

He told Sonny that just as he reached the table, he heard commotion and turned to see smoke in the foyer and people rushing for the revolving door. "We've got to get out of here," he said to his companions, and the other seven rose from the table. No one seemed in a particular hurry, because the smoke was way over on the other side of the room. As they rose and started to move, however, suddenly the room was filled with smoke and a fireball rolled through in what seemed seconds. Hewson saw people headed for an exit along the rear wall nearby, so he and the others pushed toward the door, tripping and stumbling in the darkness, having difficulty breathing but then, suddenly, finding the Shawmut Street exit door and making it outside. And Hewson said he realized that if he had lingered with his friend in the foyer for a few more seconds, he would surely have perished in the fire.

Sonny tracked down Ferdinand Bruck, who had also testified at the commissioner's hearing. Ferd was an architect in Cambridge, a dignified, articulate man who had gone to the Grove with his date, Cleo

Lambritis, as a farewell celebration, for Ferd was days from active duty in the U.S. Army. Ferd and Cleo were seated in a cramped corner of the Melody Lounge when the fire started. They noticed what appeared to be a flicker from the top of an artificial palm tree. A bartender and busboy sought to extinguish the flame, but as they tried, it suddenly accelerated.

Sonny wrote:

Because their little table was located on the Piedmont Street side of the lounge, Ferd and Cleo were among the first to start into the stairwell upward to the Foyer. It was already filling with fingers of flame. As he held Cleo close to him, Ferd hugged the wall of the stairs and the couple bent low to avoid the searing heat now burning their heads and ears. In pain, they reached the top of the stairs and turned towards the Foyer and the revolving door exit while darts of ever-increasing flame spurted over their heads.

The flames and unburned gases were now gaining control of the Foyer and Lobby seeking oxygen for complete combustion. The heat was intense! And through this tunnel of torture, Ferd, still holding Cleo tightly to his side, rushed toward the panicked crowd milling about in front of the revolving door main exit. In pain, but with purpose, the couple forced their way through the throng to the exit door which seemed to be jammed but, suddenly, as Ferd stated, "Because we were so skinny," the pair was through the exit and into the cold safety of the Piedmont Street sidewalk. Both were in shock, burned, in pain, but alive.

Ferd hailed a cab directing a hasty trip to the Boston City Hospital. On arrival Ferd, with burned hands, attempted to reach for his wallet to pay the fare. The cabby said, "Forget it, Buddy, I'm going back there to see if I can help!"

During this period Sonny was a familiar figure at Boston Fire Department headquarters. "Anything he wants," Marty Pierce had instructed one of his assistants, and Sonny felt very good about that. At one point, Sonny was having some difficulty precisely defining the street grid in the Cocoanut Grove area because it had changed during the intervening years. One of the commissioner's assistants promptly called over to City Hall, and a massive five-by-six-foot street map of the city, intricately detailed, was delivered to Sonny. He was treated with respect—treated as a member of the family.

Perhaps what pleased him most was that he had succeeded in establishing himself as an important resource on the Cocoanut Grove fire. Increasingly, he was recognized as such within the department and at the National Fire Protection Association. This was crucial for Sonny at the time. Gaining this credibility meant he was not simply a pestering retired firefighter rummaging around in the archives—he was a resource, a credible person who possessed valued knowledge about the fire.

In early 1992, there was growing awareness around Boston that the fiftieth anniversary of the fire would come that November. As Sonny looked ahead to the anniversary, he saw it as an opportunity. He anticipated that there would be press interest in the anniversary, and he knew he would be in a position to answer the questions many journalists would pose.

What excited him most about this prospect was his belief that journalists might help lead him to new information about the fire. Sonny made a decision early in the year that he wanted to make himself available to any and all journalists who wished to speak with him. But he would do so on a single condition: that they promise to share with him any new information that might come their way in the process of their reporting—or even after their work had been aired or published.

The irony of it, of course, was obvious to Sonny as the anniversary approached: He was the expert almost by default. "I was the only one doing any type of research," he recalled. "I was the only one asking any questions or evincing any interest at all."

As he proceeded with his work, he let people know that he was writing a book about the Grove, and when he did this he instinctively felt that in some places there was a subtle skepticism. He had been a firefighter—not even an officer—and he had never written anything in his life. How did he think he was ever going to write a book?

And so he decided early in the anniversary year of 1992 that he would write an article about the fire and seek to have it published. This would get his voice out there and would establish him as a credible source on the issue. This, of course, was easier said than done. Writing can be a difficult business, and finding publications willing to take work by new writers is a challenge. But Sonny made the wise decision to write an article specifically targeted to firefighters—for that was what he knew best. He sat down at his old Selectric and began pecking away. Eventually, he submitted his finished piece to Casey Grant at the National Fire Protection Association, asking whether there might be space for it in the NFPA newsletter. Casey placed it in *The Times*, a regular NFPA publication. It appeared under the headline "For Firefighters Only":

> [As] units were responding they were totally unaware that the chief of district 5 was ordering the striking of the 3rd and 4th alarm. . . .
>
> The importance of this omission of the 2nd alarm must be noted since, in the Boston Fire Department, all multiple alarm responses are not programmed, but even the multiple alarm apparatus response routes are pre-designated to avoid responding apparatus colliding with one another. Only in rare and grave situations would a Chief officer risk the simultaneous response of fire equipment that three additional alarms would bring to the streets. In the instant and accurate judgment of District Chief Crowley this, indeed, was such a situation. . . .
>
> Behind the glass paneled [revolving] door could be seen people succumbing to flames and smoke. The first three arriving engine companies directed their lines on the revolving door in an attempt to gain entry and effect rescue. Noting only one other door into the building, the deputy directed the men of Ladder 12 to force entrance through that door. With great difficulty, the door was breached and the captain of Ladder 12 reported back to the chief that the passageway was "loaded with bodies. . . ."

The supply of water posed no problem. In addition to a plentiful distribution of standard post hydrants strategically located throughout the area, the City of Boston had, in its "high value" district, a secondary system of high pressure hydrants whereby lines could be run directly from these red bonneted hydrants and, without benefit of pumpers, could supply 125 p.s.i. for immediate operation. What did, however, cause concern for the command officers was the congestion of the neighborhood. The main entrance of the fire building was on Piedmont Street which was 30 feet wide, sidewalk to sidewalk, while the rear of the building was on Shawmut Street, even narrower. . . .

On all sides of the fire building paramount concern was to gain entry for rescue purposes. On Piedmont Street, in spite of vast amounts of water being directed at the revolving door, it was many minutes before the fire companies could approach closely enough to begin removal of the charred remains of more than 100 persons stacked in the area of the revolving door. Only after Ladder 12 forced the only other door on the Piedmont Street side could 25 to 30 bodies be removed. At the sole entrance to the Broadway Lounge, Engine 22, backed by three more engine companies, was removing bodies stacked to a height of six feet in the vestibule as it attempted to move in on the fire. Only on the Shawmut Street side [where Pops had been], where a double door exit direct from the main dining room had been opened, were the fire fighting companies able to achieve early access. And it was through this exit that most survivors escaped. . . .

There is no accurate record of firefighter injuries at this fire. More than a few of the responding men were removed to area hospitals, some sustaining injuries of such severity that they were pensioned on disability. Most firefighters worked until they dropped, many being revived at the scene and remaining on duty. A pipe-man from Engine 22, having battled the fire for nearly an hour, collapsed and was carried out . . . One of the Ladder 12 crew was knocked unconscious when a Cocoanut Grove employee jumped from the second floor and landed on him. When the ladder man regained his senses, he found himself on the concrete floor of a nearby commercial garage being used as a temporary morgue. He had been assumed dead and was lying among rows of blackened corpses. He rejoined his company and continued working. . . .

For the men of the Boston Fire Department there was no post-fire trauma counseling, no psychological guidance. Every last fire fighter who participated in fighting the fire at the Cocoanut Grove carries, etched indelibly in his memory, the unspeakable horror of that November night and for each the burden is his and his alone to carry to his grave.

At the bottom of the article was: "The author, Charles Kenney, Jr., is retired from Rescue 3 of the Boston Fire Department. His father, Charles Kenney, was a member of Rescue 1 on November 28, 1942, and is believed to be the first fire fighter to enter the Shawmut Street doors of the Cocoanut Grove. He is credited with the rescue of many survivors. As a result of injuries sustained at this fire, Rescueman Kenney was retired from the fire department. . . ."

Publication of the article was a milestone for Sonny, and it appeared in a publication from the most trusted fire-prevention organization in the country, perhaps the world. It gave an enormous boost to Sonny's confidence and established him as someone who was serious— someone who could actually get something down in writing and get it into print.

At both the NFPA and the Boston Fire Department, people took note and steered inquisitive reporters working on fiftieth-anniversary stories to Sonny. Overseas newspapers and TV networks called him, and he received many interview requests from U.S. papers, particularly in the New England area. The greatest area of interest, of course, was Boston, where newspapers and TV stations put together special coverage to mark the anniversary.

As the November 1992 anniversary approached, Sonny fielded dozens of phone calls and sat for a dozen or more interviews with various news outlets. "The only thing I was concerned with was giving them all the information I had with the proviso that they would come back to me with any new information, especially about survivors because of my intent to locate more survivors."

Sonny had made a decision that his book—rather than a definitive history of the Grove, a project that seemed too daunting to contemplate—would be a series of survivor profiles. On November 27, the day before the fiftieth anniversary, an article by Carol Dumas appeared in the *Cape Codder* newspaper. It began: "Charles Kenney of Harwich was in the Navy on Nov. 28, 1942, but he can tell you almost every detail about the Cocoanut Grove fire that killed nearly 500 people that night in Boston. For the past two years, Mr. Kenney has been relentlessly tracking down survivors, interviewing firefighters, former employees and doctors, and poring over records and files . . . Within the next year he hopes to turn his research into a book of vignettes compiled from his interviews."

In the article, Sonny wondered aloud about the source of ignition and speed of the fire. "What caused [it] to blow and spread within five minutes and kill almost 500 people? Was it the leatherette . . . that generated a gas and asphyxiated people? There's a lot of conjecture."

The day before the fiftieth anniversary, Sonny drove up in the afternoon from the Cape to Boston and checked into the Fifty-Seven Hotel, adjacent to where the Grove had once stood. He was in town for the anniversary event the following day, to which he had received a special invitation. He took a stroll around the neighborhood and viewed the plaque out behind the hotel commemorating the site. He walked down Piedmont Street to the very place where the revolving door once stood. He walked slowly down Shawmut Street where Pops had been that night, rescuing all those people. It was cold in the late afternoon, a typical raw New England November day. Sonny took it all in, picturing mentally what had been there so many years before.

He recalled walking those streets as a boy on his way to his job as an elevator operator over on Warrenton Street. He remembered going out for a bite at Eddie's Lunch and as he reached the junction of Shawmut and Church Streets, Sonny saw Mario's restaurant, where a reporter had made the first call to a newspaper reporting the fire.

The next morning, Sonny awoke and reviewed the Boston papers. There, on the front page of the *Globe*, was a lengthy feature article by Jack Thomas. It began:

"Flip through this," said retired firefighter Charles Kenney of Harwich, handing over a document with 11 pages of names. "Force yourself to turn every page. It gives you an idea of what the Cocoanut Grove fire meant to Boston. Page after page of names, 492 of them, all dead. It's hard to comprehend." Few events have taken a greater toll on Boston's psyche than the Cocoanut Grove fire 50 years ago next Saturday night. Hollywood rarely provides the drama of that 15-minute fire, rarely captures the horror and never conveys the agony endured by victims and their families for days, even years.

At 1:00 PM on the afternoon of November 28, a ceremony was held just behind the Fifty-Seven Hotel at the corner of Shawmut and Piedmont Streets. So much had changed through the years. The city was a different place with its newer and bigger buildings. The old neighborhood was not what it once had been, though the change did little to dim the memories. For Sonny and many others there, most of them quite old, the vivid memories recalled terrible suffering and death, but also escape, a reminder of the most precious of gifts.

The mayor and fire commissioner both offered remarks to the gathering of perhaps a couple of hundred people. The state fire marshal and a member of the Boston City Council spoke as well. There was, appropriately, a somber note to the occasion. Honor guards from the U.S. Coast Guard, the U.S. Navy, and the Boston Fire Department presented the colors. The fire department's Gaelic Brigade played their haunting bagpipes. A priest, a minister, and a rabbi offered prayers.

Finally, the plaque was unveiled. It was laid into the sidewalk, among the bricks, adjacent to a parking lot. It reads: "The Cocoanut Grove. Erected by the Bay Village Association, 1993. In memory of the more than 490 people that died in the Cocoanut Grove Fire on November 28 1942. As a result of that terrible tragedy, major changes were made in the fire codes, and improvements in the treatment of burn victims, not only in Boston but across the nation. 'Phoenix out of the Ashes.'"

When the ceremony itself was finished, the crowd walked quietly to the Park Plaza Hotel for a reception and discussion. The panel included officials from the fire department as well as the commissioner of the city's Inspectional Services Department. A fire department chemist talked about fire codes, and a physician and nurse from Boston City Hospital discussed advances in medicine and emergency response.

Casey Grant from NFPA spoke about the history and legacy of the fire. Casey had spent countless hours researching the Grove—it had become an obsession of sorts. He talked about the speed of the fire, a subject that had proven vexing, fascinating, and terrifying, for those whose lives had been touched directly or indirectly by the event:

> The total time from the first appearance of flame until [the fire] had explosively traversed the main dining room and passed almost 225 feet away to the entrance of the Broadway Lounge [the commissioner] estimated at an incredible 5 minutes at most. At this point in time all exits normally open to the public, each of which had something functionally wrong, were useless for a safe escape.

Casey displayed a series of slides, one of which showed the exit at the top of the stairs from the Melody Lounge. "Note the panic bar on this door—but it did little good since it had slide-bolts in two spots holding it shut. When the fire department finally forced this door open [from the outside], they found bodies piled chest high against it."

With a slide of the Broadway Lounge, Casey observed: "An estimated 100 people perished in this section of the Grove trying to exit out on to Broadway through a door that opened inward and quickly became blocked."

Casey quoted a report from the *Christian Science Monitor* published the Monday after the fire. The article quoted Robert Moulton from NFPA, saying: "The Cocoanut Grove nightclub tragedy is clearly due to gross violation of several fundamental principles of fire safety, which had been demonstrated by years of experience in other fires, and which should be known to everybody. The most glaring feature of this tragedy was the lack of proper exits. Revolving doors have long been considered by the NFPA Committee on Safety to Life as a menace under fire and panic conditions [and] . . . can readily serve as a death trap."

It took this tragedy, Casey noted, to create public-safety procedures that—to this day—made millions safer than they might otherwise have been. In the immediate wake of the Grove, Casey said, fire-prevention rules were tightened across the country in cities such as Chicago, Cleveland, Detroit, Philadelphia, and many more. He noted that within days after the fire, two revolving doors at Boston City Hall were removed.

After the Grove, it became common practice that "any part of a building where [there was] public assembly should have two separate means of egress; revolving doors must be flanked by standard exit doors." Laws were passed prohibiting the use of combustible materials as decorations in places of public assembly. He noted that at the time of the fire, nightclubs and restaurants were not considered places of public assembly and therefore were not subjected to rigorous fire safety codes. The definitions were quickly changed.

"The lights fail very early in fire and this contributed greatly to the panic and chaos," Casey explained. New regulations called for emergency lighting to be "installed to allow egress from the building. These lights should be reliable and independent from the regular lighting system."

Sonny walked slowly past the displays of old newspaper clippings from the days after the fire. There was a chair from the Grove dining room on display. Sonny saw John Gill, an elderly survivor confined to a wheelchair. He had come in from a nursing home in Framingham. Sonny saw Hewson Gray and chatted with Ferd Bruck.

On the last page of the event's program was this note: "The event committee gratefully acknowledges the contributions and hard work of the following people and organizations." The list included "Charles Kenney, Author."

17
Breakthrough

I n January 1993, Sonny wrote to his contact at the fire department, District Fire Chief Joseph Fleming, with a "respectful request to be appointed 'Boston Fire Department Historian, Cocoanut Grove Fire.'"

> As you are aware I have been involved in all aspects of researching this most significant event during the past two years and will continue until all avenues of any information have been exhausted. I have amassed a great deal of information including first person interviews with employees, patrons and firefighters who were involved with the fire. . . .
>
> The appointment I seek will lend credence in the furtherance of my attempts to attain all remaining information from archivists at Boston City Hospital, Massachusetts General Hospital, Beth Israel Hospital, Waterman Funeral Service as well as news releases and pictures from Time-Life, World Wide and a host of other potential sources of record. Department Headquarters will be properly sorted, catalogued and returned. There will be no cost to the City of Boston or the Boston Fire Department. . . .

The title would also connect him more formally with the department. In retirement, Sonny struggled with having no professional identity, nothing that defined him. He had always found comfort and pride in his connections to the navy, the fire department, and the submarine veterans. He sent the letter with high hopes.

Around this time, Nana, Sonny's mother, suffered a stroke and broken hip. Sonny brought her to a rehabilitation facility not far from his home on Cape Cod, where it quickly became clear that she would never recover sufficiently to be able to return to her apartment in Roslindale and live on her own. Sonny thus had to begin the sorrowful task of packing up her apartment. This required long drives up to Boston from the Cape, and hours of sorting and packing her things—all somewhat overwhelming, for Nana had crammed six decades of furniture into three tiny rooms. Sonny discovered to his astonishment that Nana had saved all of the birthday, Christmas, Easter, and other cards that she had received *since about 1923*. She had packed them away in drawers so tightly that when Sonny opened a drawer, cards would literally pop out like a jack-in-the-box. She had been a pack rat, collecting and keeping all sorts of knickknacks through the years. The closets were so crammed with clothing—even with dresses she had worn prior to World War II—that it was difficult to remove anything.

During Sonny's regular trips to Boston, he typically spent a couple of hours packing boxes, and then before returning to the Cape, stopped at the pub around the corner from Nana's apartment for, as he put it, "a couple of stiff ones to drive home on." And once home, there would be more of the same, until he stumbled off to bed, only to repeat the process the following day.

During the long winter and spring of 1993, Sonny was so preoccupied with Nana's affairs—and drinking so much—that he was distracted from his work on the Cocoanut Grove. He had had a brief conversation with a man named Walter Hixenbaugh back in January, and Mr. Hixenbaugh said he had some things to say about the fire. In the course of their short phone call, Sonny learned Mr. Hixenbaugh had not been at the fire. As a result, Sonny had only passing interest in speaking with him. He would get to him, but was in no rush.

In the spring of 1993, Sonny, along with other active firefighters and retirees, in fact, the entire Boston Fire Department family, heard about another amazing rescue by none other than the irrepressible Eddie Loder, who had made the spectacular Ritz rescue.

This time, a disturbed man threatened to jump from a six-story building at Boston City Hospital. When Rescue 1 pulled onto the scene, Eddie scampered up the aerial ladder, fully extended to 110 feet and reaching just about six feet shy of the edge of the roof where the man was perched. Eddie stood on the top rungs, but in his haste to get up there, he had neglected to tether himself to the ladder. Eddie initiated a conversation with the young man, who said his name was Ed White and he was a Vietnam vet with all kinds of problems. He kept saying he was going to jump, but Eddie kept telling him no, he wouldn't jump, he should just keep on talking.

"Hey, listen," Eddie said, "I'm kind of tired of being up here. I'd like to get a sandwich. Come on down and let's get a sandwich and talk about this thing."

But the young man ran to the other side of the roof. He soon returned, and he and Eddie continued to chat while a crowd gathered in the streets below.

"Why don't you go back to the hospital and let's end this thing," Eddie said to the man.

"No, I'm going to jump," the fellow said. And he ran to the other side of the roof, at which point Eddie lost sight of him. After a few minutes, the fellow ran back across the roof to where Eddie Loder could see him, and he started pitching rocks off the roof down onto cars on Massachusetts Avenue.

"If you bean me with one of the rocks and I fall off this ladder, I'm going to be pretty well upset," Eddie said to the man. The humor seemed to calm him a bit.

The standoff stretched to more than an hour, and Eddie Loder was growing fatigued, hanging onto the uppermost rungs on the ladder—a hundred-plus feet in the air, untethered. He felt his legs cramping.

Suddenly, the young man climbed down from the roof on an electrical conduit pipe running down the side of the building. Standing on a thick bracket securing the conduit pipe to the building, he removed his jacket and tossed it into the air.

"I'm going to jump," he told Eddie. Then he said it again.

Then he jumped.

And just as he did so, just as he leaped a few feet away from Eddie Loder and was heading for the ground and certain death, Eddie reached out with one arm, holding onto the ladder with the other arm, and caught the man in midair, grasping his shirt with his fist. With a surge of adrenalin, Eddie clutched his shirt tightly, the man dangling in the air, the crowd gasping.

Fearful that the man's weight would pull Eddie off the ladder and both would plunge to the ground, firefighter Lawrence Holt raced up and hooked Eddie into a safety belt attached to the ladder. He then reached past Eddie and grasped one of the man's wrists.

Meanwhile, the firefighter working the aerial ladder from the platform on the ladder truck began pushing levers to lower the ladder down toward the ground, but he made a mistake and instead of lowering the ladder, he swung it around, sending Eddie Loder crashing into the building, nearly crushing his arm. Eddie cried out in pain—but he did not let go.

The firefighter quickly lowered the ladder's elevation until it was just above the roof of a one-story section of the hospital, at which point Eddie lost his grip and the man fell a few feet to the roof—unhurt.

The newspapers loved the story. Loder "snagged him out of the air with his bare hands," wrote the *Herald*. The *Globe* wrote that "A Boston firefighter, stretched to the limit of his body while standing at the end of a ladder raised to its maximum height of 110 feet, yesterday reached out and with one hand saved a man who jumped off the side of a six-story building. Firefighter Edward Loder—with the help of two other firefighters—made the dramatic mid-air rescue. . . ."

Years later, Eddie Loder reflected on the rescues he'd made through the years: "Maybe, today, those people are all right. Maybe they got the right counseling and the right medication and they're on the right track and they're saying, 'Boy, how close did I ever come to actually doing myself in and there's somebody out there who was able to stop me.'"

———

Quite unexpectedly, four months after making the request, Sonny received a letter indicating that he had been designated by Commissioner Marty Pierce as the Boston Fire Department historian of the Cocoanut Grove. The approval—bearing the commissioner's signature—was dated February 19, but for some reason had not been sent from fire headquarters until the second week of May.

Sonny was pleased, naturally, but the designation came when virtually all of his time was devoted to Nana. For it was now clear that she was at the end. Mary Florence Devlin, born March 7, 1902, died May 29, 1993.

Sonny chose St. Mary's in Charlestown, where Nana had grown up, as the location for her funeral mass, and the Carr Funeral Home for her wake. On the first night of the wake, Sonny was standing in the receiving line as friends and family members came through to offer a prayer and condolences. In the midst of this, Sonny's aunt Irene, Nana's sister, leaned over to him and said that she was disappointed he had chosen the Carr Funeral Home. The Devlins had traditionally used Sawyer's, the other Charlestown funeral home, she said. "Sawyer's is better, Sonny," Aunt Irene said, standing a few feet from Nana's casket.

It was August before Sonny got around to calling Walter Hixenbaugh at his summer residence in Brewster. Walter had been awaiting the call and invited Sonny to his home for a conversation.

On August 10, 1993, Sonny drove the short distance from Harwich to Brewster, winding along a dirt road that led to the water and Walter Hixenbaugh's home, a well-cared-for ranch, the fence and garage decorated with scores of lobster-pot buoys. In the sparkling sunshine, Sonny and Walter Hixenbaugh relaxed on the terrace. They chatted amiably about families—children and grandchildren—and then hiked back in time through the decades to the weeks and months after the fire.

"I was in the navy at the time," Sonny said.

Walter brightened. "Me too," he said.

"I ended up freezing my ass off in the Aleutians," Sonny said with a smile.

"Jesus," Walter said, genuinely surprised. "That's where I was, too."

"You're kidding," Sonny said.

Bathed in the warmth of the August day on Cape Cod, the two old men talked of having been in one of the coldest and least hospitable environments on earth. They talked and talked about the war and the elements—about the wind and waves, about the plunging temperatures, about the barrenness of the islands.

When Walter went inside to help his wife, Sonny gazed out over the bay, watching scores of sailboats in the light breeze moving artfully across the placid blue water. Walter had retired from a successful career in the commercial refrigeration business and was enjoying a comfortable lifestyle. He was a slight man with a shock of white hair and a quiet manner. Walter's wife, Jeannette, served homemade cookies that Sonny pronounced "magnificent."

Sonny's expectation was that this would be a pleasant visit with a nice man who had some sort of memories of the Grove, albeit second-hand. When the conversation turned to the fire, Walter started talking about the club's refrigeration system. He explained that from about age ten, he had worked alongside his father at National Sales Company on Massachusetts Avenue in Cambridge, between Harvard and Porter Squares. Walter explained that his dad was a refrigeration mechanic and was training Walter in the same trade. By the time he was fifteen years old, Walter was skilled enough to be hired by National Sales Company as a paid mechanic.

Walter explained that National Sales Company was next door to a company called Miller and Seddon, the firm that serviced the refrigeration system at the Grove. In fact, Walter said, the two companies, side by side, shared a back platform on their warehouse and a common work yard in the rear. Walter said the mechanics from the two companies knew each other well.

As it happened, Walter said, a couple of weeks after the fire, one of the guys next door said that the compressor-condenser from the Grove was being brought in. The mechanics from the two companies—seven or eight men—went out the back loading dock and down into the yard, curious about this piece of machinery. The condenser was on the back of an open flatbed truck. The mechanics gathered around and examined it closely. It was about six feet long and had a round tank, eight to ten inches in diameter with copper tubing.

"When was this?" Sonny asked.

"December sometime," Walter replied. "The fire was end of November, and I shipped out to the navy in January, so it was December."

Jesus, thought Sonny. There's the worst fire in the history of the city, a massive fire department investigation underway along with investigations by the state fire marshal and the district attorney, and a piece of the cooling system is removed from the site and carted off. It struck Sonny as strange.

"There were obvious leaks in the tubing," Walter said. "The refrigerant obviously leaked."

But Sonny knew very well that the original report from the National Fire Protection Association—the report from Bob Moulton—had definitively stated that the refrigerant gas in the Grove was not flammable and thus was dismissed as a factor in the fire. Sonny remembered quite clearly what Moulton had written in his initial report: "None of the commonly used refrigerant gases is flammable so this would seem to rule out any refrigerant gas being in any way responsible for the initial flash."

"But Freon doesn't burn, Walter," Sonny said.

"Freon?" Walter Hixenbaugh replied. "There was no Freon in that system. There was no Freon available then. You couldn't get it—the military had all the Freon."

Sonny was puzzled. The assumption had always been that Freon was the refrigerant gas at the Grove, and it had been discounted as a source of the fire because it did not burn.

"Are you sure there was no Freon in the Grove system?" Sonny asked.

"Positive," Walter replied. "There was no Freon available."

Sonny felt a bit disoriented. He sat back and tried to take all this in. Could it be right? Could it be that so fundamental an assumption had been dead wrong going back half a century?

"So what *was* in the system?" Sonny asked.

"Methyl chloride," Walter replied. "It was what everybody was using then."

Sonny had never heard of methyl chloride.

"What is it?" Sonny asked.

"Refrigerant gas," Walter replied.

"Is it flammable?" Sonny asked.

Walter seemed surprised by the question. "Extremely," Walter said. "Extremely. It burns with great speed and intensity."

Sonny was speechless. He could not believe what he was hearing.

"How can you be so sure it was methyl chloride?" he asked Walter.

"As I say, the company I worked for shared a dock with this company," Walter replied. "I knew directly from them what went into the Grove system. It was what was going into everybody's system. We were doing conversions from Freon to methyl chloride all the time. It was routine."

Jesus, thought Sonny.

"So no question it is flammable?" Sonny asked.

"Absolutely no question," Walter replied.

"Ever seen it burn?" Sonny asked.

"Sure. I'd burn it off intentionally all the time—get it out of a system."

"What does it look like?" Sonny asked.

"Well, it's kind of a bluish flame," Walter said. "And it flutters."

A fluttering blue flame—that was precisely what a number of witnesses in the Melody Lounge had seen. Sonny sat silently, thinking for a few moments.

"Why didn't you ever tell anybody this before?" he asked.

Walter shrugged. "I assumed people knew," he said. "It wasn't until I saw the article from the *Cape Codder* that I was aware that there was still a mystery after all these years."

As Sonny drove slowly back to Harwich, he tried to sort it all out in his mind. He couldn't get away from the notion that he had, in fact, previously heard of methyl chloride—in the context of the Grove.

Back at the house Sonny settled in and began systematically going through his files, drawer after drawer, file after file, page after page. He searched through one manila file folder after another, some with a few dozen pages, some containing 100 or more. He moved painstakingly through one after another, dust from the files soiling his hands as he worked.

Suddenly, there it was—a photocopy of an old letter he had obtained from the Boston Fire Department files. The letter, dated December 4, 1942, just five days after the fire, was addressed to Austen Lake, a columnist for the *Boston American.* The letter was written by W. Irving Russell, the proprietor of Russell Radio and Refrigeration Service in Beverly, Massachusetts. Mr. Russell had read in the newspaper about testimony before the commissioner's investigation in which one of the witnesses had referred to a "mystery gas" at the fire. The letter read:

> Dear Sir,
>
> In regard to the so-called "Mystery Gas," which so far has not been definitely identified, I believe it would be worth while to investigate a possible leak in one of the refrigeration units in the Cocoanut Grove.
>
> Since most places of this type have several units for Beer cooling, Air Conditioning, Food Storage, etc. Many of these larger commercial systems use Methyl Chloride as a refrigerant, a leak of this gas would produce conditions exactly as obtained in the Cocoanut Grove on the night of the fire.
>
> Methyl Chloride is practically odorless gas, which burns in suspension with a bluish-yellowish flame and which produces on burning a very choking acrid pungent smoke which is highly toxic if breathed in any quantity.
>
> Most modern systems use Freon, but due to the war Freon has become very scarce and Methyl Chloride has been used widely to replace Freon since their characteristics are nearly identical.

Russell wrote that he had considered the methyl chloride possibility "from the start" but only decided to write after hearing testimony before the fire department investigation suggesting the presence of a mystery gas at the Grove.

Okay, Sonny thought. *Let's say for the sake of discussion that methyl chloride was in the system and it leaked. The key question would then be where was the compressor-condenser located within the club?* Sonny knew that if it was positioned upstairs on the opposite end of the building from the Melody Lounge, then methyl chloride was not the answer, for there was no doubt that the blaze had started in the Melody. But if the condenser was somewhere nearby, then a methyl chloride theory could have some plausibility.

Sonny dug out City of Boston blueprints from his files but was dismayed to see there was no indication of the condenser's location. *But that was crazy,* he thought. He felt sure he had seen blueprints that indicated a condenser space. Why was there nothing on the official city document? Sonny went through his files for a while longer, feeling a mounting sense of frustration. If he could not pinpoint the location of the condenser, he was lost—nothing would come of the information from Walter Hixenbaugh.

Sonny reflected on it for a while and realized that he had definitely seen a second set of blueprints at some point. He went back into the files and searched until, finally, he found them. He spread them out on his desk and saw that this set had been done by the Boston architectural firm of Stevens, Curtin, Mason and Riley, drawn between December 6 and 14, 1942, within days after the fire. There was no indication of who had ordered the second set of blueprints, and Sonny supposed it could have been an insurance company or even the state fire marshal's office, seeking to gather its own independent information for its investigation.

Sonny scanned the set of plans briefly, and then his eye was drawn to a small enclosed space literally a matter of inches from the Melody Lounge that was labeled "fan compressor room."

It couldn't be closer! Sonny thought. It was tucked behind a wall of the Melody Lounge, within a matter of a few feet from where the bluish, fluttering flame first appeared. It was the very same wall, in fact, that several patrons had said felt hot just before the fire broke out.

My God, thought Sonny. *The idea of methyl chloride has been sitting there in the files all these years.* It was mentioned a matter of days after the fire, yet no one picked up on it at the time. No one pursued it—not the Boston Fire Department, not the state fire marshal's office, no one. Sonny sat alone in the quiet house in Harwich and thought about the ferocious speed of the fire. He thought about the questions through the years about how it had started and how in God's name it had accelerated so fast.

Sonny could barely contain himself. He went back to the Army Materials Testing Lab at Watertown, where he had formerly worked, and contacted an engineer. He explained the situation and said he was looking for detailed scientific information about methyl chloride and its properties. The engineer came through with a number of articles that explained methyl chloride and its behavior. The one concern he had was that methyl chloride was heavier than air and would tend to go toward the floor. How then did the fire first appear in the ceiling? Sonny talked with several scientists who said that if the gas built up in a confined space—which the condenser room certainly was—it could build up over time so that it filled the space, from bottom to top.

Walter Hixenbaugh had stated emphatically that the unit had holes through which the liquid gas could easily have leaked. Methyl chloride, upon coming into contact with open air, converted into a highly combustible vapor that may well have begun settling within the confines of the compressor space. Walter had also informed Sonny that he estimated the Grove system contained about 50 pounds of refrigerant liquid—as Walter had said, "That's an awful lot of gas."

But how had it ignited? Sonny reflected upon this and recalled testimony at the commissioner's hearings that the electrical work within the club had been done by an unlicensed individual, that investigators had discovered after the fire that there were faulty electrical switches. Sonny knew that an infinitesimal spark from an over-fused box could easily have ignited the vapor. The heat of the fire within the compressor room would have accounted for the hot wall patrons said was in that precise location. The contained fire would have pushed its way up toward the ceiling—heat rising—and first shown at ceiling height, which was exactly where Melody Lounge patrons had first seen it.

Sonny worked feverishly throughout the rest of August and into early September trying to solidify backup for the methyl chloride theory. By the middle of September, convinced he had it nailed down, he made an appointment to see Boston Fire Department Commissioner Marty Pierce on Wednesday, September 22. Sonny went into fire headquarters for his meeting with Commissioner Pierce and summarized his findings. Marty Pierce was clearly intrigued. Sonny was delighted with Marty's response and came away with a great feeling of satisfaction— that his work had been well received by the commissioner himself.

When Sonny told me about his discovery, I passed word along to a colleague at the *Globe*, veteran reporter David Arnold. David spoke with Sonny at some length and came away excited about the theory. Two days later, David Arnold's story appeared in the *Globe* with the headline, "Decades Later, Clues to an Inferno," followed by a subhead that read: "Gas Seen as Cocoanut Grove Culprit."

It took almost 51 years, but the Boston Fire Department, acting on the research of a former firefighter, now believes gas from a faulty air conditioning system may have provided the mysterious fuel for the fireball that shot through the Cocoanut Grove lounge and took 492 lives. "I have been very enlightened. The theory merits a lot of credit," said Boston Fire Commissioner Martin E. Pierce. He has forwarded the material gleaned recently by retired Boston firefighter Charles Kenney to Dr. Edward Clougherty, the department's chemist.

Clougherty is expected to make a more definitive ruling today, perhaps providing the epilogue to an event that has haunted Boston for a half-century and turned a former firefighter into a sleuth.

"It was the reported blue flash that had always nagged me," said Kenney, 68, born in Charlestown and now a resident of Harwich. "I was never content with the explanations about where it came from."

It took a 50th anniversary of the tragedy to start the mystery unraveling.

Kenney's father, also a firefighter, was among the first to respond to the fire on Nov. 28, 1942. The Cocoanut Grove story—its blocked entrances, the piles of bodies, the heroism of rescuers that frigid night—became a hobby of sorts for Kenney.

A 1960 injury forced his retirement (he had served in the firehouse at Bowdoin Square). Last year, Pierce appointed Kenney the unofficial Cocoanut Grove historian. During the flurry of 50th anniversary stories last fall, both the Fire Department and the Quincy-based National Fire Protection Agency referred reporters to Kenney.

Kenney struck a bargain with every reporter who called for his recollections of the event, which were incomplete because of the undetermined source of the fire.

He would gladly share his records—but on the condition they notify him if any readers called with new information.

What has been long reported is that shortly after 10 on a Saturday night, the club, located in what is now Bay Village, was jammed with more than 1,000 patrons, 25 percent over capacity. A band was about to begin the second show in the dining room. In the Melody Lounge downstairs, the piano player was banging out "Bell Bottom Trousers."

The source of ignition remains unclear. At first a busboy was blamed for accidentally lighting a decoration while trying to locate a light socket. The accusation was unfair and never substantiated, according to Kenney.

What witnesses did agree on during the subsequent three-week hearing was seeing a sudden burst of blue flame in the northwest corner of the Melody Lounge. They described it "rippling" over the ceiling. In less than two minutes, the lounge was an inferno. Heat and flames shot up the stairs; patrons panicked. The horror and dying inside the club would be over in less than 15 minutes. It would persist for weeks in hospitals.

Fifty years later, Walter Hixenbaugh, 69, of Clermont, Fla., read one anniversary account last fall and realized he might have information missing in official reports.

Reading the account in the *Cape Codder* newspaper mailed to him in Florida, he wondered: "Why no mention of the methyl chloride?"

Methyl chloride is a flammable gas that was commonly used as a refrigerant during the war years. It replaced Freon, almost all of which was allocated to the military. In November 1942, Hixenbaugh worked for National Sales Co. in Porter Square, Cambridge. Next door, sharing the same loading dock on Massachusetts Avenue, was the Miller Seddon Co. National handled domestic refrigeration accounts; Miller Seddon serviced the cooling system for the Cocoanut Grove.

Several days after the disaster, the 5-foot-long condenser taken from the Cocoanut Grove cooling system, known to have been located behind a false wall most likely in the northwest corner of the Melody Lounge, was brought to the loading dock pocked full of holes. It was common knowledge among workers at National Sales and Miller Seddon that the Cocoanut Grove was cooling beer, food—and people in the summer—with methyl chloride in a system with a capacity of 10 to 15 tons.

"It was dangerous stuff, but you've got to remember, there were almost no fire codes back then," Hixenbaugh said. Methyl chloride is practically odorless, and burns with the kind of bluish burst and choking, toxic smoke reported by survivors.

Late last year, Hixenbaugh called the *Cape Codder* reporter, then met with Kenney. Prior to meeting with the fire commissioner on Wednesday, Kenney spent weeks poring over 1,500 pages of 1942 testimony—looking for, but not finding, any mention of methyl chloride.

Historically, the toxic smoke and burst of flame have been attributed to paper and fabric decorations in the lounge. The record only briefly mentions refrigerants, concluding that the material was not a factor because it was nonflammable, Kenney said. He believes investigators at the time thought the Cocoanut Grove was using Freon or an older cooling chemical, sulfur dioxide.

Interviewed yesterday, Hixenbaugh had little difficulty recalling events of a half-century ago. He recalled thinking at the time: "It will all come out in the official report."

But when the report was completed in early 1943, with no mention of methyl chloride as a possible accelerant, Hixenbaugh and many of the men with whom he worked never saw it. They had gone to war.

"I find it incredible, 51 years later, that this stuff is now coming out," he said.

It was a singular moment of triumph for Sonny. He received congratulatory calls from dozens of friends, family members, acquaintances, and fire buffs.

But he was also looking forward to a more definitive word on the theory from both the Boston Fire Department and the NFPA, and it was his expectation that both would soon be forthcoming. A couple of days after the *Globe* story, both the fire department and the NFPA announced that they would conduct further investigation to determine whether the methyl chloride theory was correct. Their expectation was that it would take about a month to do the additional research needed.

There was a bit of a sour note when an article appeared in the *Boston Herald* with the headline, "Doubts Cast on New Cocoanut Grove Theory." The story quoted George (Red) Graney, of all people, disputing the theory. This was the same George Graney whom Sonny had phoned in South Boston and who had been talking with Casey Grant from NFPA about Pops and the Grove. But it was clear from the article that George had misinterpreted what Sonny was saying. George disputed the notion that the Grove was saturated throughout with methyl chloride. But Sonny wasn't saying that at all. He recognized from the evidence that the rapid spread of fire, as he later wrote, was "fueled by the tinder dryness and high degree of flammability of the cloth-draped ceilings, wall coverings and decorations." Sonny's hypothesis was that methyl chloride had been the *initial accelerant* that, he wrote later on, "provided immense force and thrust, resulting in the rapid headway and spread of fire throughout the entire structure within minutes."

Soon after his meeting with Marty Pierce, Sonny was pleased to hear that Marty wanted to sit down again to talk about the theory in greater detail. When Sonny arrived at fire headquarters, Marty Pierce greeted him and they sat chatting in the commission's spacious office. Marty said he wanted the department chemist, Edward Clougherty, to join them for the meeting and Clougherty soon appeared. Right away, Sonny felt a chill from Clougherty. There was no sense emanating from him that a member of the brotherhood had done something wonderful. This was what Sonny sought—approval, acceptance, acclimation. He wanted and needed to be embraced by this department that had always meant so much to him, that had meant *everything* to him.

Sonny had arrived expecting that this would be a triumphant meeting in which the commissioner would bless his findings and the department would announce that the mystery of what caused the initial, murderous acceleration at the Cocoanut Grove had been solved; and not only solved but solved by one of the department's very own men, by a member of the brotherhood.

But something very different was happening. The commissioner sat back as the department chemist—referred to as *Doctor* Clougherty—began what felt to Sonny to be a deliberate attempt to discredit the methyl chloride theory. There was something wrong—the tone was wrong, the approach, the whole atmosphere was somehow negative.

Sonny heard the negative message clearly, and it was coming from a chemist, not a firefighter—and this Sonny resented. He wanted to communicate with a member of the brotherhood, with a man who had been to a three-alarm fire, who had fought his way up over the stick to ventilate a roof, someone who knew what it was to stick by his partner in a fifth-floor tenement when the smoke was so thick you could chew it. Sonny was here with Marty Pierce—or as he thought of him, Marty Pierce's *kid*—and he was the commissioner. How great was that? How proud must the old man be? What a great family and what great firefighters, and here Sonny sat and listened not to Marty—not to one of his own—but to a chemist who referred to himself as *Doctor*. And now

Doctor Clougherty was dismissing the methyl chloride theory and doing so with words and a tone that suggested he was perhaps put upon to have to be going through this. And he was doing so in a clever way—with the use of scientific jargon he knew Sonny was ill equipped to comprehend. How does a retired firefighter respond to a chemist immersed in talking chemistry? How does a retired firefighter who believes he has solved the age-old mystery respond to a man who condescends to him?

Sonny was stunned. He knew the history of the Clougherty family on the department; knew a number of Clougherty men had served the department with distinction in a variety of positions; knew well the terrible tragedy when, back in 1964, Assistant Chief of Department John Clougherty arrived at the Trumbull Street fire, where his son Robert was killed. Sonny could not understand how a member of that noble family—even though he himself was never a jake—could treat a firefighter this way.

It was plain that *Doctor* Clougherty did not like the fact that news of Sonny's theory had made the newspapers. The doctor talked of the weight of methyl chloride and said there was no burning in the lower portions of the Melody Lounge or the rest of the club, for that matter. He said there was no way the compressor-condenser could have had nearly enough methyl chloride to fill a space as large as the Cocoanut Grove. Sonny was about to respond to these two points with clarity and precision, but the *Doctor* plowed on with more scientific talk that made him sound erudite—but not to Sonny. To Sonny he sounded arrogant and defensive, a man who could not tolerate the possibility that a retired firefighter might well have solved the mystery.

Sonny decided to push back, trying to explain that he saw methyl chloride as the initial accelerant. But the doctor brooked no dissent. He frowned in a way that suggested he considered Sonny's responses rather, well, naive and ill-informed. Sonny detected a note of nastiness in this response. The doctor did not like having to be here at this meeting with this retired firefighter—who was what rank? A *private*?—and having his analysis questioned in any way.

And then it occurred to Sonny what this was all about: Clougherty was trying, in the presence of the commissioner, to expose Sonny, to embarrass him. And Sonny had an impulse—though he has always been a quiet man—to say to the doctor, "Why don't you stick it up your ass?" And walk out. But Sonny did not do this of course, because he was a guest of Marty Pierce's kid, now the commissioner, and because he did not want to permit his anger to get the best of him.

Sonny felt disoriented. He was sixty-eight years old and believed he had solved the mystery of the worst fire in the city's history, believed he had done something historic. He was an old retired firefighter celebrated in the newspaper for his finding and designated the department's Cocoanut Grove historian. Yet he now sat humiliated because he didn't know the sort of scientific jargon needed to fight back against the *Doctor*. His pride was hurt, and he finally got up and left. Though he was wounded, Sonny did not allow Marty Pierce's kid or Clougherty to see it. He walked out of the headquarters of the organization that had been the most important place in his life, a place that should have been providing him with support and sustenance, beaten down.

Looking back on it years later, Sonny said simply: "I was not technically deep enough to defend myself."

Sonny urgently wanted affirmation for his theory, so he sought it from Casey Grant at NFPA. He met with Casey on September 29, 1993, barely a week after the *Globe* article had run. After the meeting, Sonny wrote a memo to his files in which he laid out his theory. He concluded the memo by stating that Casey Grant, "acting as both consultant and Devil's advocate, was in agreement with this theory."

This overstated Casey Grant's position in the matter. Casey thought the theory was intriguing—thought it might very well hold a good deal of merit—but Casey also knew it would have to be subjected to intense scientific scrutiny to be proven conclusively.

But Sonny would not be denied.

Sonny was feverish in his activity, for he could not accept the humiliation from Clougherty. He could not accept that the department had failed to embrace him and his findings because of the views of the doctor. Sonny worked the phone, calling around to various experts in chemistry. He studied *Hawley's Condensed Chemical Dictionary,* eleventh edition, and found methyl chloride described in the *Hazardous Chemicals Data Book* (revised 1978) as giving off a "sweet" odor and producing "poisonous gases" in a fire. He called Oklahoma State University in Stillwater, Oklahoma, where a well-respected fire-safety curriculum was in place. He found articles explaining that when it burns, methyl chloride gives off the toxic gas phosgene.

And he sat down and composed a letter to Marty Pierce—not to Clougherty—but to the commissioner himself. He wanted to provide the commissioner with a detailed written explanation of his research and findings. Sonny wrote at some length and then delivered his conclusion:

> . . . [It] is herewith submitted that Methyl Chloride leaked from its condenser and, undetected, changed from its liquid state under pressure to vapor stage at atmospheric pressure reaching, in the concealed space behind the wall of the Melody Lounge, a concentration within its flammable limits. When provided with an unknown source of ignition the vapor cloud flashed, providing the initial powerful impetus of heat and flame throughout the crowded lounge. Both the "whoosh" and the "blue flame" as described in the sworn testimony of bartender Bradley are in conformity with ignited Methyl Chloride in vapor stage. Methyl Chloride was the "Mystery Gas" that so disastrously fueled the Cocoanut Grove fire. . . .

Not long after sending that letter, Sonny sat down and wrote once again to Marty Pierce in October, emphasizing that

> the leaking compressor/condenser was located within a confined, concealed space. The leaking compressor/condenser was located DIRECTLY AT THE ACKNOWLEDGED POINT OF ORIGIN of the Cocoanut Grove nightclub fire.

Although, as stated to you in my initial report the actual source of ignition may never be determined the foregoing facts and statements would indicate the overwhelming probability that Methyl Chloride was the accelerant within the Melody Lounge of the Cocoanut Grove nightclub.

I await your early review and comments on this report.

18
"My Task Is Finished"

There were certain Boston firefighters who were special. Bill Shea, who had gotten hurt with Sonny and gone on later to accomplish the dramatic rescue after the Paramount Hotel explosion, was certainly among them. Eddie Loder merited particular distinction. Bobby Greene, who died in the tragic fall, fit into the special category, as did Jimmy Hardy, who had rescued young Mark Walsh in South Boston.

Lieutenant Steve Minehan held an honored place on that list of distinguished jakes. Steve Minehan had been a spark with Tom and Patrick and had broken in on the Boston Ambulance Squad with Tom, where the two had become close, bound together by their passion to become firefighters and by their family firefighting histories. Steve's father, Alfred, had rescued a number of people at the Cocoanut Grove and his grandfather, Michael, had gone on the job back in 1899, rising to the rank of district chief. Steve had grown up with six brothers and sisters, in a home where the fire-department radio was on continuously.

When Tom first met him, Steve was working as a custodian at St. Ambrose Church in the Fields Corner section of Dorchester and volunteering part-time for the ambulance squad. Steve was enough older than Tom to have begun the process of applying for a firefighting job several years earlier, before the federal court ruling. Steve, in fact, barely made it onto the job, winning final appointment just before the court ruling took effect.

After midnight on June 24, 1994, with the city bathed in the yellow light of a full moon, fire broke out in an abandoned warehouse on the Charlestown waterfront. Within minutes it became clear to the department brass that the fire—which quickly grew to a nine-alarm conflagration battled by 200 firefighters—was too dangerous to fight from within, and all firefighters were ordered out of the structure.

Deputy Chief Kevin Mochen got word that two firefighters—Darrell Johnson and Terrance Jones—were unaccounted for after the building had been ordered cleared. The two men, both just thirty-three years old, were good friends. Steve Minehan and Ladder 15 showed up just when the two men were reported missing, about 1:20 AM.

"Stevie, get in there and get those guys out," Mochen ordered.

Minehan and three other men charged inside, slowly working their way through dense yellow smoke, searing heat, and pitch darkness searching for the two lost firefighters.

It so happened that two men responsible for some of the most dramatic rescues in years were together at the fire: Eddie Loder and Jimmy Hardy. Eddie arrived early on, when the fire had barely gotten started. "It was a very, very small fire. I remember saying to myself we'll get rid of that in about fifteen minutes . . . It was very warm that night. I was thinking I'd get back and get some sleep."

Jimmy Hardy got there at the same time as Eddie and headed into the warehouse. While they were inside, however, before the call to evacuate, something happened. Whether it was the creosote buildup on the pier underneath the building or some other cause, nobody knew. All they knew was that the fire accelerated, as Jimmy Hardy put it, "like *that*."

"It was almost instantaneously," Eddie recalled. "It was like someone pulling a shade down. [The smoke was] coming down from the ceiling and coming up from the floor."

The sudden shift in conditions alarmed Eddie. "This ain't right," he remembered thinking. "This ain't supposed to be. And I remember having a face piece on my mask hanging on my coat; it wasn't attached, it should have been attached. So I remember dropping down on my knees and taking it off my coat and putting it on . . . and turning the bottle [of air] on . . . And I remember looking around saying we got to get out of here."

But when Eddie stood up and looked around, he wasn't sure where he was in relation to the exit. He did not know which way to go, and he knew that heading off in the wrong direction could be fatal. Going back over the events later on, he said:

I got back down on my knees again, figuring I would try to get out of the smoke and then I could see the fire coming up through the cracks in the floor. I'm saying I'm in trouble here . . . So I went towards what I thought was the opening. . . . I thought I was headed for it and the next thing I know I banged into the wall. So now I'm getting a little nervous and panicking, and I knew I was in the middle of the warehouse and I knew if I didn't find my way out of there that I could have possibly run out of air and that would have been the end of it.

I said to myself, try to calm down. I gather my thoughts and think about what I'm doing and don't panic because if you panic you're all done. So I said, let me find the hose they dragged in there. So I'm on the floor again looking for the hose and when I did find it, it was in a big pile of spaghetti. The only other thing you can do is find the couplings, male and female coupling because they always run the male coupling into the building . . . so if you find the male, the male is coming from the outside of the street. So I find the male and the next thing I know I'm going around the pile again. So this is not working. This is not working at all.

They say your life flashes in front of your eyes. As far as I'm concerned that's the truth. First thing I started thinking is I'm going to die in here, this rotten, lousy warehouse . . . this is it. You think of your wife, your kids, your mother, your father, and I said this is where it's going to end for me right here.

But it did not end there, because as Jimmy Hardy was making his way out of the building, he realized that Eddie was not with him and he went back inside, deeper into the building, searching. It was then that Eddie Loder heard a familiar voice—the voice of Jimmy Hardy—shouting: "Eddie!"

Eddie Loder turned around and in the thick smoke, he saw a light, a white light, and he knew it was Jimmy Hardy. And Jimmy knew exactly where he was and where the exit was, so Eddie followed as Jimmy led him out of the building and into the night.

Just as Jimmy and Eddie were getting out of the building, Steve Minehan and his Ladder 15 crew were making their way inside to search for Johnson and Jones.

Jimmy and Eddie told Steve and his crew to watch out, warning them that it was really bad in there. Just minutes later, Steve Minehan and his crew found Johnson and Jones lying on the floor, unconscious. Their air supplies had run out, and they had been overcome by the deadly smoke. Minehan instructed his crew to gather up the injured men and to follow the hose line back to the exterior. His men did that, carrying the two young firefighters outside.

They were in rough shape, having consumed quantities of smoke and suffering from carbon monoxide poisoning. It was determined that their only chance was immersion in hyperbaric chambers—airtight tubes filled with pure oxygen—which work to flush carbon monoxide from the system. The two men were flown to Norwalk (Connecticut) Hospital, the only New England location then equipped with hyperbaric chambers.

However grim their condition, Johnson and Jones both had a fighting chance. The rescue led by Stevie Minehan had been successful—in that sense at least. It would be days, perhaps weeks, before it was clear whether the two young firefighters would survive.

In the meantime, it suddenly became alarmingly clear in the wake of the rescue that when Steve Minehan's men had emerged from the building with the two firefighters, Steve was not with them.

The guys from Ladder 15 had just emerged into the night when one of them turned and said, "Where's Stevie?"

Steve had somehow gotten separated from his crew and was still inside the building.

The conditions inside were extremely dangerous, but several members of Minehan's Ladder 15 crew went back inside to search. They tried to find their way back to where they had been and raised their masks, shouting loudly in the hope that Steve would hear them. Conditions were deteriorating by the second. The smoke and heat were hellish. The building was much too dangerous now. There was no way the men could survive the smoke and heat. Everyone was ordered out.

At 1:30 AM, the radio at the Boston Fire Department's central communications station crackled with a transmission from somewhere inside the warehouse.

"Fire alarm," said the voice of Steve Minehan.

Sixteen seconds later, Minehan again: "Fire alarm."

Minehan identified himself: "Ladder 15."

Dispatcher: "Ladder 15 go ahead."

Steve Minehan: "Fifteen is trapped."

The dispatcher radioed officers on the scene: "Fifteen reports he's trapped."

Dispatcher: "Fire alarm calling Ladder 15."

No response.

Dispatcher: "Fire alarm calling Ladder 15."

Eight seconds passed, and then, in a weakened voice, Steve Minehan replied: "Fifteen answering."

Dispatcher: "Ladder 15, where are you in the building?"

No response.

Eleven seconds later, the dispatcher said: "Ladder 15, what is your location?"

There was no response for twenty-five seconds, and then, in a still weaker voice, Steve Minehan said: "Ladder 15."

Dispatcher: "Fire Alarm calling Ladder 15."

But there was no response.

The following morning, Eddie Loder and Jimmy Hardy were sent inside to try to find Steve Minehan. They moved slowly, crawling around hot spots, the fire still smoldering, the charred warehouse seeming truly vast. They had been inside about an hour, perhaps longer, when Jimmy Hardy found Steve. Eddie and Jimmy looked down at Stevie, his body laid out on the floor, the microphone still in his hand. He was not burned at all and had clearly died from smoke inhalation. There was something merciful about this, because smoke inhalation has an almost anesthetic quality about it, easing a person into unconsciousness.

Following tradition, Minehan's Ladder 15 crew was summoned to carry his body out of the building. As the men did so, the other firefighters on the scene lined up in two rows facing one another, and Steve's body was carried out past firefighters standing at attention, their helmets removed. Investigators later found that after Steve got lost within the building, he tried to kick his way through a tin wall.

Darrell Johnson and Terrance Jones remained unconscious for several days, then both started to rally. After a couple of weeks in Norwalk Hospital, the two firefighters were released and returned home to Boston.

They said that even while they were lost in the warehouse, they had confidence that their fellow firefighters would search and find them and that they would be saved. They never doubted it. In the Boston press, much was made of the fact that Steve Minehan, a white Dorchester kid, had gone into a burning building to rescue black firefighters. Darrell and Terrance soon met with Steve's family to express their gratitude.

Steve Minehan was forty-four years old when he died. He was survived by his wife, Kathy, and four children—Kelly, seventeen; Joseph, fifteen; Meagan, thirteen; and Caitlin, eleven. Years later, Kelly went to work at Fire Alarm. Joseph, Steve's only son, became a Boston firefighter, the fourth generation of Minehans to serve on the Boston Fire Department.

On a warm summer day in the first week of August 1994, Sonny retrieved the mail and was surprised to find a Boston Fire Department envelope containing a typewritten document, one and one-half pages long. Oddly, the document bore no name, no note or cover letter, no date or signature—nothing to identify the sender. The document was a photocopy with the heading: "BFD Report of Presence of Flammable Refrigerant at Cocoanut Grove." Sonny had read no more than a paragraph before he knew it was from *Doctor* Clougherty.

In the fall of 1993 new evidence was presented which indicated that methyl chloride . . . was used in an air conditioning unit in the vicinity of the Melody Lounge where the fire originated.

In order for the methyl chloride to be involved in the ignition and spread of the fire a flammable explosive mixture with air (8.1 to 17.2 volume per cent methyl chloride) would have to be present along the path of the observed fire. Calculations performed for a release of 50 pounds of methyl chloride into the combined volume of the partition and the Melody Lounge yield an average room composition of 1.7 volume percent, well below the lower flammable limit. Since the methyl chloride gas is heavier than air, the concentration of flammable gas would be lower at the ceiling level.

Consideration of the characteristics of gas fires in confined space is also not consistent with the observed spread of fire along the ceiling. If a flammable mixture of methyl chloride and air was ignited in a confined space such as a separated area within the partition, an explosion would occur.

The Fire Department has continued to investigate reports of factors responsible for the origin and rapid spread of this tragic fire and will release pertinent information upon verification.

In other words, your methyl chloride theory is full of shit.

Sonny was so angry he did not know what to do. No note, no date, no "thanks for bringing this to our attention." Just technical bullshit that amounted to: GO AWAY AND DON'T BOTHER US WITH THIS METHYL CHLORIDE CRAP ANYMORE.

It was not only the manner in which he was being treated. Worse, Clougherty had entirely missed his technical point. Sonny's theory was that methyl chloride was the *initial accelerant*, the agent that got the fire going in an explosive way. Sonny had explained that to Clougherty and had enunciated it in writing to the commissioner. Clougherty's calculations were based on the Melody Lounge having been drenched with methyl chloride—not even close to what Sonny's theory was.

For three weeks, throughout the rest of August, Sonny stewed. He hated this, being made to feel small by Clougherty; he hated that his relationship with his department had been reduced to this by some chemist. On August 30, Sonny wrote a letter to Clougherty in which he expressed "my thanks and appreciation for the recently received report . . .

> Unfortunately, in spite of the effort expended in the production of this report, the original premise, as submitted to the Boston Fire Department in September of 1993 has not been examined, evaluated or addressed.
>
> The original explicit premise, i.e. THE REFRIGERANT, METHYL CHLORIDE WAS THE INITIAL ACCELERANT IN THE FIRE WHICH WAS INITIATED IN THE MELODY LOUNGE OF THE COCOANUT GROVE NIGHTCLUB ON NOVEMBER 28, 1942 . . .
>
> . . . It is suggested. . . that the existing Report be reconsidered and re-evaluated.

While he waited for such a reevaluation—which he doubted would ever come—Sonny worked feverishly to find support for his theory. He called the DuPont Chemical Company's fluoro-chemical laboratory in Wilmington, Delaware, and found a chemist who talked about methyl chloride with him. He followed up the phone call with a letter on September 15, in which he enclosed a written version of his hypothesis, hoping for feedback. He telephoned Oklahoma State University and managed to speak with the head of the School of Fire Safety. He followed up the call with a written version of his hypothesis, saying in the letter that "comments and/or criticisms from you, your associates or students are respectfully requested and will be most gratefully received."

It was around this time that Sonny read a recent article that blamed Stanley Tomasczewski for the fire. Stanley had died a year or two earlier, and Sonny found it disturbing that Stanley was blamed yet again—unfairly in Sonny's view—and after he had any ability to defend himself. How had Stanley been able to stand it, Sonny wondered, being blamed all those years? How did he handle the unceasing pressure of having been targeted as the cause of the catastrophe? Sonny had thought of Stanley often through the years, but he had made it a point not to seek an interview with Stanley, for he wished not to add to the man's burden. Besides, it was eminently clear from the original investigation that Stanley was *not* the cause of the fire. The fire commissioner and state fire marshal had both exonerated Stanley in their reports. But the initial publicity had been so sensational and ferocious that the idea of Stanley as scapegoat carried through the decades.

Although Stanley could no longer defend himself, Sonny thought he could. He thought perhaps he could write something that might, in some small way, comfort Stanley's wife, children, and grandchildren. And so Sonny sat down and drafted an article sympathetic to Stanley, trying to set the record straight. He sought help from my brother John, who was then a writer living in New York, and together John and Sonny worked the piece into shape. The article was published on Sunday, December 3, 1995, in the *Middlesex News*, a paper whose circulation area included Stanley's hometown. The article carried the headline "Cocoanut Grove Busboy's Legacy of Pain, Suffering." Sonny's article recounted the story of Stanley, at age sixteen, working weekends at the Grove, and reviewed the facts of the boy's life: his father unemployed, his mother sickly, his older brother, a GI, off in the war. The article recalled that Stanley's friend Joe had helped him get the job at the Grove and that after the fire, Stanley had wandered from hospital to hospital searching for Joe through much of the night, only to learn when he returned home that Joe had died in the fire. Sonny wrote about Stanley's trip to the police station the next day, where Stanley had told the story of the sailor unscrewing the lightbulb and Bradley the bartender telling him to go over and replace the bulb. Sonny wrote about the police immediately leaking the story to the press—instantly making Stanley the focus of mob fury throughout the city, so useful in keeping the heat off public officials who should have been scrutinized more closely. It had been so bad that Stanley had been taken into protective custody by the police, brought to an undisclosed hotel, and protected round the clock for weeks.

Sonny noted that a year after the fire, the Boston Fire commissioner wrote in his official report to the state fire marshal that "after a careful study of all the evidence and an analysis of the facts presented before me, I am unable to find the conduct of this boy was the cause of the fire."

Yet it wasn't enough. Stanley received anonymous phone calls all his life from people accusing him of murder. During an interview around the time of the fiftieth anniversary of the fire, Stanley told a reporter: "I've suffered the tortures of the damned. I don't like to talk about it because I still get the calls. Even after a big fire somewhere else some nut will call me and start blaming me for the Cocoanut Grove. I've got three kids and three grandchildren and I don't want some kook going after them because they still blame me after 50 years."

Sonny was discouraged. He had gone to the experts but received little information in return. He had asked the fire department to look at it again, but there had been no response. And so Sonny yielded to a sort of bitterness about it and drowned his sorrows in scotch whiskey, going back to his supplemental strategy—nips. He bought them by the bagful. That way, he could make sure he had plenty around whenever he needed them. He could drink secretly, although there was no indication that Theresa ever bothered him about his drinking. But by the middle of the 1990s, it was out of control—worse than ever. But then a man named Jack Deady came along and Sonny was reenergized.

Jack Deady was in his mid-sixties at the time, a retired IBM sales executive living in southern New Hampshire. He was a robust man of average height and husky build. He had thinning hair and wore glasses. He was affable and spoke in an articulate, precise manner—

just what one would expect from a successful IBM sales manager. A couple of years earlier, Jack had begun his own work looking into the Grove. Jack's interest, much like Sonny's, was personal—Jack's father had been the chief investigator for the state fire marshal's office on the Grove.

The night of the fire, Jack was nine years old, an only child, sitting in the living room of the family home in the Brighton neighborhood of Boston. It was late and Jack was playing Parcheesi with his father. At around 11:30 PM, there was a phone call, and when he got off the phone, Detective Lieutenant Philip Deady said to his wife: "There's been a fire at the Cocoanut Grove nightclub."

"Oh, my God," she replied.

He asked her to throw some things in a bag, and within minutes Philip Deady had said good-bye to his wife and son and was out the door, driving into Boston to begin the investigation that was to consume his life for months to come. Jack Deady's father worked night and day on the investigation, interviewing virtually every survivor of the fire. He also interviewed numerous public safety officials in the city, particularly those responsible for code enforcement.

As part of his research, Jack Deady went back and read—just as Sonny had done—the transcripts of the Boston Fire Department hearings that began the day after the fire and continued daily for nearly two months, concluding on January 20, 1943. During this time, when Detective Lieutenant Deady was intensively investigating the matter, Jack suddenly noticed that there were police officers outside his home. He later learned that there were credible threats made on his father's life. For a period of time a police officer accompanied Jack to and from the Winship grade school in Brighton.

Jack went through the few files his father had left behind when he died. But Jack also knew that his father had taken most of his files on the Grove and burned them some years earlier. Jack and his dad had not spoken often of the Grove, but his father had said to Jack on a couple of occasions that justice had not been served in the case, telling him that corruption in Boston had been rampant and that the corruption had been covered up throughout the investigation.

A fire chief Jack knew gave him a copy of Sonny's article about Stanley Tomasczewski. "I read it and said this article really has a soul," Jack recalled. "It's sensitive. I've got to meet him."

Jack called Sonny, and they quickly bonded over their interest in the Grove. Jack grew progressively more interested in Sonny's theory about methyl chloride. He drove down to the Cape, and he and Sonny enjoyed a long lunch together. Jack said his father had been convinced the fire started with a short circuit. This made perfect sense to Sonny because a short circuit in the area of the methyl chloride would surely have ignited the blaze. Jack said that during the investigation, several master electricians examined what had happened and concluded that there had been a massive short circuit, that the boxes were over-fused. And the hearings had revealed that the man who had done the electrical work for the Grove on the cheap was not a licensed electrician.

Jack had studied the photographs of the Melody Lounge, and he said it seemed obvious that the fire had come from inside the wall and ceiling rather than from where Stanley had lit the match. Jack showed Sonny a picture of the corner of the Melody Lounge that he had dug out of the files. It showed a triangular piece of plywood laid high in the corner of the room, just below the ceiling. A speaker had been positioned on the plywood, which was covered by fabric. The photograph revealed extensive charring on the top of the plywood—but little or none underneath—which indicated that the fire had come from behind the wall at ceiling height, not from underneath.

Sonny found Jack's energy infectious and became energized by his involvement. He was pleased that Jack's work—though not confirming the theory—found no experts poking holes in it. Thus encouraged, Sonny sat down and cobbled together an article for submission to *Firehouse Magazine* about the methyl chloride theory. He sent the article to *Firehouse* on March 3, 1998, with the explanation that this was "the final chapter of the yet-unpublished book 'Of Undetermined Origin,' the story of Boston's Cocoanut Grove fire."

In the meantime, at Jack Deady's urging, Sonny had submitted information to *Yankee Magazine*, which was published in the fall of

1998. The *Yankee* article posed the question, "How did it start?" and offered the following explanation:

> Although investigators blamed a busboy who, while trying to replace a light bulb, struck a match near the paper decorations on the ceiling of the Melody Lounge, former Boston firefighter Charles Kenney of Harwich, Massachusetts, believes the club was rapidly engulfed in flames because of the presence of methyl chloride gas in the cooling system . . . According to Kenney, investigators in 1942 mistakenly concluded that the refrigerant was not a factor because they assumed the system was filled with either Freon or sulfur dioxide, both non-flammable substances. Witnesses have recently come forward confirming that the Cocoanut Grove was using methyl chloride in the system that cooled their beer and food that fateful night.

Sonny was not aware the article had appeared until Jack sent him a copy. Sonny was more focused on *Firehouse Magazine,* which carried a certain prestige within the firefighting community. In April 1999, Sonny wrote to Jack:

> I have talked personally with the editor of *Firehouse*, explained that there was to be a presentation re: the C.G. Fire at the N.F.P.A. annual meeting in Baltimore this coming May. He did not want to be scooped . . . and he stated that the methyl chloride story would be in the May issue of *Firehouse*. (I hope so!) . . .
>
> Please stay in touch. You know that I will give you any information that I have regarding what research has been done. When and if, *Firehouse* magazine really publishes the article in early May I honestly feel that a major part of my job will have been done!!!! And, truthfully, I'm getting tired.

The May 1999 issue of *Firehouse Magazine* did, indeed, carry Sonny's article. The headline read: "Did A 'Mystery Gas' Fuel The Cocoanut Grove Fire?" Sonny explained his findings concerning methyl chloride, writing that "there can be little doubt that an accelerant initially provided immense force and thrust, resulting in the rapid headway and spread of fire throughout the entire structure within minutes."

It was a wonderful coup for Sonny to be published in *Firehouse,* a publication read in firehouses across the country. And it preceded a meeting of the NFPA, where Doug Beller, an NFPA engineer working in the fire analysis research division, was scheduled to make a presentation about the Grove. Jack Deady traveled down to Baltimore, where Beller made his presentation to the World Fire Congress (organized by NFPA) in May 1999. Beller was assisted in his work by Doug Carpenter and Jennifer Sapochetti. The presentation—"Using The Scientific Method in the Analysis of the Cause and Origin of the Fire at the Cocoanut Grove: Development of a New Hypothesis"—said essentially that the Grove case should be reopened and studied more closely, and that, in fact, Beller intended to do precisely that. Beller wrote that "there are a number of significant factors that suggest a need for reexamination" of the fire, including:

- The official cause of the fire is still listed as "undetermined,"
- The magnitude of the tragedy was almost unparalleled in the United States with more than 492 persons perishing in a relatively short period,
- As a result of the fire, major changes to fire codes were adopted even though no complete and valid theory has been put forth that can explain all the events of the fire,
- Important and relevant information may have been overlooked from the original origin & cause investigation,
- There is always a need to fully understand the events of such a fire so we can understand past fire experience and prevent similar events.

None of these points was even remotely new, of course, except the second-to-last one: "important and relevant information may have been overlooked." Beller was clearly referring to the information about methyl chloride. In fact, one of Beller's points was that the "hypothesis involving methyl chloride is consistent with observations"—the sweet smell, the flickering blue flame, and so on.

This was a hugely significant moment, for here was an NFPA engineer—at a major NFPA event—saying that he intended to delve into the study of the fire more deeply, *as a result of Sonny's work.* The plan was for Beller, Doug Carpenter, and Jennifer Sapochetti to collaborate on a study and to publish their findings in the *NFPA Journal.*

This was an extraordinary moment: It meant that the most prestigious fire protection organization in the world was taking Sonny's theory seriously. These professionals saw enough merit in what Sonny was saying to be willing to undertake an intensive study of the matter. If Sonny was wrong—if he had overlooked something or if his analysis was fundamentally flawed in some way—the NFPA inquiry would surely find it. Any weakness in his analysis would be exposed, he knew, but he welcomed the scrutiny.

While work was proceeding at the NFPA, Jack Deady suggested something a bit less formal—a small summit meeting, of sorts, about the methyl chloride theory. Jack's idea was to pull together a small cadre of experts, to hash over the evidence, talk it through, and come to some sort of conclusion, if possible. Sonny embraced the idea, and a meeting was set for August 4, 1999, to be held at the Harwich Fire Department. The participants were: Sonny, Jack, and Casey Grant from NFPA; Walter Hixenbaugh; and John Vahey, a retired Boston district fire chief who had long been a student of the Cocoanut Grove fire.

The meeting was held at 10:00 AM on a Saturday in the Harwich firehouse in a conference room supplied by the Harwich chief. Sonny opened the meeting by saying that the idea was to explore the question of whether methyl chloride was the initial accelerant. Sonny said he believed it was but that it had not been proven to the satisfaction of technical experts.

Casey Grant said the paper Beller and his colleagues were working on would be pivotal. "Getting it into a peer review journal gives it credibility," Casey said.

The Grove fire was unique, Casey added. "When you look at all big fires we've had in the U.S. and around the world the Cocoanut Grove is unique not only by the large number of people who died, but it really is still a mystery. Unlike other fires where it's relatively clear exactly what happened," the question here remains "why did the fire spread like it did? That question has never really been answered."

At most fatal fires, Casey observed, the fatality rate ran around an average of 5 to 10 percent. But at the Cocoanut Grove, the statistics were so horrific they were difficult to grasp. "For every four people who went into the club that night," Casey said, "two died, one was injured and one got out safely."

A deeply intriguing new piece of information—Casey and other others agreed—was Walter Hixenbaugh's firsthand account of having seen the compressor-condenser. The men gathered around a table and listened for some time as Walter explained precisely what he had seen on the back of the truck by the rear loading dock fifty-seven years earlier. "It came in on the back of a truck exposed, laying in the back of the truck backed up to platform," Walter said. "We were all standing around looking at it. There was no fire marshal, no police, no nothing. It was the mechanics next door; my boss, my father was there."

There was no question it was from the Grove, he said; he knew that because the mechanics next door at Miller Seddon had brought it directly from there. Walter said it was clear that the unit had corroded somewhat over time and leaked. He said the unit was undamaged by the fire—there were no signs of burn or heat damage anywhere.

Casey, Sonny, Chief Vahey, and Jack questioned Walter for an extended period of time about the mechanics of the cooling system and about how various elements worked. Walter answered all the technical questions with confidence and the air of authority that comes with decades of experience. He explained that the unit removed from the Grove was the water-cooled condenser-receiver. Copper tubing carried water snaking through the tank filled with methyl chloride to cool the gas and, in turn, cool the air.

Walter estimated that the tank held twenty pounds of methyl chloride—"an awful lot of gas." He said he was aware that methyl chloride was heavier than air, but he said he had worked with it frequently and that it was "not very much" heavier. "I'm very familiar with it. I've burned if off. I'm very familiar with methyl chloride and how it works. . . ."

Walter explained that because it was winter, the system was almost certainly not running. In winter, he said, such systems were drained of water and the drain left open, while the methyl chloride remained within the tank. What appeared to have happened, Walter explained, was that the methyl chloride in the tank, very gradually, had seeped through holes corroded through the water tubing snaking throughout the tank. The methyl chloride had then most likely leaked out through the water tubes—coming out the open drain intended for the water.

Walter said that when methyl chloride was ignited—which he had done many times to burn it out of a system under controlled circumstances—it burned in a flickering blue flame that danced around the room. Walter said that if there were flammable materials in a room, methyl chloride "would spread a fire very quickly." Walter said he felt there was no doubt that methyl chloride was the initial accelerant.

Casey Grant said it was possible that methyl chloride had "kick-started the fire," and that with such a powerful start, various decorations and ceiling material burned with ease and ferocity. When Casey returned to NFPA, he wrote a memo to Doug Beller on August 25, 1999, saying he left the Harwich meeting "with the strong belief that the flammable refrigerant was a potential contributing factor for the rapid initial fire growth in the Melody Lounge . . . it appears that MC may have kick-started fire in Melody Lounge, but other contributing factors then added in, i.e., leatherette, drapings and palm tree decorations, adhesive for ceiling tiles in Broadway Lounge, etc. . . ."

At the Harwich meeting, there was some discussion of the hot wall precisely where the condenser was located—supporting the theory that after the methyl chloride leaked, building up in the confined space, it then ignited. The men agreed that it was impossible to be sure what had ignited the gas, but they speculated that it had been some sort of electrical spark. As they all knew, the electrician working in the Grove had been unlicensed and it was believed the Melody

Lounge had been overfused—allowing a wire to short out more easily.

As the meeting wound down, Casey Grant reiterated that he felt it was critically important to get an article about the methyl chloride theory into a professional, peer-review journal. This had to be done right, Casey emphasized, because the Grove had shattered so many lives. There were still many people out there who had lost their brother or sister, their best friend or fiancé, their mother or father. It was a defining event that countless people carried in their sorrowful hearts for a lifetime.

19
"I'm Going Back Again Tomorrow"

That fall, not long after the meeting at the Harwich firehouse, Sonny was informed by an orthopedic specialist that he needed a knee replacement that would require extensive surgery and a lengthy period of rehabilitation. Just as he was about to schedule the operation, however, Sonny and Theresa went in for their annual flu shots. While they were there, the doctor drew some blood and ran some routine tests on both of them, among them the newly recommended PSA test to screen for prostate cancer. Sonny's test revealed the presence of cancer in his prostate. Further testing revealed it had not spread and was eminently treatable.

Theresa was not so fortunate. She was diagnosed with cancer of the liver. Soon after the diagnosis, Theresa underwent surgery to determine the extent of her illness. The news was grim: The cancer had spread and was inoperable. The prognosis was that she had two years to live.

It was not long before Theresa's cancer metastasized. She became unable to climb stairs, so she slept in a hospital bed in the living room. Sonny slept in the living room as well, to be near at night when she called out for a glass of water or just to be reassured. In time, Theresa could no longer be cared for at home and had to be moved into a hospice. Sonny visited in the afternoon, and then, on his way home in the early evening, he would stop for a few belts. At home he would continue drinking.

Sonny had lost one wife to cancer and now he was about to lose another. Theresa died on October 22, 1999, at the age of seventy-four.

———

It was a few days before Christmas and eight weeks after Theresa's death. My youngest brother, Tim, wanted to get Sonny out of the house, so he planned to take him out to lunch with Tom's daughter, Meaghann, home from college for Christmas break. After lunch Tim intended to drive Sonny up to Boston to my house for the holiday.

The appointed day and time arrived, and Tim drove down to the Cape. When he arrived, Sonny's tongue was thick with drink, his words slurred, then repeated and slurred some more. Sonny spoke in fragments, making no sense. He was incoherent, but Tim wasn't sure what to do—he still needed to pick up Meaghann in Hyannis. He considered taking Sonny back to his house, but he didn't want to leave him alone in that condition. In the end, Tim pressed on with Sonny in tow, picking up Meaghann in Hyannis, and they took Sonny out to lunch. It was a surreal scene: Sonny so drunk he could barely speak, Tim and Meaghann trying to pretend all was well.

When they arrived at my house, Tim came in pale and trembling.

We went out to Tim's car and there was Sonny, wearing an old pair of jeans and a plaid shirt, trying to mutter a Christmas greeting, his words difficult to decipher. Tim and I guided him into the house and sat him down in the living room next to the fireplace. Tim was working that night and had to leave.

As I sat there across from Sonny, who was slumped in a chair crying, I wondered what had happened. How had it all come to this?

I thought about those summer evenings out beside the house when he would throw me one ground ball after another with such patience, hour after hour—right side, left side, straight on. He would throw me intentional short hops, or throw them hard and soft, seeing whether I could barehand a slow roller. He would mix in towering pop-ups and nasty line drives. And I remembered how we stopped only if the mosquitoes got too bad or if it grew too dark.

I remembered all of us piling into the car and going to Nantasket beach. Michael and I in particular were amazed at Sonny when he dove under in waist-deep water and swam submerged for what seemed like three or more minutes, emerging hundreds of feet away.

"Submarine training," he would say.

I recalled the night he sat at the kitchen table at Wedgemere Road, that sultry summer night when he wore a necktie loosened at the collar. He was smoking a Lucky, the smoke drifting lazily out through the window, the polished brass fire extinguisher with the 500 silver dollars on the table. That made me recall the silver dollars the commissioner had handed to each of us on the cold March morning when he arrived at our house. And I remembered going into Mass General and being frightened to see my father lying listlessly in bed, a tube running up his nose, his head and hands swathed in thick white bandages.

I sat in the living room with him and watched as he cried. I looked out at the bare trees, at the dark December evening, remembering everything. The way he used to sit in the hallway on Wedgemere at night, his soft voice telling us stories about Smokey and Joe. How he created a model train set for us one Christmas, a masterful Currier and Ives village with HO scale trains running through tunnels, over bridges. As I watched him, I calculated that was probably forty Christmases ago. I remembered very clearly how he stood off to the side, enjoying our amazement when we first saw the set that Christmas long ago. There were four boys then, all of us in our pajamas early in the morning, speechless at the wonders of the train set. And Sonny stood back, smiling a crooked smile. As those thoughts went through my mind, it occurred to me that at that moment he looked like a man who had captured true happiness, a man who knew what mattered in his life, for he had found it.

In my living room, I looked over at Sonny in the chair and wondered how it had come to a point where he was so drunk he was unable to muster a coherent thought. I made coffee and he took a tiny sip, but that was all. After a while he fell asleep. Then I did something I had never done before, something I wish I had never had to do. I slid my arms under my father's body and lifted him, carrying him like a child up the stairs to the guest room. He was 170 pounds of dead weight, and for a moment I thought maybe he was gone, but his breathing was audible as he lay stretched out on the bed. I removed his shoes and covered him with a down quilt.

That was the terrible December of the Worcester fire. Two homeless people, living in a vast abandoned warehouse, tipped over a candle and set the place ablaze. Six firefighters were lost in a raging inferno, and Worcester called out to other departments for assistance.

Tom and his FEMA crew were dispatched to provide equipment and support. The scene was bleak, with the enormous warehouse burned and six firefighters missing, presumed dead. Tom's crew had a team of search dogs that they pressed into service. He told me later how tough it had been:

Of all the things I'd ever been to, it was probably the one I felt the most helpless . . . It started on Friday night and then on Saturday it was in the news. Saturday night was our union Christmas party, and that's when I got a call from FEMA that said, "Hey, they're going to do a partial deployment to the team to Worcester. We want you to go as one of the rescue managers."

But, now, I'm a fireman and this is six firemen that are missing, and you can tell by the guys' faces from Worcester, you know, that this is going to cost more than six firemen by the time this thing is over. I mean mentally those guys—it was an incredibly difficult thing. It was like walking on eggshells the whole time that you were there. And you knew, no matter what you did, the outcome wasn't going to be good just taking a look at the building. You knew, for sure, that all six guys were dead. It would have been just a miracle of miracles to find some-body alive in that thing. It was just—it wasn't a survivor situation. Of all the things I've worked at, that's probably [the one that] was the most personal because, now, these are the same guys that I am, or at least, theoretically, you know, they're firefighters. And it happened in Worcester, but it could happen anyplace. It doesn't have to be a big city. Fire is just as hot in New York City as it is in Worcester, as it is in Boston, as it is in Hyannis or anyplace else.

There are plenty of buildings like that throughout the country where firefighters can get lost. And it doesn't have to be as big as that one. It just so happened that in that particular one, things turned to shit real fast. And those guys literally didn't have a chance. They made rescue attempts and then finally [the chief] had to stand in the door and say nobody else is going in.

By New Year's Eve of the new millennium, Sonny's deterioration be-gan to bottom out. John drove down to Sonny's on that bitterly cold afternoon to take him out for dinner. And with darkness falling fast, there was Sonny, standing motionless in the driveway, holding onto his car door, with mail scattered all around him.

"What's wrong?" John asked.

Sonny struggled to speak and finally managed to come out with: "I can't move . . . trying to get in the car."

Whatever the circumstances had been, Sonny, very drunk, had got-ten himself stuck outside in the cold. His skin was deathly pale, his eyes moist and cloudy, the rims all reddened. He was unsteady on his feet, struggling to say something, fighting to get the words out. John did not hear what he was saying and leaned closer, asking him to repeat what-ever he had said.

"Help me," Sonny implored. "Help me."

John had to carry him into the house, which was by now in a state of filth and total disorder. With Theresa gone, no one had cleaned in months. Sonny was crying and saying how much he missed Theresa. John made him something to eat and gave him some tea. When Sonny was able to speak again, John tried to find out what had happened and asked him about his drinking. Sonny denied he was drinking, despite John's confronting him with a large bagful of empty nip bottles. After staying with him for the evening, John put him to bed.

That night John stayed with friends not far away. In the morning he bought a sandwich, newspapers, magazines, and cigarettes. "He ate some of the sandwich and a few chips but he had no interest in the papers or magazines. We chatted for a while. I didn't know what to do. He seemed so alone—an old guy alone."

Sonny moved out of the house that spring and bought a two-bedroom ranch on a lovely wooded lot in East Harwich. It was a spacious place with a kitchen and a large sunroom in the back that looked out over a stand of scrub pine. It was an ideal little spot for him, yet at the same time, here he was alone in a sleepy Cape Cod village. Sonny had always loved being part of something, but now he was alone—and he hated it. Some nights on the telephone he was clear and sensible. Many other nights, though, his words were slurred. He would repeat himself over and over again, rambling on randomly.

Then a few months after he moved into the new house, Sonny hit his head badly in a fall. Luckily, John called around this time from New York to check in. Sonny said he'd had an accident and might need to go to the hospital. Alarmed, John called Tom right away.

"I was about to leave for work when John called so I called Dad right away," Tom recalled, "and he said, "Well, I had a scare." So I said, "What kind of scare did you have? Was there a ghost?" "Well, no, I fell down and I cut myself. And I should probably go to the hospital." And then, "Well, no, I really don't need to go to the hospital. I'll probably go tomorrow."

"So I'm thinking what do I do now? I'm going into work. Kathy [Tom's wife] said she would go down there with Meaghann and Lauren [Tom's daughters]. So Kathy goes down there and from there comes directly to the firehouse and I can see she's pretty upset. She said it looks like there was a murder here. You can tell by the blood and the trail what happened. He probably had to take a pee. He got up in the middle of the night. He stumbled because he was shit-faced. He fell, smashed his head, laid there for a while, bled. Probably got up, took his pee, put a towel on his head and went back to bed. I mean it's readable. Every drop of blood, everything else is all readable. When she came home she had even brought all the dirty bed clothes home to wash them. And it's like—she says, 'This is beyond even washing—we've got to throw it out.'"

Tom called me right after it happened, and I had never heard him so upset. "What are we going to do?" he asked. "He could kill himself alone in that house. We have to do something!"

But what? We had talked with him dozens of times. We had begged him to quit. We had tried to cajole him. We had been positive and supportive, and we had been savagely critical. What else was there to do?

It was terrifying, though. He was seventy-five years old now, alone in a house on the Cape where he could get drunk any day or night, have a fall, and lie there unconscious until he died.

A month or so passed. We called Sonny each day to make sure he was okay. Some days he was sober, some not. It was discouraging, and I believed that he would never change. I believed that he was bent upon this self-destructive course and the course could not be reversed. I think my brothers believed that as well, at least for the most part.

John was a dissenter. He was single, living in New York, and had tried through the years to maintain a strong relationship with Sonny. John worked at Ogilvy & Mather, one of the world's leading advertising agencies. Sonny loved to hear John's stories of traveling to Los Angeles or London or Paris to make a commercial. On one shoot in LA, John described the routine, and Sonny had said to him: "You're living like a millionaire."

John was tormented by what had happened to Sonny, and he was fearful of what the future might hold. Something terrible seemed all but inevitable, he thought. He was haunted by that image of Sonny standing frozen by the car when he had gone to pick him up on New

Year's Eve. What would have happened if John had not shown up that time? As darkness fell, Sonny would have been overcome by the cold, and falling to the ground, would quite likely have expired during the night. John thought about the fall Sonny had taken inside the house, smashing his head open. John knew that another such fall—one that rendered Sonny unconscious—could be fatal.

———

The article, by Doug Beller and Jennifer Sapochetti, was published in the May–June 2000 edition of the *National Fire Protection Association Journal,* under the title "Searching for Answers to the Cocoanut Grove Fire of 1942." By the time the article was published, Sonny had been at his Cocoanut Grove research for nearly fourteen years—longer, in fact, than he had served on the Boston Fire Department. At the outset, Sonny's approach had been essentially anecdotal, but along the way he had encountered Walter Hixenbaugh and the methyl chloride theory had been born. If someone had said to Sonny back at the start of it all that his work would result in a prominent scientific journal reporting what appeared to be the likely start of the fire, he surely would not have believed it. It would have seemed too grand a goal, an act of hubris on his part as he stood before the gods of fire.

But, incredibly, that was precisely what happened. While it was true that Beller's article was not absolutely conclusive—a nearly impossible standard, six decades after the fire—it was as close to a legitimate scientific endorsement as was possible. Beller briefly considered the possibility that the fire was caused by pyroxylin (also known as cellulose nitrate), but almost as quickly as he raised the theory, he shot it down, writing that there was not a sufficient quantity of the material at the Cocoanut Grove. Beller turned to the methyl chloride theory, citing information contained in the David Arnold article in the *Globe.* It was clear that for Beller, this theory was the heart of the matter. He wrote that he had developed "a fairly realistic fire model of Cocoanut Grove in terms of time and fire spread. . . ." And Beller applied computational fluid dynamics models to the Cocoanut Grove fire computer model. This model was constructed by Doug Carpenter of Combustion Science and Engineering in Maryland.

. . . [F]urther investigation has shown that methyl chloride, the assumed refrigerant, releases the toxic gas phosgene when it burns. It's also described as having a sweet smell at concentrations and it is water soluble. The effects of phosgene on the human body could cause the symptoms many patients displayed. . . .

Beller's article called for further investigation and study, but it was a remarkable triumph for Sonny, for it was the closest any scientific publication came to acknowledging the legitimacy of the methyl chloride theory. This recognition and legitimacy was a magnificent affirmation of Sonny's work. It was unfortunate that nowhere in the article was Sonny or his work mentioned. Nowhere—not in the body of the article, not even in a footnote—did Beller acknowledge Sonny's work on methyl chloride, or the work that Jack Deady and Walter Hixenbaugh had done. But the larger and more important point was the NFPA affirmation of Sonny's theory.

It changed Sonny. The work and the cumulative weight of his success served as a kind of lifeline for Sonny. For some time he had not fully appreciated or recognized what he had been able to accomplish, but after the *NFPA Journal* article, so much seemed to fall into place. The *Globe* article had been great and the Harwich meeting had been a critical moment of affirmation, as well. But the NFPA was the gold standard—to get taken seriously in the *Journal* was immensely fulfilling for Sonny. After the Beller article appeared, Sonny recognized all that he had accomplished. We were talking one day, reflecting on his Cocoanut Grove work, and he seemed to take a quiet pride in what he had achieved.

During his years on the project, he had become perhaps the leading expert anywhere on the Cocoanut Grove fire. He had been an important commentator and analyst for the news media during the fire's fiftieth anniversary back in 1992. And for a man who had never published a word of his own writing before in his life, he had managed to get his work into the NFPA newsletter, *Yankee* and *Firehouse* magazines, and the *Middlesex News*. And, of course, Sonny had connected with Walter Hixenbaugh and brought the methyl chloride theory to light. The *Globe* had the wonderful David Arnold article—in which the fire commissioner himself said he had been "enlightened."

As he reflected upon it, Sonny saw, I think for the first time, the totality of what he had achieved. He allowed himself to take a deep breath and feel an authentic sense of pride and accomplishment. The achievements imbued him with a sense of pride and self-worth that had been missing for a while. He had contributed in important ways to keeping the Grove story alive and honoring the memories of those who had been victims, survivors, and rescuers. His own father included.

It was not long after this that John picked up the phone in his office at Ogilvy and called Sonny. John was very calm, his voice soft but certain.

"I want to talk to you about something," John said. "We've talked about this before, all of us with you many times. But you're at a point now where the drinking is killing you. Dad, you're going to die if you keep this up and you're going to die alone." John kept saying "You're going to die" over and over again in a quiet voice. This was the stark truth and Sonny was struck by it.

"You can be happy again," John told him. "This isn't who you are. You're better than this. You're a better man than this. You're a veteran of World War II, a firefighter, a father of six sons. You're a good man. But you're going to die alone if you don't do something."

There was a silence, briefly, when John had finished. And then Sonny said: "I want to change."

John was struck by this, struck by the honesty of Sonny's tone, the rawness of it.

I want to change.

"You have to go to AA," John said.

"I want to change," Sonny repeated.

"I told him I loved him, and I don't know if I had ever done that before."

John called AA and found the meeting time and place in Harwich—it turned out it was ten minutes from Sonny's house. John then called Sonny and told him where and when the meetings were held. "You don't have to say a thing," John said. "Just show up, you get a free cup of coffee and listen."

A few days later, John called Sonny to check in. They exchanged pleasantries. *Interesting*, John thought, *he sounds sober*. John asked about the weather and Sonny filled him in. John asked whether he had seen the Bruins game on TV the night before and they discussed it.

And then, as John sat in his office in Manhattan, Sonny said: "I'm going to the meetings."

John's heart pounded.

"Excuse me?"

"I'm going to the meetings that you told me about. Noon and five."

"Two meetings?"

"Two meetings, three days in a row," Sonny said.

"Wow, that's great—what happened?"

What happened was that Sonny had discovered a new world—one in which people who had faced terrible demons had struggled to regain control. Sonny had gone down to the meeting place in Harwich—a nondescript wooden building—and found men and women from a range of ages and professions who were also unable to control their drinking. Sonny sat mesmerized, consuming endless cups of coffee, listening to one story after another: stories of terrible car accidents, of drinking and gambling, of job loss, of divorces and estrangement from children. He sat and listened to real stories from people who had been grievously harmed by their addiction to alcohol. In time, Sonny came to call this his social club. He began to feel a deep attachment to a number of these people. He looked forward to and enjoyed his meetings. But for now, he was learning about it—learning that there were others just like him who fought the battle each and every day of their lives.

"I liked it a lot," Sonny replied to John.

"Geez, Dad, that's great."

"I'm going back again tomorrow," Sonny said.

20
Rescue Man

On September 11, 2001, my brother Tom was at the Hyannis Town Hall securing a permit to do some work on his property. Like all of us, he could clearly recall the details of where he was when he heard the news.

And when I got to the window, a lady said to me, "My goodness, did you hear about the plane crash?" And I said, "No." She said, "Well, there's been a plane crash." So I instinctively reached for my pager to see if it was on, thinking she was talking about Barnstable Airport in Hyannis. And she said, "No, it's not in Hyannis. It's in New York. A plane hit the World Trade Center." I said, "So what did they say?" "Well, nothing much, the news is still breaking." So I kind of thought it was going to be like a small Piper Cub—some nitwit crashed into the building. So I left Town Hall and got in my truck and I don't even know if I put the radio on or not, but the firehouse is only two blocks. So I was at the firehouse in a blink of an eye.

When I walked in the firehouse, the guy on the desk watch was standing up and he's got a glass partition around him and I can see him waving to me. So I came in; and the first tower was on fire and the second one had been hit. And he said, "you're going to be going to New York." I said, "No, we won't go." I said. "It's a fire in New York City, biggest fire department and best fire department in the world. They'll put that out."

And then the first building fell. And he looked at me and said, "Now you're going." I said, "Geez, I could be." So I got in my truck, immediately drove home, and when I got there, the phone was already flashing eight or nine messages. So I started playing the messages and the team was on standby for New York City. "Get your stuff; call your people." So I finished that message, skipped to the next one. "Hey, this is the Task Force; we're not on the standby; we've been activated. We're going to New York. Get your people and get up here as quick as you can."

Tom called his squad members, then drove up to the group's base in Beverly, Massachusetts.

We get up to Beverly and the trucks are being loaded; guys are funneling through to get their physical exam. I get in there and the press was already lining up. And the Task Force leader said to me, "As soon as you get squared away, can you handle the press?" I said, "Yes, I can do that." He said, "Well, I want to talk to you before you do it, because there are certain things we don't want them knowing." So he gave me a list of things I was not to talk about. And then I spoke with the reporters, told them what was going on, that we were being deployed to New York and that kind of thing.

Then the vehicles are moving. A whole bunch of state police cruisers and motorcycles waiting for us to escort us onto the Pike, take us to the Connecticut line and then had the Connecticut State Police pick us up and then the New York State Police pick us up. I actually rode down in about a nine-passenger van. It was myself and Bobby Better, who's a rescue team manager. Then there were four physicians in the van also.

I was riding down thinking about seeing certain guys I knew, especially Ray Downey. I knew Ray would be one of the leaders down there, front and center, as chief of rescue operations, and it felt good that I'd know somebody down there pretty well. Ray had helped me—with training down in Maryland, and he'd also pushed us to get our FEMA team in Massachusetts going and pushed me to be part of it. It was an amazing brotherhood—an amazing connection. I had worked with Ray down in Atlanta when our FEMA team was deployed for the Olympics. He had even come up to Beverly for one of our training sessions.

When we arrived in New York, we went directly to the Javits Center, not directly to the scene, because we had the whole team and all our equipment. And they'd already told the Task Force leader—he's in communications with them; and they said that's where you're going to be staying. We got there around five thirty or six o'clock the evening of September 11.

We were the very first team to get to the Javits Center and it was nobody but staff, the bull gang, the setup guys. We started unloading our equipment and the two Task Force leaders went off to find whatever information they were going to get about when our people were going to go down to the scene. And in the meantime, we had to unload our equipment, get all our trucks emptied out of our living stuff so that we could set up a living place to be inside of the Javits Center. So we got our living quarters established and made provisions to feed the Task Force.

And the first night I saw John O'Connell from New York's Rescue 3 and he's been very involved in the FEMA and the whole collapse thing since its inception. And I went right over to him and of course, he looked like death warmed over and talked with him and asked about different guys I knew. I said, "Where's Ray?" And he kind of just looked at me and said, "Well, Ray's gone."

I said, "What do you mean he's gone?"

And he said, "Tom, Ray was killed. He was in the lobby of one of the buildings."

And I said, "Well what about so-and-so and so-and-so" and I asked about other guys I knew, five or six different guys and every time I would mention a name he would shake his head and say, "He was killed, too." He looked at me and he said—"See, we lost almost every guy on all five rescue companies. *They're all dead.*"

Three hundred and forty-three New York City firefighters dead.

We tried to sleep but we really didn't sleep well. I think eventually I dozed off. And probably about the time I dozed off, somebody was waking me up to say, "Let's go; we're out of here."

So we got up in the morning. They didn't have any coffee or anything. We just loaded into the trucks with all our stuff. We had the trucks and a school bus. And there was a New York State Trooper vehicle. And those two guys were heavily armed and they were going to be our escort down. So we just got on the bus and we left the Javits Center with our trucks following us and drove the West Side Highway.

And eventually we came up Church Street, and literally, as soon as we got off the bus, I started walking up to where the FDNY had a command post. And as soon as I walked up to the command post, the first person I saw was a FDNY battalion chief.

"You guys got one of those sound detection things for voices and noises in the collapse?" I said, "Yes." "We need it right away." So we didn't even have our stuff off the thing. So I called back by radio and spoke with Mike Gomes and said, "You know, we got a spot up front here. You need to move the equipment up. I've already got a task for search."

So the search guy went and got his stuff; and I met them right at the edge of the collapse. And they moved all our equipment right up to where we ended up staying for the whole time that we were there. Right at Church and Dey Street was where they stacked up all our stuff. Then we operated from there.

I wasn't sure how bad it was going to be. From what we were hearing, the thing kept getting bigger and bigger and bigger. Like when we left Massachusetts, you know, there might be 500 people in that building. And then it was 1,000. But the time we got to Connecticut, it was 15—by the time we got to the Javits Center, they were saying it could be as many as 3,000 people.

So we're kind of figuring, when we got off the bus, we're going to be tripping over these people. I mean, 3,000 in a collapse—they're going to be everywhere. When we got off the bus and you started to see the destruction even before you get to where you were going, the thing that impressed me is when I got off the bus, I put my foot on the ground and it was like walking in flour. Like the first snow that you get every year and you step on it and it just kind of floats away, that's what the street was covered with, this white-gray powder. Everything was the same color no matter what you looked at.

Yes, we're trained for collapse; but I just thought the collapse would be just like one building, not, you know, two blocks by two blocks by two blocks by two blocks. Two hundred stories of building spread all over the place. But it had to be the magnitude of what I saw was the most impressive thing. Everybody just looked at each other going, holy shit. It was so much worse than we could ever have imagined.

Then we started looking, we were finding people immediately. But the ones that we found were all dead. And then after a couple of days into it, we weren't even finding that. It was just, you know, there was nothing left to a lot of people, and the size of the collapse and the amount of fire that had burned there.

And that was the other thing. There were fires everywhere. There were fires that you'd like to be at it to put it out; but there were just so many of them burning all over the place. The priority was search and rescue.

The first day people stayed pretty pumped up because we had found a bunch of people. Real early on we found two Port Authority police officers almost side by side. They had been killed. We found some civilians, and we worked well past where we were supposed to. We were supposed to swap out about like 6:00 PM, and I think we ended up there until like nine-thirty or ten o'clock at night. But people were still pretty gung ho that we were probably going to have some good results in this thing because there was still a huge amount of area to be covered. And because there were so many void spaces, we thought, there's probably going to be a chance that somebody's going to be getting out of this alive.

I'm not sure exactly what day it was, but I came back from work, and it might have been at the end of the first day or the second, I'm not sure. But we came back and there were some PR guys there from FEMA who wanted me to do an interview. I said, "Okay, is it authorized?" and they said it was all set.

So we get down there and there's this nice young woman from some program, I didn't catch the name. While we were waiting for the interview to start she got a call on her cell phone and it was evidently from her father. He was obviously asking her what was going on and she was telling him about the interview with me. And then she says something like, "You want to speak with him?" So she looks at me and says, "Would you mind talking to my father?" I said, "Yes, sure." So I got on the phone and said, "How are you doing?" He says, "Good." He says, "I just want to thank you guys so much for everything you're doing for our country." And it's like, but, sir, it's just, I mean, we're here to help.

"No, you got to know how proud people are of you guys and the fabulous job you're doing down there." Here's a guy I've never met before; I have no idea; you know, I met his daughter fifteen minutes ago but there was something very real and genuine about it. I could tell it was an emotional moment for him. He said to me, "I was in the service. I served, and I know you guys are doing the right thing." It meant a lot to him to tell me that, and I have to say I really appreciated it. It meant something to me, too.

While Tom was in New York, I was at home watching television news about the attacks. John called frequently from New York to talk about what was happening. On September 11, he had gone to give blood, but so many people showed up he was turned away. He encountered a group of people a few blocks away who had taken it upon themselves to build wooden stretchers, thinking there would be a need for hundreds, perhaps thousands. John joined in, nailing them together, one after another until all the wood had been used up and there was nothing else to be done. He walked the city, back downtown, as close to the site as he could—but still a half dozen blocks away—and then walked home to Brooklyn Heights over the Brooklyn Bridge.

John was trying to get in touch with Tom, but it was very difficult because Tom was working at Ground Zero, searching the rubble for survivors. We were all wondering whether Tom was okay, and as we were worrying, watching television, suddenly there was Tom, his face filling the screen. Tom was at the Javits Center and Dan Rather, at the CBS studio in midtown, introduced Tom and asked him: "What are you seeing, and as you see it what are you feeling?"

> **Tom:** We're currently one of the first teams that was deployed to support the city of New York for this disaster and I think the first thing that struck the task force members was the magnitude of the situation. We've had the opportunity during down time to see it on television, but I can assure you that the television press is not able to deliver the size of the operation and the area of disaster that this encompasses.
>
> **D.R.:** Mr. Kenney, do you feel a sense of real and present danger as you're going about your work?
>
> **Tom:** Yes and no. And what's going on is that we're operating in areas that are dangerous, but the training that FEMA has provided to the task forces throughout the United States will get us through this. Nobody is being placed in jeopardy for this operation. However, it's still being conducted as an actual rescue.
>
> **D.R.:** As an actual rescue. Is that because you still believe or just simply hope that there may be some people alive in that rubble?
>
> **Tom:** No, we believe there is. Experiences in this country and other countries have shown that people can last for days and possibly even weeks under this kind of situation. So all the efforts now are still focused on a rescue operation.
>
> **D.R.:** And looking at it, based on your experience, is this likely to take a month, two months, what's your own personal estimate?

Tom: Normally, task force members are deployed for two weeks, but my best guess estimate is that this is going to take months before that whole area is cleared and the last person is taken out.

D.R.: Tom Kenney, thank you very much for taking time out from your work. Good luck. Take care of yourself out there.

Tom: Thank you.

———

The story ends on December 16, 2003, right where it all began—at the Cocoanut Grove nightclub. Or, more accurately, at the site where the Grove once stood.

It is a gloriously clear, frigid day. The sun is high in the sky, bright and radiant. I am standing alone on Piedmont Street in Boston, looking at a hotel that now occupies much of the site. I saunter along Church Street and then down Shawmut, where Pops arrived that night around 10:30 PM and began pulling people out of the building.

I can see it all in my mind quite clearly—I can see my grandfather, short and wiry, quick on his feet, lightning fast with his hands, pulling people out, carrying them to safety. I can see the mayhem bleeding out of the club and into the cobblestone streets—patrons fortunate enough to have gotten out sprawled on the ground, gasping for breath; police and firefighters tending to them; hundreds of rescue workers and volunteers rushing to the scene, no one prepared by experience to grasp the enormity of the event. I can see Pops laboring, fighting for breath as he penetrates the building by only a matter of feet, but it is enough to force the gaseous fumes down his throat and into his lungs, and in time he collapses at the scene and is carted off to Boston City Hospital where he witnesses a scene from Dante, from Hell.

As I stand still on the street corner, I can see the mayhem and hear the sirens filling the night sky of the city: The firefighters are shouting out to one another, the patrons are wailing as they learn the fate of their loved ones.

I stand on the street corner for some time waiting for the image to fade, but it does not. I feel the image has been with me always, and I do what I have done in the past—simply push it back into my memory and force myself to move on.

I walk through the sharp, wintry air through Park Square and over to Tremont Street. I follow Tremont up toward Beacon Hill, past Boston Common on my left, up to where Tremont and Cambridge Streets meet in what was once known as Bowdoin Square. It is no more than a ten-minute walk from the Grove. Here, I stand and gaze across the street at a crescent-shaped office building that curves with the street all the way along the block. But I do not see the office building anymore—I see the Big House. I see the Bowdoin Square firehouse with its seven bays, with its engine companies and ladder companies and the Lighting Plant and Tower 1 and the district chief—and the Rescue.

I imagine the shiny brass poles inside the cavernous firehouse. I see the men assigned here—Harold Matulitis, Dan Moynihan, and Nelson Pittman. I am hoisted into the air by John Jameson, my father's friend, who will lose his life in the Hotel Vendome fire.

I walk with my Dad as he collects his pay—a thick wad of cash folded in thirds and slipped into a small brown pay envelope that he tucks into the breast pocket of his denim work shirt.

I walk slowly back along Cambridge Street to Tremont and turn left about where I judge Cornhill Street once was. Now it is a vast brick plaza surrounding Boston City Hall. I walk down a couple of hundred feet and stand where I suppose the fire was that frigid March night in 1959. And I can see it: I can see what happens that night—Sonny racing into the burning building. I can see the fire blow out from the rear, rip through the front of the building, and I realize: My father is inside that inferno. And then there are three men coming out, and the second is my dad. He hits the top of the ladder, then tumbles through the sheet of flames and somersaults down through the night, landing on the pavement.

I stand for a while watching the scene in my mind's eye and when I look up, I see dozens and dozens of firefighters in the present, hurrying across City Hall plaza with wives and children. They are in dress uniforms and from departments all across Massachusetts. They are headed where I am headed—just a block away to Faneuil Hall.

When I arrive, there are hundreds of firefighters already inside and hundreds of family members filling the venerable old building. My brother Tom's wife, Kathy, has saved me a seat, and soon the ceremony begins. The Boston Fire Department bagpipe section enters; the thunderous sound of the pipes and the drama and power of these instruments fill the hall, sending out the signal that a moment of import is upon us. The colors are presented. We all sing "The Star Spangled Banner."

It is not often at awards ceremonies such as this that a public official will get it right, offering remarks that carry real meaning, but on this day, the governor of Massachusetts, Mitt Romney, rises to the occasion.

I don't know why it is that firefighting has long been associated in my mind and in the public's mind with being American and with patriotism. Why is it somehow that being a firefighter is so appropriate in this hall? Why is that this music and the singing of the National Anthem and the flag are so associated with firefighting? What is that connection?

I thought that it has something to do with the fact that in America we value so highly people who give of themselves for others, people who sacrifice of themselves. It's part of our culture. It's part of our heritage.

Yes, that's true in other cultures as well, but there is something unusual about the American sacrifice. And that is that we value so highly the life of one person. That we will go to great lengths, take great personal risk, make enormous sacrifice to protect the life of one person. We are a nation built upon the principle that our creator has endowed each person with inalienable rights that they are "children of God," if you will. And by virtue of that, men and women who don the uniform of a firefighter take upon them responsibility of protecting that life and for that reason we salute them and we identify them with the core of what it means to be an American ... Many of us don't recognize the kind of risks which firefighters take on as they go into those buildings. Until of course we see conflagration and we see an individual rushing in, and in some cases never rushing out.

There are other speakers and then names of firefighters are called, and they rise from their seats and move forward, many of them awkwardly, self-consciously, and mount the stairs to this historic stage, where they are handed an award.

I hear my brother's name being called—Thomas Kenney of the Hyannis Fire Department. I am sitting in Faneuil Hall, this comfortable colonial-era building, beautiful in its simplicity, a building as rich in history as any in America, and I hear my brother's name echo off the walls where Jefferson and Adams and Washington once spoke.

His award is for work in the winter of 2003. It was around 7:00 in the evening, dark and cold, a light snow falling in Hyannis. An old warehouse behind a liquor store was ablaze, in a setting eerily like the Worcester warehouse. The building was actually three buildings connected lengthwise, old and vacant for some years. A call has come in, a homeless woman reporting that her friend was caught inside. She said she knew this because she was also inside with him but managed to get out.

When Tom arrived there was heavy smoke showing. The trouble was that the owner of the building fortified it like Fort Knox, to keep homeless people out. But of course they managed to find their way in anyway. The fortifications meant to keep the homeless out now threatened to trap firefighters inside.

Several firefighters managed to get into the building in the spot where the homeless had entered and exited, a good distance from where Tom was. He went to work trying to breech a door, but each door he tried had been barred or welded shut.

Inside, the firefighters found the homeless man and were moving closer to Tom, who had to get the door open to keep them all from getting into trouble.

Tom and his team worked the door with their Halligan tools, but with no success. Tom grabbed a power saw, wielding it expertly, his immensely powerful hands driving it through the steel of the door. But the steel was thick and heavy, and the saw was moving too slowly. Tom willed it to move faster, driving it, willing it. The crew became silent as Tom continued to work, sweating profusely in the frigid night air.

On the radio, Tom could hear the crew inside yelling for him to get the door open. Inside were six firefighters and the homeless man. Six of Tom's brethren, his friends, and a man who needed their help. They could see the sparks from the saw and began to move in the direction of the light. Tom worked feverishly. At six feet, three inches tall, he is thin and wiry, but enormously powerful. And suddenly he broke through and the doorway opened—just as it had on Shawmut Street at the Cocoanut Grove—and Tom was helping to rescue the homeless man, just as Pops rescued those people so long ago.

I look up on the stage and I see my brother Tom receive his award. I watch him as he walks slowly across the stage and back down the steps and returns to his seat. He stands tall and erect in his handsome blue uniform with crisp white shirt and black tie. There are the bugles of a lieutenant on his lapels. He is an officer, a firefighter. Like his grandfather, Pops; like his father, Sonny, he is a rescue man.

Epilogue

"**Y**ou fight fire the same way today as 300 years ago," says Tom's friend, Fire Captain Paul Carey of Boston. "You get close to it, get to the source and put water on it. Technology has not solved it."

This is remarkable in a world where technology has altered so much of our landscape. There is a sense of continuity in firefighting, a powerful connection to history. Modern alarm systems, protective gear, and, particularly, communications systems have made firefighting more efficient, but at the heart of the matter is the need to have firefighters get at the source and put it out. And that has meant firefighting is a relentlessly low-tech occupation, one in which personal skill, courage, and teamwork—and humility in the face of the power of the elements—are valued.

"Firefighters are action-oriented people," observed Paul Carey. "Maybe adrenalin junkies. Every firehouse you go to, no matter where it is, has the same characters."

Whereas certain aspects have changed little or not at all, others have changed significantly. In Boston, the fire department responds with greater force than it once did. The Boston Fire Department response to a first alarm is so aggressive that some people like to say they scare the fire out. There are many cities where municipal accountants dictate slimmed-down departments—places where the first response is a good deal more modest than in Boston. But here we recognize the threat posed by the age of the city and the plethora of old wooden structures. Perhaps our sense of caution is also part of the Cocoanut Grove legacy—a haunting recollection that fire can move with murderous speed. The theory is that it is better to be safe than sorry, and that the firefighters are in quarters anyway, available to respond, so why not send them?

Other advances have helped as well. Improved construction with fireproof or fire-retardant materials has made a difference (particularly fireproof mattresses). Alarm systems in commercial buildings (which are directly linked to fire headquarters) and residences have resulted in faster notification of the fire department, meaning more fires are controlled before they get out of hand. Sprinkler systems in commercial structures have made a huge difference in preventing fires from getting a head start. Communication systems—radios, cell phones, automatic alert systems—have improved greatly through the years. Other factors have made a difference as well, including the increased values of urban property generally, a trend that has resulted in a dramatic decline in arson. With a shrinking percentage of the population smoking cigarettes, accidental fires from smoking materials have declined. And firefighters have benefited from advancements in self-contained breathing apparatus, which enables them to operate under severe conditions they could never have risked before.

In Boston, the most significant change involves the racial and ethnic makeup of the department. In 1974, when the original federal court ruling was handed down, blacks and Hispanics made up 23 percent of the city's population but only 1 percent of the firefighting force.

Twenty-six years later, blacks and Hispanics constituted 38 percent of the population and 40 percent of the firefighting force. By the turn of the new century, the racial antagonism of the 1970s and 1980s was largely forgotten. Firefighters throughout the city had moved on. Certainly there were some men, old-timers, mostly, who could not move on. Some were racists, of course, but others were too pained by the fact that their son or nephew or grandson could not get on the job—too pained to let go. For these men, the Red Book was the only way to go, the only path to fairness. With time, the separation of the races that had been routine in firehouses melted away. Firefighters of different races got to know one another as fellow professionals and as friends.

The department had changed so much that in 2003, a federal court threw out the 1974 ruling. Twenty-nine years after the federal court ruling that blocked Tom and Pat from following in Sonny's footsteps, a federal appeals court ruled that the Boston Fire Department had achieved racial balance and that the affirmative-action hiring mandate would be dropped. The court ruling came after five white men had sued the department, hoping to win jobs as firefighters. Their attorney, Harold Lichten, had argued that since 40 percent of the city's firefighters were black and Hispanic, racial balance had been achieved.

"There no longer can be a quota system for entry-level hiring at the Boston Fire Department," Lichten told the *Globe* in response to the court ruling. "The court has said you must pick based on merit." He added: "My clients are salt-of-the-earth, wonderful guys who weren't out to change the world or make a political statement. They just have been trying for many years—in some cases 10 years—to become firefighters. It was their lifelong dream."

The five firefighters had scored 98 or better on the Civil Service exam but had never been hired, even as black applicants with significantly lower test scores were selected. The *Globe* reported that "since 2000, no white applicant who scored lower than 100 has been hired as a Boston firefighter, unless he or she was a veteran or the son or daughter of a firefighter killed or disabled at work . . . Even some white candidates with scores of 100 were not offered jobs. All slots available for white applicants went first to those with preferences, then to those who scored 100, in alphabetical order. The department ran out of jobs before it reached some candidates with perfect scores."

It was a miracle, in a way. Sonny would go to the meetings Monday through Saturday, often twice a day—in the early afternoon and again in the evening. Back when he had started going, my brothers and I had been wary, but days passed and then weeks. Soon it had been a few months, then a year—and all that time—except for a slight slipup—he was sober and in control.

He sounded different on the phone of course—coherent, sharp like he used to be. And he looked different, as well. He got a fresh haircut and a couple of new shirts and pairs of pants. He was cleaner, neater, much more together looking. John had a goose-down coat shipped from L. L. Bean, and that was perfect for Cape Cod winters.

Sonny loved talking about his meetings and the new friends he had made at AA. When I called in the evenings, he told me stories he had heard that day, and each tale seemed more harrowing than the one before. There were stories of alcohol and drugs and of people losing their jobs, their businesses, their homes and families. There was no tale of degradation or humiliation that couldn't be matched or exceeded by others in the room. Sonny marveled at the mix of people: men and women of all ages; lawyers, truck drivers, bankers, doctors. He laughed as he recounted how at one of the first meetings, he saw the owner of the local liquor store, who of course knew Sonny rather well.

Over time, Sonny's friendships with a number of the members of his social club deepened. There were friends who came over to do odd jobs around the house, to shovel his walk and mow his grass. He now had friends who would pick him up and drive him to and from meetings, friends who would run all sorts of errands for him. With his newfound sobriety, Sonny became involved in town politics, serving for a while on a public safety committee.

Sustained sobriety changed his life. He was more lively and mentally active, and he managed to connect with some old friends and acquaintances. He was quite proud of what he had accomplished, and over time it became clear that his Cocoanut Grove work with methyl chloride, in combination with his sobriety, restored to him the confidence and self-esteem he had possessed so many years earlier. He had been through a hellish time, but he had managed to survive. Not everyone could say that; not everyone who went into a dark tunnel was able to come out the other side. But he had, and he felt good about that. He would joke about his drinking once in a while, just making an occasional crack. But he never talked about it with any of us. He never explored why he had done it. Introspection, self-analysis—this was not his way.

One of the great blessings of sobriety came when he met Christine, a lovely woman his age who lived in Florida. When she visited family in New England, they spent some time together, and then, a bit later, Sonny went down to Florida and spent a couple of weeks at her house. Like Sonny, she had lost her spouse. A few months after Sonny's trip down there, she sold her house and moved up to Harwich. A few months later, they married. Sonny was seventy-seven years old.

The Grove was a kind of force field within our family—a natural magnet in a way, a sort of true north. Sonny, following Pops, was drawn to the profession that had brought Pops to that door on Shawmut Street. In another of the many ironies within the story, it was the parallel experience of Sonny getting injured and, like Pops, being forced off the job that brought father and son together in work for twenty years—an amazing gift for both.

Looking back through the years, it is clear that the Cocoanut Grove fire was at the center of Sonny's life. Ultimately, ironically, it proved to be his salvation. When Sonny's life got out of control, he was drawn back by the magnetic field, back to the Grove. In the course of his work, as he interviewed survivors and firefighters, Sonny rediscovered himself and his own abilities. He groped and stumbled at some moments, but at others he was razor sharp. He gathered a treasure trove of information. And, of course, he quite likely solved the mystery by developing the methyl chloride theory.

All of us, to one extent or another, still feel a connection to the Boston Fire Department. Mike, Tom, and Pat have friends on the job. One of Tim's closest friends from growing up is now a lieutenant. Even though John lives in New York where he works as a writer and filmmaker, he still feels the connection. Back on the twenty-fifth anniversary of the Vendome fire, John wrote a public service ad commemorating that event. The ad showed a black-and-white photograph of four firefighters on a ladder fighting a blaze. The headline read: "We ask that they walk through fire for us. And sometimes they don't walk out." He sent it in to the *Globe* and suggested they run it as a tribute. *Globe* executive Rick Gulla loved the idea. The *Globe* ran John's work as a full-page ad on the anniversary and then offered the ad as a poster to subscribers and nonsubscribers alike. A copy of the ad hangs in the outer office of the commissioner of the Boston Fire Department.

After the attacks on the World Trade Center, John was so captivated by the massive loss of firefighters' lives and by Tom's involvement that he set out to produce a documentary film about Tom's experiences at Ground Zero. The film, *Looking for My Brother*, was screened at the Boston Film Festival. John wrote and directed the film and worked closely with two friends—Rick Knief and Eric Carlson—to bring it to life. The result is a graphic and moving portrait of Tom and his work.

Tom once suggested to his older daughter, Meaghann, that she consider taking the firefighting exam for a position in Hyannis. But Meaghann is a photographer and visual artist, not a firefighter. Sonny's other grandchildren, like Meaghann, seem headed in directions other than firefighting.

In 2006, there are 1,600 members of the BFD and I am related to none of them. Yet as I travel about the city of Boston, I see them and I feel as though I know them. I admire what they do, respect them, and understand their work. Sometimes I pray for them. Once in a while I feel an urge to stop in front of a firehouse on a warm summer evening when the men are sitting outside. I would like to stop and make the connection, feel the kinship; I want to tell them about my mother's father on the Rescue and about Pops at the Grove; I want to tell them the stories about Sonny at Cornhill Street and about Tom and that little girl in the car crash under the truck, or about the guy with the crowbar through his head, or about Ground Zero. But I never do. Instead I smile and nod, say hello, and keep walking as I wonder whether there will ever again be a Kenney on the Boston Fire Department.

Acknowledgments and Source Notes

The great bulk of the material in this book comes from discussions with my grandfather (Pops), my father (Sonny), and my brothers (Mike, Tom, Pat, John, and Tim), as well as my own recollections. During countless conversations through the years with family members—particularly my father and grandfather—I absorbed numerous anecdotes about the fire department. When I decided to write this book, I conducted a series of interviews with my father and my brother Tom about specific events through the years and found both possessed an excellent memory for detail.

I am indebted to numerous others who helped me along the way, including Stephanie Schorow, who conducted both library research and interviews with Eddie Loder and Jimmy Hardy. I also relied upon Stephanie's book *Boston on Fire: A History of Fires and Firefighting in Boston* (Commonwealth Editions, 2003) for certain historical sections. For certain information about the Cocoanut Grove fire, I relied upon several books, including one of Stephanie's: *The Cocoanut Grove Fire* (Commonwealth Editions, 2005). The others were *Holocaust! The Shocking Story of the Boston Cocoanut Grove Fire,* by Paul Benzaquin (Henry Holt, 1959); *Cocoanut Grove,* by Edward Keyes (Atheneum,

1984); and *Fire in the Grove: The Cocoanut Grove Tragedy and Its After-math,* by John C. Esposito (Da Capo Press, 2005). For certain details about Boston's history, I relied upon *The Hub: Boston Past and Present,* by Thomas H. O'Connor (Northeastern University Press, 2001).

I am indebted to others who provided a variety of help or advice, including: Boston firefighter Bill Noonan, former Boston fire commissioner Marty Pierce, former Boston firefighter Joe Nee, photographer Bill Brett, and Sue Marsh at the National Fire Protection Association. Paul Christian, the former commissioner of the Boston Fire Department, was generous with his time and provided important insights and an excellent historical perspective on firefighting generally and the Cocoanut Grove fire in particular. Mark Spartz took time out from his own work to read the manuscript and offer helpful suggestions. I am indebted to Jackie O'Neill, the Harvard University marshal, for reading the manuscript with a critical eye and providing important feedback. Casey Grant at the National Fire Protection Association is a true expert on fire and possesses a keen understanding of the Cocoanut Grove history. He is smart, thoughtful, and articulate, and I am grateful for his time and thoughts. Jack Deady has produced volumes of research on the Grove in general and the methyl chloride theory in particular, and I am grateful to him for his time. I am also grateful to Bill Shea, retired rescue man, for sharing his recollections of several fires, most notably the one where Sonny was injured. Fire Captain Paul Carey of Boston, a friend of my brother Tom, was generous with his recollections and insights about a variety of people and incidents in the book. I have been fortunate through the years to work with the literary agency Sterling Lord Literistic—for many years with Flip Brophy and more recently with Rebecca Friedman. I am thankful to Peter Meade and John Schoenbaum for reading the book prior to publication and sharing their thoughts and insights with me.

As always, I received crucial support throughout from my daughter, Elizabeth, my son, Charlie, and my wife, Anne.

I consider myself particularly fortunate to have been published by both the past publisher at PublicAffairs, Peter Osnos, and the current publisher, Susan Weinberg. I consider it a great blessing to work with two of the smartest, most visionary people in publishing.

Robert Kimzey, my editor at PublicAffairs, nurtured this book from the start. I am grateful to Robert for seeing the possibility here and for working closely with me throughout the process. Robert's intelligence and vision helped make this a much better book. I am also grateful to Michele Wynn, who did an excellent job copyediting the manuscript.

I owe an enormous debt to my brothers. Mike, Tom, Pat, John, and Tim all read the manuscript carefully and offered important comments. Tom spent hours discussing various parts of his career with me. Pat assisted with important library research. And John, who is also a writer, offered a number of helpful editorial comments.

Most of all, of course, I am indebted to my father. Throughout the process he remained affable, thoughtful, and generous with his time and his memories—even when those memories were sometimes painful. This book would have been impossible without him.

PublicAffairs is a publishing house founded in 1997. It is a tribute to the standards, values, and flair of three persons who have served as mentors to countless reporters, writers, editors, and book people of all kinds, including me.

I.F. STONE, proprietor of *I. F. Stone's Weekly*, combined a commitment to the First Amendment with entrepreneurial zeal and reporting skill and became one of the great independent journalists in American history. At the age of eighty, Izzy published *The Trial of Socrates*, which was a national bestseller. He wrote the book after he taught himself ancient Greek.

BENJAMIN C. BRADLEE was for nearly thirty years the charismatic editorial leader of *The Washington Post*. It was Ben who gave the *Post* the range and courage to pursue such historic issues as Watergate. He supported his reporters with a tenacity that made them fearless and it is no accident that so many became authors of influential, best-selling books.

ROBERT L. BERNSTEIN, the chief executive of Random House for more than a quarter century, guided one of the nation's premier publishing houses. Bob was personally responsible for many books of political dissent and argument that challenged tyranny around the globe. He is also the founder and longtime chair of Human Rights Watch, one of the most respected human rights organizations in the world.

For fifty years, the banner of Public Affairs Press was carried by its owner Morris B. Schnapper, who published Gandhi, Nasser, Toynbee, Truman, and about 1,500 other authors. In 1983, Schnapper was described by *The Washington Post* as "a redoubtable gadfly." His legacy will endure in the books to come.

Peter Osnos, *Founder and Editor-at-Large*